EXPLAINING INSTITUTIONAL
CHANGE IN EUROPE

Explaining Institutional Change in Europe

ADRIENNE HÉRITIER

OXFORD
UNIVERSITY PRESS

Great Clarendon Street, Oxford ox2 6DP

Oxford University Press is a department of the University of Oxford.
It furthers the University's objective of excellence in research, scholarship,
and education by publishing worldwide in

Oxford New York

Auckland Cape Town Dar es Salaam Hong Kong Karachi
Kuala Lumpur Madrid Melbourne Mexico City Nairobi
New Delhi Shanghai Taipei Toronto

With offices in

Argentina Austria Brazil Chile Czech Republic France Greece
Guatemala Hungary Italy Japan Poland Portugal Singapore
South Korea Switzerland Thailand Turkey Ukraine Vietnam

Oxford is a registered trade mark of Oxford University Press
in the UK and in certain other countries

Published in the United States
by Oxford University Press Inc., New York

British Library Cataloguing in Publication Data
Data available

Library of Congress Cataloging in Publication Data
Data available

Typeset by SPi Publisher Services, Pondicherry, India
Printed in Great Britain
on acid-free paper by
Biddles Ltd., King's Lynn

ISBN 978–0–19–929812–9

To my son, Peter Windhoff

Preface and Acknowledgments

This book represents the outcome of a number of years of research and teaching on institutional change in Europe conducted at the European University Institute in Florence and the Max Planck Institute on Common Goods in Bonn. In the course of this work I have accumulated debts of gratitude to a number of persons. An important part of the argument on institutional change developed in this book is owed to discussions over joint research carried out with Henry Farrell. This research on institutional change focused on the co-decision procedure in European legislation and found its way into several co-published articles. It also gave rise to a larger research project, generously funded by the Swedish Institute for European Policy Studies (Sieps) in Stockholm, in which we extended the scope of research beyond co-decision to include other rules of European decision-making. My book has profited from the discussions held in this wider project context, in particular from the exchanges with Jim Caporaso and Joe Jupille. Crucially, this book has also benefited from the legal expertise brought by Carl-Fredrik Bergström. The discussions with him allowed for a truly constructive interdisciplinary exchange.

This interdisciplinary cooperation is reflected in the co-authored chapter on the institutional rules governing the implementing powers of the Commission (comitology). It is based on Bergström's analysis of the long-term development of comitology (OUP 2005). The second co-authored chapter in this book investigating the Parliament's right of investing the Commission relies on the empirical materials collected by Catherine Moury. I am indebted to her for carefully and scrupulously gathering documents on the decision-making processes.

Further debt of gratitude is owed to my colleague Christine Chwaszcza who was willing to invest time and energy to carefully read my theoretical chapter and to offer constructive and critical comments. Stefano Bartolini, in a moment when I was daunted by the order of the task, gave excellent advice about how to make it manageable. My work also gained from the multiple conferences with practitioners of European decision-making organized by Helen Wallace at the Robert-Schuman Center for Advanced Studies. They offered welcome opportunities to listen to first-hand descriptions of the European decision-making processes. And, of course, I am enormously grateful to the numerous interview partners I talked to over the course of the years which made it possible to gain a direct insight into the everyday practices of decision-making in the European Parliament, Council of Ministers and the Commission. It is in particular Michael Shackleton and Jean-Paul Jacqué who I would like to thank.

Finally, I am also indebted to my students and the participants of my seminars on theories of institutional change at the European University Institute. They allowed me to discuss different theories of institutional change from different angles, and also acted as sounding boards for new theoretical attempts at explaining institutional change. Several of my supervisees, aware of my work on the book, drew my attention to relevant publications. I would like to thank Christine Reh who, inspite of a quite distinctive theoretical inclination, gave useful references. I am also indebted to Yannis Karagiannis for giving numerous useful suggestions and, as my research assistant, offering many valuable criticisms of my work. Simon Boucher passed on some empirical material from his interviews with EU decision-makers for which I am grateful. I also have to thank Falk Daviter for his assistance in putting the references together and Chiara Steindler for careful proof reading. Last but not least my work has been eased enormously by the excellent secretarial assistance of Sylvie Pascucci and Maureen Lechleitner. All errors of fact and interpretations are of course of my own responsibility.

Adrienne Héritier
Florence, 30th October 2006

Contents

List of Tables

1

Introduction

How and why do institutions change? Institutions, understood as rules of behaviour created by actors, constraining and facilitating social interactions (North 1990*a*: 3; Sened 1991), may be subject to very different forms and processes of change. On the one hand, a change may be designed intentionally on a large scale in a process specifically foreseen for that purpose and then be followed by a period of only incremental adjustments to new conditions and relative stability. These incremental changes extending over a longer period of time, however, in their sum, may amount to substantial institutional changes. On the other hand, institutional rules must not be created as 'grand designs', but may also emerge as informal institutional rules and as such persist over a longer period of time. They later may be formalized, but not necessarily so. Why? The causes, processes, and outcomes of institutional change raise a number of conceptual, theoretical, and empirical questions. While we know a lot about the creation of institutions, relatively little research has been conducted about their transformation once they have been put into place. Analytical and empirical attention has mostly focused on politically highly salient processes of institutional change, such as represented by the Inter-governmental Conferences (IGC) in which the European treaties have been revised. In focusing on such grand events of rule generation, we miss out on numerous inconspicuous changes of European institutional rules that are occurring on a daily basis between the large-scale treaty revisions. These small-scale changes may have important consequences for the overall change of institutions, albeit not occurring in 'a big bang' institutional change, but in small steps. To give an example: an important rule of coordination of decisions among the member states of the European Union, the European Council, has never been intentionally created, but has slowly emerged and acquired an important function, that was subsequently formalized as an institutional rule. Or, to mention another instance, the European Parliament, step by step, has acquired a right of investing individual Commissioners. This de facto right has never been an issue in the negotiations of formal treaty revisions. Yet another example is the decision-making rule(s) under which the European Parliament takes part in the European legislative process. These rules have drastically changed over the last decades starting from a modest right of consultation

ending up in a formal right of co-decision. How can the astonishing extension of legislative power of the European Parliament be accounted for? This
development has not occurred in leaps and bounds. It was sometimes slow
and incremental, sometimes more spectacular. What were the typical phases
of change and typical sequences of different forms of change? What were the
underlying causes and processes of change, under which conditions did they
occur and how can they be accounted for theoretically?

These are the questions that are at the centre of this book. Why—once an
institutional rule has been established—does it change in a particular way?
And how and why do different types of institutional change link together over
a longer period of time? Which theories lend themselves best to account for the
change of an institutional rule in a particular stage? Are different theories apt
to account for particular stages and can they plausibly be linked sequentially?
Which is the particular process driving the change of an institutional rule
and how do past choices of institutional rules impact on the prospects of
subsequent choices? Does—for instance—a relatively loose cooperation under
a particular institutional rule regularly increase the confidence among actors,
inducing them to deepen their cooperation or may the process work the other
way round?

2

Plan of the Book

In the theoretical part, I first outline the definition of institution as used in this book. Institution is understood as an actor-created rule of behaviour guiding human behaviour (North 1990a, 1990b). In a second step different variants of rational choice institutional theories are discussed that account for institutional change. Each theoretical strand will be scrutinized from the viewpoint of the particular explanations and hypotheses it offers on how institutional change comes about. At the same time, the typical limits and restrictive assumptions of these theories will be pointed out. This will help identify the particular scope or boundary conditions under which the explanatory power of the theory seems to be most promising. The book focuses on theoretical explanations of a 'soft' rational institutionalist variant based on the assumption of rational actors seeking to maximize their objectives within cognitive and information constraints and the context of given macroinstitutional structures.[1] Other, non-rationalist explanations of institutional change derived from sociological institutionalism will be employed as a critical foil and source of critique of the rationalist institutionalist arguments thereby helping to mark the limits of the explanatory power of each theory.

In the second, empirical part of the book a number of important institutional rules governing the decision-making process (procedural rules) in the European Union are discussed in the light of the theoretical hypotheses on institutional change developed in the first part. It will be scrutinized which theories lend themselves best to account for the particular development of the institutional rules in question in particular stages of time and over time. Most of these rules have been subject to considerable change in the decades since the foundation of the European Economic Community (EEC). The five institutional rules governing European decision-making processes that will be studied in their long-term development are (a) the institutional rule governing the role of the European Parliament in legislation; (b) the institutional rule governing the role of the Presidency in the decision-making process of

---

[1] 'Hard' rationalists stay strictly at the microlevel, reduce macroconditions, such as institutions and other conditions, to individual preferences and beliefs and assume perfect information (for a discussion see for instance Lichbach 2003).

the Council of Ministers; (*c*) the institutional rule governing the composition of the Commission; (*d*) the institutional rule guiding the control of the implementing powers of the Commission by the Council (comitology); and, finally, (*e*) the institutional rule to be followed in the investiture of the Commission.

All these institutional rules are collectively binding decisions determining how individual actions are aggregated into collective decisions, who and what is included into a decision situation, how information is structured, and what actions can be taken and in what sequence (Kiser and Ostrom 1982: 179).

3

Theories of Institutional Change

3.1. INSTITUTIONS: DEFINITION

The concept of institution employed in this analysis is institution as an actor-created rule of behaviour, restricting and enabling actors' behaviour (North 1990*a*, 1990*b*). This definition of institution is not the only one applied in political science. Thus Greif distinguishes different notions of institutions: rules of behaviour, as used here, organizations, beliefs, and norms. Institutions understood as *rules of behaviour* forbid, permit, or require some action or outcome and are actually used, monitored, and enforced (North 1990*a*, 1990*b*). Crawford and Ostrom in their syntax of a grammar of institutions map out different crucial dimensions of 'institutions as rules'. The first dimension ('Attribute') indicates to whom the institution applies; a second dimension ('Deontic') indicates whether the institutional rule implies a may (permitted), must (obliged), or must not (forbidden); the third dimension ('Aim') describes the action or outcomes to which the 'Deontic' applies; a fourth dimension ('Conditions') describes when, where and how and to what extent an 'Aim' is permitted, obligatory, or forbidden; and finally, the dimension of 'Or Else' specifies the sanctions to be imposed for not following a rule (Crawford and Ostrom 1995: 584). These different dimensions are helpful in empirically identifying more fine-grained aspects of institutional changes in concrete cases.

Institutions defined as *organizations* as opposed to institutions understood as *rules of behaviour* are social structures, such as parliaments, or universities (Homans 1950; Granovetter 1985) consisting of persons, funds, and buildings that are meant to fulfil a particular organizational task. They are 'composites of participants following rules governing activities and transactions to realize particular outputs' (Kiser and Ostrom 1982: 193). Institutions understood as organizations are not the topic of institutional change discussed here.

Institutions defined as *social norms* contain all elements of an institutional rule (i.e. 'Attribute', 'Deontic', 'Aim', and 'Conditions' as described above). They, too, convey standards of behaviour that are internalized by members of a society and influence behaviour (Elster 1989*a*; Parsons 2001; Greif 2006). They differ from institutional rules as rules of behaviour in that they do not include the dimension of 'Or Else', that is the explicitly specified sanctions for not following a rule (Crawford and Ostrom 1995: 584). Moreover, institutional rules unlike social norms entail the introduction of 'man-made' rules that change the incentive structure of the involved actors (Ostrom 1986; Taylor 1987). Social norms and their changing nature are not the topic of this analysis.

Finally, to mention the last dimension of institutions distinguished by Greif (2006), that is institution understood as *shared beliefs*, it expresses beliefs about the behaviour of others and internalized beliefs about the structure of the world, as well as actions and outcomes (Greif 2006). Sabatier and Jenkins-Smith differentiate between 'deep core beliefs' about the state of the world, 'core beliefs', and 'instrumental beliefs' about actions and outcomes (Sabatier and Jenkins-Smith 1993). Again this dimension of institution is not the object of analysis here.

The different notions of institution, that is rule of behaviour or *institutional rule, organization, norm and shared beliefs*, Greif emphasizes, have a common overlapping core. This common core is that institutions are regularities of behaviour among actors in particular *social* positions, that are *created* by actors, and that are *outside* the choice of *individual* actors. As such they are *guiding* and *motivating* human behaviour. On the one hand, they provide information that makes it possible to take action and to coordinate behaviour; on the other hand they induce behaviour by offering rewards, threatening punishments, or instilling beliefs (external or intrinsic to the individual) (Greif 2006).

In short, institutions defined as rules of behaviour or *institutional rules*, as I call them throughout the book, are at the centre of the analysis of this book. Institutional rules are commonly known to individuals, articulated by them and transmitted among individuals (Greif 2006). They are exogenous to individual actors in that they are not created by *individuals*, but by *collectivities*. They are 'external solutions' (Taylor 1987: 21–2) or 'man-made rules' (Ostrom 1986: 6) that change people's possibilities, attitudes, or beliefs. They create a common understanding of a situation and thereby coordinate behaviour in this situation. They may be formal, that is written down and subject to third-party dispute resolution such as laws and constitutions, or informal, that is not written down, and/or not subject to formal sanctioning in case of non-abidance (Stinchcombe 1968), such as conventions and self-imposed codes of conduct. They may be specific or relatively vague and always cover only certain aspects of concrete action 'by providing a general schema which is then adapted to the particular circumstances' (Hayek 1967: 56).

Limiting the analysis to *institutional rules*, disregarding institutions as organizations, social norms, and beliefs, comes at a cost. It only allows to account for the motives of rule-abiding behaviour by emphasizing the positive and negative sanctions that are linked to the (non)-observation of an institutional rule (Greif 2006). However, we know that institutional rules may be followed due to deeply held beliefs and internalized social norms. Moreover, the relationship between organizations and institutional rules only enters the analytical picture in a simple way by assuming that actors seek to maximize their institutional power. This does not fully grasp the complex relationship between organizations and institutional rules. Thus the change of an institutional rule may be strongly influenced by the vested interests actors have in their own positions in an organization needed to apply the institutional rule. As a result, they would resist any change of the institutional rule questioning their relative weight and organizational position under a revised institutional rule. The price of conceiving of motivation and organization as elements of institutions in that simplified sense, however, needs to be paid for methodological reasons. To focus on all possible dimensions of institutions simultaneously would overload the explanatory design of institutional change by trying to accommodate too many variables at the same time (Greif 2006).

In sum, institutional rules as used in this book are rules of behaviour in a society or constraints created by human actors that shape, reshape, and constrain social interaction (North 1990*a*: 3). Together with their enforcement characteristics, they define the incentive structure of societies (North 1996: 344). The fact that institutional rules are shaped by human actors, but at the same time restrict and influence human behaviour, constitutes the *dual face of institutions* (North 1990*a*: 3). This means that when we seek to explain institutional change, institutions may be causal factors. But at the same time institutions are also the object of explanation. At the moment of the *initial* institutional design, institutions do not constrain actors. They are chosen in the light of existing alternatives. But once institutions exist, in the processes of subsequent change, they do constrain actors. 'They are both, exogenous and endogenous to actors' choice' (Snidal 1996: 127).

3.2. INSTITUTIONAL CHANGE

What happens once an institutional rule has been established? Does it change over a longer-term period, and if yes, why, how and with what outcome? Two perspectives are taken throughout the book: a 'process perspective' and a 'structural perspective'. The process perspective looks at the factors driving institutional change, the underlying causal processes and their outcomes and tries to theorize them. It also seeks to identify typical sequences of distinct types of changes. The structural perspective, by contrast, looks at the different *levels and arenas* of decision-making across which change occurs. It also focuses on the *types of (organizational) actors* involved in the process, distinguishing between actors designing and implementing these rules.

From the process perspective different types of *processes of change* are addressed, conceptualized, and theorized. How does the change happen? What are the underlying driving forces? Thus, just to mention a few possibilities, the process driving change may be a process of bargaining of explicit nature, that is the negotiators are sitting around a table and are bargaining over an institutional change; or they may bargain in a more implicit way (Sebenius 1992) in which actors are engaged in strategic interaction without making explicit offers and counter-offers, but nonetheless bring their power to bear in the interaction in order to achieve particular outcomes. A different underlying process of institutional change may be a competition among different institutional forms. The competitive process may 'crowd out' some institutional rules because actors opt for rival institutions that are on offer. This may lead to the disappearance of some institutional rules and the persistence of others. It is one objective of the book to discuss and empirically illustrate under which scope conditions different theoretical accounts of institutional change are more or less powerful in explaining particular stages in a longer-term institutional development of selected institutional rules in the European Union.

A question directly linked to the analysis of the process concerns the factors triggering a change of institutions. Are these causal factors *exogenous* and constitute an *ex ante* defined changed parameter (such as a completed round of enlargement of the European Union by x new members), that is a change of preferences of the designing actors, or a change in the institutional environment which is itself not due to the process of institutional change to be accounted for? (Jones 2001: 194). Or is it *endogenous* in the sense that the institutional properties at t1 set into motion a causal process producing altered institutional properties at t2 without outside influence? (Caporaso forthcoming). Because '. . . institutional rules are not infrequently ambiguous, and individual participants can, in effect, take advantage of this ambiguity to redefine the institution "on the fly"?' (Jones 2001: 194), such an endogenous change may occur.

Another process-related question addresses the question of typical links between distinct types of institutional change over a long-term period. Is, to mention just one possibility, a period of redesigning of institutions triggered by a new external problem pressure, followed by a period of endogenous rebargaining of an institutional rule to adjust it to the needs of implementing actors? If yes, how could this be captured in theoretical terms?

The *structural perspective* focuses on *levels, arenas, and types of actors*. Institutions structure behaviour at different levels: actors at the higher-order or constitutional level establish institutional rules about collective choices at the lower-order rule level (Kiser and Ostrom 1982: 209–10; Ostrom 1990). The question is whether institutional change cuts across two different levels or arenas and what is the nature of the link between the two? Does the cutting across levels/arenas have an accelerating, slowing-down, or compensating effect on institutional change? One level can also have a constraining impact on choice at other levels (Kiser and Ostrom 1982: 213). Thus, higher-order or constitutional rules determine, enforce, or alter the institutional rules at a lower level and define the set of acceptable strategies and the ways to deal with deviators of all kinds (Sened 1991: 385). But, as we will see, the interpretation and specification of higher-order rules at the lower level may also feed back into higher-order changes. Another mechanism linking levels is conflict resolution: higher-level adjudication may solve conflicts between lower-order rules (Stone Sweet 1998, 1999). The adjudication outcome then guides the subsequent application of lower-order rules. Another structural perspective relates to the *types of actors* involved in the rule-making: which actors are 'designing actors', that is formally responsible for the adoption of an institutional rule; and which actors are 'implementing actors' (or affected actors), that is charged with and affected by the daily application of the institutional rule?[1] Institutional rules are the result of a process of collective choice of the designing actors, that impose their rules on the implementing actors (and affected actors) (Moe 2005: 220). A discrepancy between the designing actors of an institutional rule and its distributive implications and the implementing actors (and those affected by the rule in society at large) may constitute an important source of institutional change.

The *process* perspective, that is process (exogenously or endogenously driven), and sequence, and the *structural* perspective, viewing change across levels, arenas, and distinguishing designing from implementing actors, are taken throughout the book when discussing the different rational institutionalist theories of institutional change and the empirical cases in the light of the theories.

Which are the major rational institutionalist theories accounting for institutional change? What are the underlying arguments accounting for change and under which particular conditions are they particularly apt to explain a particular type of institutional change?

---

[1] As Jones emphasizes 'A major reason that institutional reforms fail to perform as well as expected is that designers do not pay much attention to how the incentives they create or alter are likely to be received by participants in the institution' (Jones 2001: 194).

3.3. INSTITUTIONAL CHANGE: RATIONAL
CHOICE INSTITUTIONALISM

Rational choice explanations for institutional change may roughly be divided into a *functional (intentional)*[2] approach which views institutions as an efficient and stable solution to a particular collective action problem (Williamson 1975; Keohane 1984; Weingast and Marshall 1988); a rational (non)-intentional evolutionary approach viewing the outcome of institutional change as a selection and adjustment process; and a *power-based political bargaining approach* considering *distributional outcomes* (Knight 1992; Moe 2005) in order to account for institutional change.[3] Actors are assumed to be self-interested and goal oriented (individual rationality assumption), to engage in repeated interactions with other actors and to have enough information to assess the likely outcomes of various strategies.[4] The functionalist and the distributive bargaining-oriented approach further assumes that rational actors intentionally choose institutional rules, while the evolutionary approach is based on an assumption of non-intentionality.[5]

[2] As opposed to the spontaneous emergence notion of convention/institution which is a non-intentional outcome of repeated social interaction (see Knight 1992; Schotter 1981).

[3] Since the topic of this book is the change of institutional rules governing political decision-making processes, the literature on property rights is not included. Property rights define the rights of actors to use valuable assets. It is true that the property rights literature also recognizes that individuals seek to improve their positions not only by 'investing in economic activity within a given framework of institutions, but also, in the long run through altering the institutional framework' (Eggertsson 1996: 17). The economics of institutions uses the term property rights differently from law to define the rights of an actor to use valuable assets (Alchian 1965). Property rights enable private persons or groups to control resources that might otherwise be controlled politically. To guarantee that these rights to use, sell, rent, profit from, and exclude others from particular resources, are recognized, requires that rulers allow persons other than themselves to exercise control over valuable resources (Riker and Sened 1996: 283). The property rights of an actor may be expressed in formal rules and in social norms and customs. The ability of an actor to use valuable resources derives both from external control and from internal control. External control depends on the property rights of an actor or how her 'institutional environment'—constitutions, statutes, regulations, norms, enforcement and sanctions—constrains and directs both the actor in question and outsiders. Internal control is established by the actors themselves through various investments aimed at gaining control over scarce resources, involving monitoring, fencing, hiring private guards, checking reputations, and other measures. The term transaction costs refers to an actor's opportunity cost of establishing and maintaining internal control of resources' (Eggertsson 1996: 8).

[4] Rationality is understood as intentionality as opposed to non-intentionality. Intentionality may in a minimal way be understood as consistency of goals. The consistency of goals attribute may distinguish between process-oriented and substantive rationality. The substance-oriented rationality may be divided into materially oriented as opposed to non-materially oriented maximizing of goals (see, e.g., Elster 1989*a*, 1989*b*).

[5] However, this assumption is contested to some degree within the evolutionary approach; see p. 15. We need to differentiate between functional design and *intentional* rationalist accounts

What are the basic arguments presented by the different strands of rationalist institutionalism with respect to the change of institutional rules? These questions will be tackled from the perspectives of the underlying *causal process* driven *by exogenous or endogenous factors*, the *sequence* of distinct types of changes, the *levels and arenas of decision-making* and the *types of actors* (*designing or implementing*) involved in the shaping of the institutional rules. While the *process* perspective and, linked to it, the *exogeneitiy/endogeneity and sequence* aspects are discussed as inherent elements of the theories, the *levels/arenas and type of actors* perspective are discussed separately in special sections.

3.3.1. Functional Rationalist Explanation

The functionalist approach to institutional change conceives of institutions as an outcome of an attempt to solve a collective action problem. Institutional rules are created to guarantee efficiency and stability in the solution of a particular collective action problem. I will start with the notion of institution as an equilibrium and, therefore, self-enforcing rule in dealing with coordination problems, then outline the need for institutional rules in order to prevent defection in solving a cooperation problem.

In a first step, institutions are created or designed by actors that view institutions as an efficient and stable solution to a particular coordination problem (where all stand to gain from collective action) (Williamson 1975; Keohane 1984; Weingast and Marshall 1988). The goal-oriented actors are states, or

for institutional change on the one hand and non-intentional *evolutionary* accounts on the other. Thus Dowding (2000) distinguishing between evolutionary explanations and intentional explanations defines an evolutionary explanation as 'specifying any non-intentional selection mechanism by which policies are generated' (Dowding 2000: 75). Evolutionary rational choice theory as a theory of institutional change combines a selection model with an adjustment model. Change is assumed to be 'blind', i.e. the product of a constant interplay between actors and their social, political, and economic environments. Nelson, in his evolutionary theory, criticizes the theory of the pure profit-maximizing theory of firms in a market and emphasizes that firms make decisions based on routines representing 'good enough' (Simon 1957) adjustments to the given economic environment. The best routines, in our case the best institutional rules, will spread among collectivities by an increasing imitation of the successful rules and selecting out of the unsuccessful ones (Nelson and Winter 1982; Kay 2003: 108). Kerr, too, considers evolutionary explanations as a corrective to intentional explanation in political science, however, argues that no clear distinction is possible and that both adaptation and selection, the key mechanisms in the evolutionary approach, can be intentional, too. This version of evolutionary theory brings it very close to functionalist institutionalism. Thus when Kerr argues that evolutionary theory places actors '...within their structured context and...emphasise(s) that this context places limitations on the choices, preferences and autonomy which agents have...' (Dowding 2001; Kerr 2003: 124).

individuals. They are considered to be unified actors that are clearly defined and assumed to be given in the analysis. Their level of information and the degree of certainty about likely outcomes are specified. Actors are assumed to have symmetrical power. The institutional issues to be decided on are well defined. In its most simple form the design of a new institution involves searching alternative institutional options, linked with costs of information. The (deductive) explanation of an institution as an outcome begins with a description of an anticipated social event or collective action problem, and the rules of strategic interaction (the game), that is the set of players involved, the strategies/actions they can undertake and the outcomes, or payoffs associated with each strategy undertaken by the participants (Schotter 1981: 11). The outcome of the strategic interaction is an institutional solution which for the involved actors represents an equilibrium[6] (Sened 1991: 394)[7] and as such is stable. In repeated interactions, actors continue '...to change their planned responses to the actions of others until no improvement can be obtained in their expected outcomes from independent action' (Crawford and Ostrom 1995: 582). The *underlying causal process* bringing an institution about is strategic interaction leading to an equilibrium. All players, by definition, are interested to maintain the institution once an equilibrium has been reached. For, given the strategies of all other players, no player would be better off with another institution than the rule that has been established. The institutions-as-equilibria approach (Riker 1980; Schotter 1981; Calvert 1992: 17) focuses on the stability that can arise from mutually understood actor preferences and optimizing behaviour (Crawford and Ostrom 1995: 582). They do not require outside enforcement nor a commitment to some value to follow the rules (Crawford and Ostrom 1995: 583) because all actors have an incentive to cooperate because they all gain equally from abiding by the rule; no institutional provisions of control and sanctioning are necessary to secure coordination.

   Going, in a second step, beyond this notion of institutions as equilibria and, therefore, self-enforcing institutional rules solving a coordination problem

---

   [6] An equilibrium includes three different aspects: the technologically determined external constraints, humanly devised external constraints (rules of the game), and constraints developed within the game through patterns of behaviour and the creation of expectations (equilibrium conception of institution) (Snidal 1996: 128).
   [7] Sened (1991: 394) and Greif and Laitin stress that an equilibrium behaviour is self-enforcing. If members of a society share the beliefs that the institutional rule will be observed, each actor is motivated to follow it as well. Equilibrium analysis thus represents the interdependencies between one actor's optimal behaviour and the expected behaviour of the others actors. A self-enforcing institution comprises shared beliefs that correspond to a self-enforcing behaviour and expected behaviour (Greif 1994; Calvert 1995).

from which all participant actors gain, it has been emphasized that many collective action problems, while *overall* efficiency increasing and allowing actors *in the aggregate* to gain the benefits of joint activity, are confronted with the problem of defection. A cooperation problem emerges in solving the collective action problem because individual actors may be tempted to freeride on the contributions of the other actors. In order to prevent freeriding, explicit institutional rules are adopted, spelling out the rules of cooperation in order to make defection or other forms of opportunistic behaviour more unlikely. These rules provide information on actors' likely behaviour, punish defection, or shift authority from one actor to another to reduce the incentives or opportunity not to observe the rules. It is the mutual gains from cooperation that drive actors to create institutional rules that bind their own hands and limit opportunism (Lake 2004: 3–4).

Thus, the functional approach draws the attention to different types of problems with which collective action is confronted (see, e.g., Martin 1992). Attributes of events and goods[8] shape individuals' decision-making incentives (Kiser and Ostrom 1982: 195). Thus in a situation where individuals might be tempted to freeride on the contributions of others (prisoners' dilemma), institutions are needed to monitor compliance and impose sanctions in case of defection. Or in the case of 'assurance' problems, where all want to cooperate in principle, but actors are not certain of the other participants' intentions because they do not have the necessary information about the other actors' intentions (Martin 1998; Snidal 2004); or if actors agree to cooperate in principle, but cannot agree on the best way to achieve the agreed on goal (game of the sexes). In all cases institutional rules are needed to provide necessary information about actors' intentions, controlling actors' behaviour, and applying sanctions in case of defection.

Given a particular collective action problem, there usually are a number of ways in which social interactions among the involved actors may be structured. By establishing one of the possible institutional rules as *the* authoritative institutional rule (Knight 1995: 98), particular constraints and

---

[8] See also Kiser and Ostrom distinguishing between attributes of events of decision situations specifying the nature of goods at stake. Public goods (non-rival consumption and accessibility), common pool resources (rival consumption and accessibility), club goods (non-rival consumption and limited accessibility), and private goods (rival consumption and limited accessibility) are linked with different incentives as regards individual provider and user behaviour, hence also a need of different institutional rules to secure cooperation (Kiser and Ostrom 1982: 195). Olson (1965) has shown that non-subtractable (i.e. non-rival consumption) and non-excludable public goods (free access) present serious problems for collective action. Individuals are more likely to choose a freeriding strategy in large-group situation than a small-group situation.

possibilities are introduced. Thus Krasner (1991) has developed a functionalist argument for the establishing of international institutions. The latter
facilitate cooperation among states, moving states from the status quo to the
'Pareto frontier' on which all involved actors, given the strategies available
to the other actors, could not choose a better institutional solution than
the existing institutional rule. Optimal institutions lie on the Pareto frontier and the rationalist functionalist explanation seeks to identify variables
that move states closer to the optimal or overall efficiency-increasing solutions on the Pareto frontier (Haas 1958; Keohane 1984; Lake 1999; Mattli
1999).

   Which explanation of institutional *change* can be derived from this first
model of rationalist functional institutional theory? *Institutional change should
ensue when at least one actor has an incentive to reconsider the existing institutional rule and propose an altered rule that is more advantageous for her than
the existing one* (Lake 2004: 3). The reasons why one actor or several actors
press for such a change of the existing institutional rule may be manifold.
One reason could be a change of the capabilities of an individual actor, such
as an increase in population or wealth of an individual member state in the
European Union inducing the state to ask for more votes in the European
decision-making process. The causes of the change in capabilities are not
itself accounted for by the model explaining the institutional change, but
exogenously defined as a revised parameter.

3.3.2. Including Transaction Costs

The new economic institutionalism has widened the functional rational choice
model (of neoclassical economics) by including transaction costs. Coase
(1960) established the link between institutions, transaction costs, and neoclassical theory.[9] Efficient markets and actors' agreements in market processes
are reached only when it is costless to transact, that is to bargain. However, in
reality the informational and institutional requirements necessary to achieve
such efficient results are considerable. Actors must have objectives and know
how to realize them. At the outset this is frequently not the case. Rather
actors go through information feedback movements and correct their initially
wrong action-objective models (North 1990*a*: 344). Thus, a more gradual
functionalist view of the emergence of institutions was developed, distinct
from the perfect-information based, efficiency-oriented functional rationalist

---

[9] See among many others Furubotn and Richter (1997), Foss (1995), Eggertsson (1996),
Alchian and Demsetz (1972), North (1981, 1990*a*), and Demsetz (1988).

theory. Because of actors' lack of information and uncertainty about the environment, institutional rules are unlikely to work exactly the way they were designed to work.[10] Thus, North, assuming bounded rationality and emphasizing the costs for the search of information, takes transaction costs into account and views processes of institutional change as occurring in repeated interactions. Information is deepened and learning takes place that leads to merely incremental change of institutional rules. Transaction costs, however, are not only taken into account by modifying the assumption of a high level of actor information, that is introducing bounded rationality[11] or incomplete information, emphasizing the costs for the search of information (Stigler 1961; Alchian 1965). Rather, transaction costs also arise from the choice process itself. There are costs of communication, bargaining, and securing compliance because of the divergent preferences of the involved actors and indeed actors' opportunism, that is the strategic misrepresentation of information and intentions in order to secure a better outcome for themselves (Williamson 1985; Petersen 1995).

What triggers institutional *change* from this view of institutional change including transaction costs? Again a process of change would be initiated if one or more actors seek alternative institutional rules that are more favourable for them. The changed view of the extant institutional rule may be caused by changes in the external environment which indicate serious gaps of information about external circumstances that need updating. The improved information may commend another institutional rule and therefore initiate the search for a new institutional solution for collective action problems. Or a particular institutional solution may have proved to be difficult to monitor and secure compliance with, that is the transaction costs of monitoring the rule have proven to be excessive.

Depending on the particular problem type at hand—as distinguished above—institutional solutions call for a higher or lower extent of monitoring or sanctioning. Thus Martin's analysis (1992) shows that different types of problems demand different institutional rules: 'only' the provision of information and communication in the case of coordination problems; monitoring and enforcement in the case of cooperation problems where there is a problem of defection. Transaction costs are particularly high in the case of collective

---

[10] Lohmann argues that 'if it is hard for us to correct institutions once they are in place, it makes sense for institutions to be designed to self-correct or break down when appropriate' (Lohmann 2003: 99; see also Koremenos 2005).

[11] The Simon—Williamson approach of bounded rationality focuses on the decision process but retains the assumptions of purposive action and (limited) rationality (Simon 1957; Williamson 1985).

action problems of the type of the prisoners' dilemma, where actors have an incentive to defect on the agreed institutional solution in order to achieve short-term individual benefits. To give an example, although actors may have decided to abolish trade barriers in the form of tariffs to increase trade among themselves, individual actors may be tempted to reintroduce hidden trade barriers during implementation and thus benefit from the rule abidance of others without contributing themselves to the production of the collective good (i.e. a free trade area). This poses serious enforcement problems that can only be dealt with by carefully designed monitoring and sanctioning mechanisms (Mitchell and Keilbach 2001: 894–5). Coordination problems, by contrast, as mentioned above, are not only easily agreed on because all gain from an institutional rule, but are also self-implementing, hence do not cause enforcement costs. A case in point is technical norms, where it does not really matter around which norm, or focus point (Bates 1988) coordination occurs as long as coordination occurs at all. Since all gain from the coordination, there is no incentive to defect during implementation (Krasner 1991; Martin 1992).

To reiterate, from a functional efficiency—and transaction cost oriented— viewpoint, the factors explaining the (re)designing of institutions are the wish to seek mutual gains from cooperation and make actors bind their own hands and forsake opportunism. The desired effects of an institution are directly linked with their emergence and persistence (Pierson 2000*a*, 2000*b*). But how does this theory account for institutional change? The very factors responsible for the initial creation of an institution plus the consideration of the transaction costs caused by the redesigning of the existing institution, that is seeking information, engaging in a bargaining process, will explain *changes* in existing institutions. However, as Frieden argues, proponents of this argument should not work back from identifiable institutional effects to determine the initial preferences of the actors engaged in the shaping of the institutional rule (Frieden 1999: 49; see also Elster 1989*a*, 1989*b*). In order to avoid *ex post* hypothesizing when formulating a functionalist hypothesis and to wrongly derive preferences from outcomes, it is crucial to *ex ante* define the preferences of the involved actors.

In short, the functionalist rationalist explanation of institutional change that includes transaction costs argues that actors will change an existing institutional rule if the prospective benefits of the new institutional rule minus the costs of developing the new rule (bargaining and information costs) and the costs of securing compliance with the new rule exceed the benefits of the existing institutional rule (minus its transaction costs). The costs of creation are already 'sunk' (Lake 2004: 2). The estimation of the costs of change sums the institutional options in comparison, taking into account that actors must '...exit an institution, write a new set of rules, and suffer the uncertainty of an untested design' (Lake 2004: 2). Information and incentives resulting from the prior operation of the institutional rule are compared to the prospective, changed institutional rule (Jupille 2004*b*: 14).

But why, from this theoretical viewpoint including transaction costs, would there be discontent with the existing rule in the first place? The trigger of change may lie in increased transaction costs of bargaining, collecting information, and securing compliance. But why would the bargaining, information, and compliance costs increase? The reason for the altered transaction costs are not explained by the model itself, but are caused exogenously. To give an example: transaction costs in solving a collective action problem under unanimity rule are likely to rise if an increasing number of actors with divergent preferences are involved who have a say in solving the collective action problem. As a result, bargaining becomes more lengthy and complicated. Implementation becomes more costly, too, because the higher number of involved actors renders compliance control more difficult. Take the example of a rule governing the use of a common pool resource.[12] It is obvious that an increasing number of actors with different preferences participating in the joint use and deciding on the basis of unanimity will make decision-making more lengthy, that is the transactions costs in terms of negotiation time increase (Ostrom 1990; Gardner and Ostrom 1991). With increasing transaction costs, the overall benefit of solving the collective action problem based on unanimity rule decreases. The changed cost–benefit relationship of the use of the unanimity rule may lead to a questioning of the viability of the institutional rule under the changed circumstances and give rise to a call for institutional change, for example the adoption of a qualified majority rule. The ultimate reason for the increase of the transaction costs, that is more actors who are participating in decision-making process, is *exogenous*. The increase in number is not explained by the model accounting for institutional change (Rittberger 2003*b*).

Increased transaction costs of negotiations may also derive from a value shift that has occurred in the social environment. This value shift may make the rule seem outdated or not viable any more. The implication is that the costs of monitoring and enforcement will rise if the rule is to be observed. To use an example: a particular rule allowing for private ownership of natural resources (e.g. access to a water body) has lost in societal support because of a value shift emphasizing the importance of public access to natural resources. As a result, the transaction costs for securing the implementation of the rule

---

[12] Characterized by free access and at the same time exhaustibility of resources, i.e. rival consumption.

will rise and lead to a reconsideration of the validity of the institutional rule. Rising transaction costs of monitoring compliance with a rule and sanctioning non-compliance may also flow from changed technical or physical circumstances in the external environment. Altered external conditions may offer a temptation to defect from the existing institutional rules, and actors will either 'bolster their ability to sanction cheaters or, potentially, abandon cooperation entirely' (Lake 2004: 3–4). For instance, if one actor experiences a drastic rise in economic wealth, she might consider not to abide by the community rules because unilateral action might seem more beneficial. In consequence, the other actors, in turn, might consider a change of the valid rules in order to force the defecting actor to comply with the existing institutional rule.

In summary, if the number of actors with divergent preferences involved in the negotiation of institutional solutions has increased (exogenous change), one would expect higher transaction costs and in consequence steps to revise the existing institutional rules. Or if a change in values regarding the observation of existing rules has occurred (exogenous event) and the control of rule abidance has become much more costly, there is an incentive to engage in renegotiations of the existing institutional rules. Similarly, if external conditions have changed in such a way as to facilitate defection, actors will seek to engineer more stringent rules allowing for controlling the compliance with the rules, or abandon cooperation altogether. The trigger of the wish to change the extant institutional rule, the altered transaction costs, in all cases lies outside the explanatory model, that is is exogenous.

The above theoretical arguments based on the functionalist institutionalist argument including transaction costs lead to the hypothesis

H: Functionalist transaction cost-based hypothesis
'If an external event has decreased the gains of institutional rule A (benefits minus transaction costs), the rule will be changed if the net gains expected of a changed rule B, including the transaction costs of negotiating the institutional revision, collecting information and maintaining the new rule are higher than the net-benefits of the existing institutional rule A.'

Or in simpler words:

'If, due to an external event, the benefits of rule A have decreased, the rule will be changed, if the gains of the proposed altered rule B including the transaction costs will be higher.'

Taking a longer time perspective an exogenous shock would trigger the wish to redesign the existing institutional rule. This event would be followed by a phase of relative institutional stability. This period of stability, in turn, might be disturbed by new exogenous changes forcing a redesigning of the existing institutional rules (Krasner 1988). According to this punctuated equilibrium type of sequence argument one would expect

H: Exogenous shock inducing institutional change
'An exogenous shock exerts pressure to redesign the existing institutional rule after considering transaction costs.'

and

'An event of institutional redesigning is followed by a period of relative stability.'

and

'A new external shock forces to reconsider the extant (redesigned) institution taking transaction costs into account.'

The attempt to buffer the influence of external shocks on institutional rules is described by Koremenos. In her theory of *flexible institutional design*, she shows that introducing flexibility clauses into an institutional rule/contract allows for the adjustment to unanticipated exogenous shocks. She argues that since cooperation is plagued by uncertainty, actors tend to conclude the best agreements they can using available information. However, there are events beyond their control after the agreements have been signed that cannot be predicted. Therefore, actors tend to insure themselves against uncertainty concerning the distribution of future gains from an agreement.[13] In order to meet the concerns of uncertainty, clauses of flexibility are introduced that make it possible to adjust to shocks and to correct the changes in the distribution of gains caused by external shocks. Koremenos distinguishes between

---

[13] With respect to institutional rules such shocks would mainly be of political nature. Koremenos assumes that the actors know the distribution of gains in the current period, but know only the probability distribution for the distributions of gains in all future periods. 'The distribution of gains in each period equals the distribution of gains in the previous period and a random shock. These random shocks are cumulative. Put simply, a shock to the distribution of gains occurs in each period. As a result, either the gains to one state increase relative to that of the other or, possibly, there is no change, if the shock equals zero. These shocks have two important features. First, they are completely random. Each shock is independent of every other, both before and after. They are also independent of everything else that the states can observe, which implies that they cannot be predicted, either at the time an initial agreement is made or later on. Second, the shocks add up over time, i.e. the gain for a state in any one period is the sum of its initial gain plus each of the subsequent changes. Because the random shocks are cumulative ... it is possible to the states' relative shares to evolve in a different way that differs quite substantially from the assumed equal division at the start of the agreement.... The extent or importance of the uncertainty about the distribution of gains is summarized by the variance of the shocks. The larger the variance, the greater and more important is the uncertainty. Moreover, the larger the variance, the farther the distribution of gains will depart from its initial value, on average, over a given time. Finally, I employ a standard assumption in international relations that states are risk averse' (Koremenos 2005: 550).

escape clauses, renegotiation clauses, and provisions of finite duration of a rule. Escape clauses allow actors to temporarily opt-out of the institutional rule without leaving the agreement entirely; renegotiation clauses provide for a renegotiation of the entire contract at a pre-defined point in time; and finite duration provides for the expiration of the contract at a pre-defined point in time. Thanks to such provisions institutional rules can adjust to changing external circumstances during the duration of an institutional rule (Koremenos 2005: 550–2).

From these theoretical considerations one would expect that

H: Institutional rules with in-built flexibility
'If institutional rules have in-built flexibility clauses, an external shock does not induce a change of the institutional rule.'
'With an opt-out rule, an external shock does not lead to a change of the institutional rule.'
'With a re-negotiation clause, by contrast, an external shock will lead to a change of the institutional rule.'

While Koremenos accounts for a stability of rules due their in-built flexibility or their renegotiation within the existing rule framework, a more *gradual view of continuous change* is taken by North (1990a, 1990b). He contends that rule change is an incremental process, in which information regarding the environment is improved leading to small institutional modifications, a gradual learning process. Since actors' knowledge is imperfect, the learning of actors, according to North, from new knowledge and new information constitutes the most important source of institutional change. He also argues that the rate of learning[14] is higher when there is a competitive relationship among actors[15] (North 1990a: 346).[16] Information is continuously renewed and adjusted into strategic interactions. Institutional change is a consequence of the choices that individual actors and entrepreneurs of organizations make everyday on the basis of an improved information feedback from the environment. While the vast majority of these decisions are routine, some also involve important institutional rules of collective action of individuals and organizations. Sometimes the redefining of these rules can be accomplished within the existing institutional rules. But sometimes an explicit reform of

---

[14] Learning 'is an incremental process filtered by the culture of a society as the stock of accumulated knowledge that determines the perceived pay-offs' (North 1990a: 349).

[15] Competition, reflecting scarcity of resources, induces actors to learn in order to survive (North 1990: 346).

[16] North argues that 'it is necessary to dismantle the rationality assumption underlying economic theory in order to approach constructively the nature of human learning' (North 1990: 346).

the rules is necessary (North 1990*a*: 346). The trigger of institutional change lies in the additional and new information drawn from the external environment.

H: Updating of information and increasing knowledge as sources of gradual institutional change
'New knowledge in the environment of an institutional rule (external and behavioural)[17] leads to a gradual transformation of this rule in the light of newly gained information.'

Based on the same assumption of actors' limited information on their environment as well as the behaviour of interacting partners, Abbott and Snidal (2000) develop a longer-term model of gradual institutional change for the context of an anarchic environment in international relations. Given the 'anarchic nature' of the international environment, institutional rules tend to be more open-ended and have more of a framework character. This is because actors are not willing to commit themselves to the same extent as they would in a well-known environment, such as the nation state. Therefore, they argue, in international relations choosing an institutional rule is initially more a decision to follow a particular *procedure for developing institutional rules* than a substantive rule. Accordingly, they distinguish three paths to arrive at institutional rules. In the case of the first path (that they call 'framework conventions'), actors agree on legally binding institutional rules that cover however only limited substantive areas, but include a wide range of participants of a limited 'Aim' (actions and outcomes to be applied to), but widely defined 'Attribute' (actors targeted) (Crawford and Ostrom 1995). In the case of the second path (that they call 'plurilateral agreements'), actors agree on binding institutional rules defining significant substantive commitments, but include only few actors a widely defined 'Aim', but a narrowly defined 'Attribute' (Crawford and Ostrom 1995). In the case of the third path (that they call 'soft law'), the actors agree on significant substantive content, a widely defined 'Aim', that is however not legally binding, a 'must' Deontic without an 'Or Else', that is sanctions linked to the prescription (Crawford and Ostrom 1995) targeted at a large number of actors (Attribute—Crawford and Ostrom 1995; Snidal 2004: 12). All three pathways have modest beginnings: the framework convention is 'hollow' because it does not contain much substance, the soft law rule is weak because it is not mandatory, the plurilaterally agreed institutional rule is limited to a small number of members. Limited cognitive capacity and different types of uncertainty explain why actors move to cooperation along

---

[17] 'External' refers to external events, such as enlargement, 'behavioural' refers to the behaviour of other actors.

different pathways in particular stages. If actors do not know enough about the problem in a technical sense, they hesitate to engage in full cooperation. If actors do not know if the other participants are truly interested in cooperation and would comply with an institutional rule, they would equally be reluctant to commit themselves. If actors are uncertain about the reactions in the domestic political arena, they equally hesitate (Snidal 2004: 13). With some modifications, they would engage in the following sequence of institutional rules of cooperation.

In a first phase, they decide to cooperate in principle without fleshing out substantive areas of cooperation. Through the gradual accumulation of knowledge regarding their cooperation partners' behaviour they gradually start trusting each other if the partners prove to be reliable. In a next step, they proceed to a phase in which they design areas of substantive cooperation without binding rules; in another stage, with even deeper knowledge about each other, they extend substantive areas of cooperation and make rules of cooperation mandatory. The point is that, an initially weak institutional rule might get a cooperative process going because actors face only a limited loss of autonomy by subjecting themselves to the institutional rules. Over time—with increasing knowledge about actors' reliability, decreasing technical uncertainty, and decreasing political uncertainty, the 'soft' institutional rules may turn into 'hard' institutional rules (Snidal 2004: 13). According to this argument we may therefore expect that

H: *Decreasing uncertainty and deepening rules*
'With decreasing uncertainty (actor related, technical, political) soft institutional rules of cooperation tend to be changed into more constraining institutional rules.'

3.3.3. Contract Approach and Principal–Agent Theory

One important variant of the functional approach to institutional change which includes transaction costs is the *contract approach* of institutions. The contract, the institutional rule, is based on a voluntary agreement, an exchange among actors that facilitates mutually beneficial outcomes. Again there are transaction costs in the establishment and enforcement of the institution. The higher the transaction costs involved in an exchange, that is negotiation, information, and securing compliance, the lower the level of benefits enjoyed by the contracting actors (Knight 1995: 105). The pressure to change the existing institution again originates in the external environment. If the relevant external conditions remain stable the institution will remain viable. If they change, the relative benefits of the contract will be affected. As a consequence, the involved actors will consider a change of the existing institutional rule that will produce larger aggregate benefits. If these additional benefits are not lower than the transaction costs involved in changing the present contract, the rule will be changed (Knight 1995: 106). As with all voluntary exchanges, contracts are most likely to emerge when potential benefits are high and the transaction costs of developing, negotiating, monitoring, and enforcing the political contract are low (Heckathorn and Maser 1987; Taylor and Singleton 1993; Lubell et al. 2002).

One of the most prominent theories of the functional contract theory of institutions is *principal–agent theory* (McCubbins and Schwartz 1984; Moe 1982, 1984; Lupia and McCubbins 2000).[18] According to this theory at least two actors, the principal and the agent, draw up a contract. The principal engages the agent to perform some task on her behalf because the principal lacks the expertise to perform the task and wants to secure credibility in task performance over time. To this end, she delegates some decision-making authority to the agent. It is assumed that the individual rationality of the actors is bounded (Aghion and Tirole 1997) and that information between the principal and the agent is asymmetric. It is also assumed that it is too costly for the principal to directly monitor the agent's actions ('hidden actions'— Arrow 1985: 38) and that the principal cannot acquire knowledge of the agent's unique observational information (hidden information—Arrow 1985: 38; Furubotn and Richter 1997: 148). Therefore, by delegating the principal faces two risks of 'agency loss': adverse selection and moral hazard. The principal, before contract conclusion, may select the wrong agent because the latter withholds information about herself and her skills (adverse selection). After contract conclusion, the information asymmetry implies that, since the agent's actions are not directly observable by the principal, the agent may engage in 'shirking', that is go beyond the tasks specified by the principal. Or 'slippage' may occur, that is the agent behaves differently from what the principal would wish (Pollack 2003: 26). Both constitute moral hazards due to asymmetric information that emerge *after* contract conclusion.

Aghion and Tirole (1997) develop the cost–benefit calculations that the principal engages in when interacting with the agent. In fulfilling the contract, the agent pursues and screens 'projects' for the principal. In pursuing 'these projects', there are benefits for the principal, but also private benefits for the agent. There is no necessary congruence between the benefits of the principal and the agent. The principal seeks to make the agent converge towards her own preferences by setting the 'right' incentives. In doing so the principal has to consider whether she should in non-routine decisions try to find out about the projects the agent is engaged in or leave them to the agent. The costs for collecting information are decisive in this context. If the principal collects all

---

[18] For a critique of the use of principal—agent theory in political science see Karagiannis (2006).

the information to pursue the projects himself, there would be no need of delegation. But the principal also has to consider the incentives of the agent. If the agent collects a lot of information on projects and is then overruled by the principal, his incentives to collect information for projects in the future will weaken (Aghion and Tirole 1997).

By devising various institutional devices the principal may establish appropriate incentives for the agent to comply with the contract, such as 'police patrol' and 'fire alarm' mechanisms (McCubbins and Schwartz 1984). The principal may also create loyalty through bonding, that is the providing of pecuniary and non-pecuniary incentives to commit the agent to trustworthiness (Jensen and Meckling 1976: 308). Agency costs, in sum, result from monitoring expenditures, and bonding expenditures (Jensen and Meckling 1976: 39; Furubotn and Richter 1997: 148).[19] Analysing the costs of various institutional devices to contain agency costs,[20] McCubbins and Schwartz (1984) conclude 'police patrol', based on the regular control of the agent's activities, is rather costly, whereas 'fire alarm' mechanisms, rely on the ringing of the fire alarm by third actors (i.e. courts, the press, and non-state actors) to reveal non-compliance behaviour of the agent (McCubbins and Schwartz 1984) and are therefore less costly.[21]

[19] And the residual loss, i.e. the difference between the profit which could have accrued to the principal in the first-best solution, and the actual profit when transaction costs are positive and the agent does not truly maximize the welfare of the principal (Jensen and Meckling 1976: 39).

[20] In a comparative historical context see Margaret Levi's *Of Rule and Revenue* (1988).

[21] The functionalist contract view of institutional design based on a principal–agent relationship is extended in Lohmann's notion of 'audience' costs (Lohmann 2003: 97). This argument bears some resemblance with the monitoring activities of a principal over an agent through 'fire alarm', but goes into more detail regarding the particular aspects of the actors monitoring the agent. Lohmann argues that an institutional commitment is made between the actors shaping an institution. At the same time 'an audience' is present which observes the application of the institutional rule, watches over its observation and 'can and will ... punish institutional defections' (Lohmann 2003: 97). Committing an institutional rule to specified audience costs makes the institutional rule more credible (Lohmann 2003: 97). However, institutions are frequently monitored by audiences with different stakes, attention cues, and information sets (Lohmann 2003: 97), such as a mass audience on the one hand or a specialized functional elite on the other. A mass electorate would have information and coordination problems, therefore their punishment strategies may be less effective. By contrast, this would be easier for a functional elite (Lohmann 2003: 102–3). According to Lohmann an optimal institutional design requires that an institution is set up 'close to an ideal audience: the guardians of the guardians should have the ability and will to inflict an audience cost on the policymaker in the event of an institutional defection, thereby generating credibility; but they should also have the ability and will to excuse defections when extreme shocks or unforeseen contingencies occur, thereby allowing for flexible policy responses while minimizing the probability and cost of costly institutional breakdown' (Lohmann 2003: 103). An approximation of the 'ideal audience' can be put together by giving an institutional rule varied audiences with different stakes, attention cues, and information sets. 'Collectively, these differentiated audiences create a complex menu of audience cost' (Lohmann 2003: 105). What accounts for institutional change under this 'audience cost' theory of

Institutional change, that is the correction of the contract agreed on by the principal and the agent, is to be expected if the principal faces extensive agency loss and seeks to correct the original contract in order to reduce it. The mechanism underlying agency loss is an inherent element of principal–agent theory when it is argued that the agent—due to her function as an agent—makes empirical observations that are not accessible to the principal, hence may develop divergent preferences from the principal. To that extent one could consider a theory of institutional change based on principal–agent contract theory as containing an element of *endogenous* explanation of institutional change. The elements that account for a necessary change of the contract are incorporated into the explanatory model.

H: Agency loss as a cause of institutional change
'If the divergence between the principal's and the agent's preferences has become too large, the principal will redesign the contract, i.e. change the institutional rule in order to rein in the agent.'

As emphasized until now, all functionalist explanations of institutional change—except principal–agent theory—resorted to an *exogenous factor* to identify the factor setting off the process of change.[22] Only the principal–agent model of change by arguing that the principal's and the agent's preferences systematically tend to diverge, thereby inducing the principal to revise the contract, proposes an endogenous explanation of institutional change. However, there is also an exogenous element in this explanation since the causes of the increasing divergence in preferences of principal and agent, such as a change in the empirical observations (Furubotn and Richter 1997) of the agent in fulfilling the delegated task, are rooted in external factors.

3.3.4. Endogenizing Factors of Change: Quasi-Parameters

An attempt to systematically *endogenize* the explanation of institutional change within the functionalist approach has been developed by Greif and

institutions? Assuming that an institution has several specific audiences, the discontent of these audiences would be the trigger inducing institutional change. However, institutions should allow for some flexibility, too. As long as this flexibility of the institutional rule can be exploited by the agent without triggering a sanctioning mechanism by the audience, there will be institutional stability. If this is not the case anymore, high audience costs and imposed sanctions would force an alteration of the institutional rule. Hence it would be important to define the threshold beyond which this flexibility would not be acceptable anymore. Since it would be difficult to define this threshold in absolute terms, it very likely would depend on a possible conflict among the different audiences of an institution; the causes of these conflicts in turn are not part of the model, therefore constitute an external cause.

[22] 'Institutions change following environmental changes that is, changes in parameters exogenous to the institutions under study' (Greif and Laitin 2004: 633, 1–2).

Laitin (2004). The authors first establish under which conditions institutions are stable or self-enforcing.[23] They argue that they are self-enforcing when the actual and expected behaviour of all concerned actors generate the institutional rules that enable, coordinate, and motivate other individuals to follow the behaviour associated with the rule (Greif and Laitin 2004). This 'equilibrium' situation, as discussed above, suggests that institutional change occurs if one of the parameters as defined *ex ante* are changed (Greif and Laitin 2004). In order to endogenize institutional change within the model, the authors propose a 'dynamized model' of institutional change based on the concept of 'quasi-parameters' and the processes of institutional 'reinforcement' and 'undermining'. Institutional rules, thus the argument, over a longer period of time may influence the given parameters of the rules of the game, such as actors' information and capabilities (material wealth). The marginal changes in these parameters do not necessarily lead to a change in the institutional rules and the expected behaviour associated with these rules. For if the value of a relevant parameter only *marginally* changes, the behaviour associated with a stable institution is *not* likely to change because in such an instance actors are likely to rely on past institutions to guide them. This argument is, as the authors emphasize, closely related to the notion of path-dependence (Mahoney 2000; Pierson 2000*b*; Crouch and Farrell 2004), which states that if the environment (marginally) changes, institutions will not necessarily be altered. Rather, existing institutions may be reinforced.[24]

The crucial question, of course, would be: when is an institution reinforced? Greif and Laitin argue that an institution is reinforced when the behaviour and processes it entails, through their impact on quasi-parameters, *increase* the range of parameter values in which the institution is applied and more individuals in more and different types of situations adhere to the particular institutional rule. In the language of Crawford and Ostrom (1995), it would be an extension of the ('Attribute') dimension of an institutional rule indicating to whom the institution applies and ('Aim') dimension describing the action or outcomes to which the prescriptions of the rule apply (Crawford and Ostrom 1995). The most important mechanisms of reinforcement, according to Greif and Laitin, are of a social nature, that is through habitual action and ideology,

---

[23] Greif and Laitin only talk about institutional rules that are self-enforcing, i.e. do not have to rely on monitoring and sanctioning in order to persist. But as we have seen, some authors restrict the usage of institution to rules that require monitoring and enforcement through sanctions because there is a risk of actors not abiding by the collective action agreement.

[24] Moreover, sunk costs associated with coordinating behaviour around the existing institutional rule, free-rider problems, distributional issues may prevent coordination around a new institutional rule (Greif and Laitin 2004).

of political nature, that is laws and regulations, and of economic nature, that is through increasing returns of existing capabilities and learning (Greif and Laitin 2004). Moreover, those who benefit from existing institutions will seek to ensure their preservation.[25] The outcome is institutional stability. In short, given a marginal change in quasi-parameters of information and capabilities, an existing institutional rule may be reinforced and apply to additional new situations and individuals and *no* institutional change occurs.

But changes in quasi-parameters may also undermine existing institutions. An institution undermines itself when the changes in the quasi-parameters that it entails have the consequence that the behaviour associated to the institutional rule will be applied in a *smaller* set of situations. Gradual changes in relevant quasi-parameters and their cumulative impact eventually lead to an inconsistency between the institutional rule and the associated behaviour. The underlying mechanisms are social utopias and counter-hegemonies and a decrease in the value attributed to the future gain of cooperation (Greif and Laitin 2004). The predicted outcome under these circumstances is institutional *change*. The institutions are self-undermining and the behaviours they entail can cultivate the seeds of their own demise. But institutional change will endogenously occur only when the self-undermining process reaches a critical level such that past patterns of behaviour are no longer self-enforcing (Greif and Laitin 2004: 633).

Again, the change of the institutional rules taking place, that is a restriction or extension, may be empirically mapped along the dimensions of 'Aim' (to which actions or outcomes does the rule apply?) and 'Attribute' (to whom does the rule apply?) as described by Crawford and Ostrom (1995).

Greif and Laitin discuss the example of a small community with a rule of collective sanctioning. The rule is self-enforcing because it is a small community and members have an incentive to prove themselves to be 'good' community members. They therefore abide by the rule of behavioural prescription. The community prospers and enjoys economic success, thereby attracting new members and the community grows. However, in the larger community self-implementation of the institutional rule does not function as smoothly any longer. Information about behaviour spreads more slowly and gradually the rule stops to be self-enforcing. The very success of the application of the rule of behaviour in the context of a small community undermined its viability. The size of the community and its economic wealth are the quasi-parameters that were influenced by the institutional rule and the change of which, in the long

---

[25] In pointing out the distributional impact of institutions, Greif and Laitin take a step from a functional rationalist argument to the power-oriented distributional argument of institutional change that will be discussed in the next section.

run, led to the demise of the self-implementing rule of collective sanctioning (Greif and Laitin 2004).

This argument of endogenous institutional change leads to the hypothesis

H: Endogenous change of an institutional rule through the rule's impact on quasi-parameters
'A rule may induce a marginal change in quasi-parameters of information and capabilities and thereby reinforce the existing rule by making it applicable in new situations and additional actors. A change occurs in the Attribute and Aim dimension of the institution.'

or, on the contrary:

'A rule may induce a marginal change in quasi-parameters of information and capabilities and thereby undermine the existing rule by making it applicable to less situations and less actors. A change occurs in the Attribute and Aim dimension of the institution.'

So far the discussion of functionalist theoretical arguments in their different variants have focused on the causes and *processes* of institutional change and their theorization. What insights do we gain if we consider these theories of institutional change from the structural perspective of level/arena and types of actors?

3.3.5. Structural Perspective: Level/Arenas and Types of Actors

Considering functionalist explanations of institutional change from the *structural perspective of level/arena* it emerges that these explanations operate at one level/arena of lower or higher-order institutional rule-making, but that they may also cut across *two or several levels of rule-making*[26] and cut across arenas. This gives rise to the question: What exactly is the nature of the relationship between the rule-making at the different levels or arenas and how might a process of institutional change be affected by the nature of the link between levels or arenas?

One translation mechanism between levels pointed out by functionalist theories is the possibility of the selection among multiple lower-order rules which ensues in a *competition* among lower-order rules as the underlying motor of institutional change. The contract approach of institutional rules focuses on such a mechanism of competition. Individual exchanges produce a variety of institutional rules that may translate into a higher scale of generality

---

[26] In the terms of Kiser and Ostrom across the collective choice level and the macroinstitutional or constitutional level.

at the entire polity level. A particular form of institutional rule among all the possible options may be selected more frequently than others and therefore 'crowd out' the others and prevail over them at the higher-order level (Knight 1995: 106). Thus, Spruyt (1994*a*, 1994*b*) investigates the competition among different institutional forms, that is sovereign states, city states, and city leagues as competing institutional rules for organizing political, social, and economic life in early modern Europe. He argues that the emergence of the institution of state sovereignty reflected a selection process in the course of which the sovereign state proved to be economically efficient by facilitating credible commitments and economic exchange (Spruyt 1994*a*). This would hold only if certain preconditions are given, such as a market-like competition among institutional rules, sufficient information about the availability of alternatives and low transaction costs (Knight 1995: 107).[27] This suggests the claim

H: Competition among rules as motor of institutional change
'Given a possible choice and competition among different lower-order rules, the institutional rule most frequently selected will "crowd out" other rules and become generalized across a polity, thereby turning into a higher-order rule.'

A different functionalist argument of institutional change that is based on the fact that change cuts across levels and arenas refers to an actor's intentional change of a venue of decision-making (opting out—Oye 1992) in order to maximize the likeliness of an outcome according to her preferences. It presupposes that there are two or more possible arenas/levels for decision-making with different rules (and actor constellations) and hypothesizes that the shift from one arena to another opens prospects of obtaining a favourable outcome. Thus, Jupille conceives of a possible 'market for institutions' in international politics (Jupille 2004*b*). If on the supply side there is an increasing number and diversity of institutional options, they will compete with each other. Actors would select the institutional rule that maximizes their benefits (after considering transaction costs), that is influence and policy outcomes. As the diversity of institutional options increases one would expect stronger incentives to select the most advantageous arena with the most advantageous institutional rules and a willingness to engage in a conflict over the selection of the rule (Jupille 2004*b*: 10). This argument leads to the contention that

---

[27] Competition serves as a selection mechanism that determines the survival of various institutional forms 'on grounds of reproductive fitness. This is the logic behind the Alchian (1950) model of evolutionary competition employed by most economic analysis of institutional emergence' (Knight 1995: 106).

H: Shifting levels/arenas to accelerate institutional change
'Given a choice between different levels/arenas of decision-making, an actor, by opting out of one arena and shifting the decision to another, may improve his prospects of obtaining an institutional change according to his preferences.'

From the *type of actors' perspective*, finally, all the functionalist explanations of institutional change discussed here focus on 'designing actors', that is on the actors formally engaged in the original design and then redesigning of the institutional rule. Thus the initiative for a change of rule may result from a designing actor's change in capability. Or if the transaction costs of controlling the rule application rise, it is because the designing actors do not comply with the rule. In the functionalist delegation model, the contract between the principal and the agent is part of the original design of the contract which subsequently may be renegotiated and corrected between the contracting parties. There is a coincidence of the actors designing and re-designing the institutional rule. As we will see, the distinction between designing actors and implementing (and affected) actors will be important to explain a particular dynamic of institutional change set off by discontent implementing actors under the distributive power-based institutionalist theories.

Summary of Functional Rationalist Explanation of Institutional Change (see also Table 3.1)

H: Functionalist transaction cost-based hypothesis
'If, due to an external event, the benefits of rule A have decreased, the rule will be changed, if the gains of the proposed altered rule B including the transaction costs will be higher.'

H: Exogenous shock inducing institutional change
'An exogenous shock exerts pressure to redesign the existing institutional rule after considering transaction costs.'

and

'An event of institutional redesigning is followed by a period of relative stability.'

and

'A new external shock forces to reconsider the extant (redesigned) institution taking transaction costs into account.'

H: Updating of information and knowledge as source of gradual institutional change
'New knowledge in the environment of an institutional rule (external and behavioural)[28] leads to a gradual transformation of this rule in the light of newly gained information.'

[28] External refers to external events, such as enlargement, behavioural refers to the behaviour of other actors.

H: Agency loss as a cause of institutional change
'If the divergence between the principal's and the agent's preferences has become too large, the principal will redesign the contract, i.e. change the institutional rule in order to rein in the agent.'

H: Endogenous change of an institutional rule through the rule's impact on quasi-parameters
'A rule may induce a marginal change in quasi-parameters of information and capabilities and thereby reinforce the existing rule by making it applicable in new situations and regarding different actors. A change occurs in the Attribute and Aim dimension of the institution.'

or on the contrary:

'A rule may induce a marginal change in quasi-parameters of information and capabilities that thereby undermine the existing rule by making it applicable to less situations and less actors. A change occurs in the Attribute and Aim dimension of the institution.'

From the longer-term/sequence perspective:

H: Exogenous shock inducing institutional change
'An exogenous shock exerts pressure to redesign the existing institutional rule.'

and

'An event of institutional redesigning is followed by relative periods of stability.'
'A new external shock forces to reconsider the extant (redesigned) institution.'

H: Institutional rules with in-built flexibility
'If institutional rules have in-built flexibility clauses, an external shock does not induce a change of the institutional rule.'
'With an opt-out rule, an external shock does not lead to a change of the institutional rule.'
'With a re-negotiation clause, by contrast, an external shock will lead to a change of the institutional rule.'

H: Updating of information and increasing knowledge as sources of gradual institutional change
'New knowledge in the environment of an institutional rule (external and behavioural)[29] leads to a gradual transformation of this rule in the light of newly gained information.'

H: Decreasing uncertainty and deepening rules
'With decreasing uncertainty (actor related, technical, political) soft institutional rules of cooperation tend to be changed into more constraining institutional rules.'

---

[29] 'External' refers to external events, such as enlargement, 'behavioural' refers to the behaviour of other actors.

Table 3.1. Functionalist theories of institutional change from process and structural perspectives

Perspective	Process: causal mechanism	Source of change: exogenous/ endogenous	Links in time	Structure: level(s) arenas	Type of actors
Efficiency including transaction costs	Strategic interaction	Exogenous	Punctuated equilibrium	One	Designing actors
In-built flexibility	Bargaining	Exogenous	Adjustment through flexibility	One	Designing actors
Limited information	Updating and adjustment	Exogenous	Constant updating of info and adjustment of institutions	One	Designing actors
Decreasing uncertainty/transaction costs and change of rules	Bargaining	Endogenous	Linking different stages of institutional change	One	Designing actors
Principal–agent, contractarian including transaction costs	Negotiation	Endogenous	Agency loss leads to rule change, leads to new agency loss, leads to rule change, etc.	One	Coincidence of designing and implementing actors
Rule-induced change in parameters (quasi-parameters)	Strategic interaction	Endogenous	Rule changes quasi-parameters: q-p change rules	One	Designing actors
Decreasing uncertainty/transaction costs and change of rules	Bargaining	Endogenous	Linking different stages of institutional change	One	Designing actors
Competition among rules/selection of institutional rule	Competition	Exogenous	Crowding out of some rules, prevailing of others	Two	Designing actors
Shifting levels accelerate institutional change	Strategic interaction	Exogenous	Punctuated equilibrium	Two	Designing actors

H: Agency loss as a cause of institutional change
'If the divergence between the principal's and the agent's preferences has become too large, the principal will redesign the contract, i.e. change the institutional rule in order to rein in the agent.'

H: Endogenous change of an institutional rule through the rule's impact on quasi-parameters
'A rule may induce a marginal change in quasi-parameters of information and capabilities and thereby reinforce the existing rule by making it applicable in new situations and regarding additional actors. A change occurs in the Attribute and Aim dimension of the institution.'

or on the contrary:

'A rule may induce a marginal change in quasi-parameters of information and capabilities and thereby undermine the existing rule by making it applicable to less situations and less actors. A change occurs in the Attribute and Aim dimension of the institution.'

From the structural (level/arena and type of actor)s perspective:

H: Competition among rules as motor of institutional change
'Given a possible choice and competition among different lower-order rules, the institutional rule most frequently selected will "crowd out" other rules and become generalized across a polity, thereby turning into a higher-order rule.'

H: Shifting levels/arenas to accelerate institutional change
'Given a choice between different levels/arenas of decision-making, an actor, by opting out of one arena and shifting the decision to another, may improve his prospects of obtaining an institutional change according to his preferences.'

3.3.6. Critique of the Functionalist Explanation of Institutional Change

As we have seen, a functional explanation of institutional change focuses on the consequences of an institutional rule that are favourable, or functional, for some actor(s) who observe that institution. A successful functional explanation requires the indication of a mechanism by which the consequences uphold or maintain the institution one wants to explain (Elster 1989b; Kay 2003: 102ff). The functionalist rational institutionalist approach has been criticized on several grounds, such as

— the unrealistic assumptions of rationality, full information and the knowledge of the objective of the institutional rule;
— functionalism as an 'institution-free' theory;

— the disregarding of power and distributional effects in the decision-making process on institutional rules;
— the neglection of intended inefficiency;
— the neglection of the unintended consequences of institutional designs.

The assumption of rationality, full information, and the knowledge of the objective: While the basic rationalist account of change of an institutional rule relies on these strict assumptions of full rationality, full information, and knowledge of the objective of change, most of the present function-alist models of contract theory of institutional change and principal–agent theory[30] have released these assumptions and take into account transac-tion costs, that is the costs of collecting information, uncertainty about the objective of the change process and a more comprehensive or 'soft' notion of rationality as goal-oriented action with a prioritization of objec-tives as opposed to a strict material cost–benefit calculation based notion of rationality.

As we have seen, North criticizes that the stringent conditions that are deemed necessary to reach efficient solutions in a market are seldom given in politics. Actors are characterized by bounded rationality rather than full rationality. Actors do not know all the solutions to the problems they face, are unable to calculate the possible outcomes of these solutions, and cannot perfectly order these outcomes in their space of preferences (Simon 1982, 1987). In 'political markets' constituents exchange votes, that is electoral sup-port against policy promises of the office-holders. However, the voter has little incentive to become informed,[31] because the influence of one vote is very small. Moreover, 'the complexity of the issues produces genuine uncertainty' (North 1996: 345). Therefore, delivering on the promises is rather unlikely. Precisely because of a possible uncertainty about outcomes in the medium and longer term, the functional theory appears to be somewhat mechanistic when it predicts that a negative cost–benefit balance of an institution unavoidably leads to a change of institution. Since the *ex ante* computation of pay-offs over a longer period of time is fraught with uncertainty, it is more likely that actors learn from repeated interaction that lead to incremental change within overall stable institutions (North 1996). Therefore entirely abolishing an institution and choosing an alternative 'design' to an existing institution

[30] Or evolutionary models.
[31] In some simple, 'easy-to-measure, and important-for-constituent-well-being policies, constituents may be well informed, but beyond such straightforward policy issues ideological stereotyping takes over' (North 1996: 345).

may involve 'the opening of a Pandora's box of instability...' (Sened 1991: 398). As shown above, the releasing of the perfect information assumption and the inclusion of transaction costs take this criticism into account. In sum, the research that North has instigated insists that if only the complexity of human motivation and problems of information processing are taken into account (see, e.g. Mantzavinos 2001), the limits of the functionalist argument could be overcome. However, this argument contains a blind spot in that it neglects the power of actors (Moe 2005: 223). In a world with transaction costs bargaining strength affects the outcomes. Therefore institutional rules do not reflect efficiency, but the superior bargaining power of those who create and change the rules.

Power Considerations

One important point of criticism levelled against the efficiency-oriented functionalist view of institutional change is that cooperation under a particular institutional rule or defection from an institutional rule does not include distributive issues and power (Sebenius 1992; Knight 1995; Snidal 1996) and that it is based on the precondition of a functioning 'market' in politics. A change of institutional rules in terms of an efficient and stable (equilibria) solution may be likely under the condition of a competitive market. However, this is less likely to occur in politics. Knight argues that in the case of rules that structure social interactions in which we are involved ourselves they do not lend themselves easily to be interpreted as market-like exchange processes. We not only produce the rules, but we also consume them (Knight 1995: 116).[32] Moreover, institutional rules are often related to activities in which the actors are not interchangeable (Knight 1995: 116). The efficiency orientation is reinforced by the public goods perspective of functional theory that views the provision of a collectively optimal level of a good as the central problem and pays less attention to the distributive implications of a particular institutional rule, that is the question of which actors are benefiting from it (Snidal 1996: 129). However, existing institutional rules and the opportunities they offer will favour particular actors and disadvantage others (North 1996: 346). These distinctly affected actors, in turn, will influence the negotiation over institutional change. For these reasons and on account of the high transaction costs that are involved in politics, *power* plays an important role in changing

---

[32] This has implications for the number of actors who can produce rules. There are fewer producers than consumers of rules, hence fewer competing offers and the set of possible institutional rules governing social interaction (again compared to goods) are finite (Knight 1995: 116).

institutions. And power is not distributed equally. Institutional change should not be depicted as 'the new institution somehow "fits better"—solution' (Lake 2004: 6).[33]

A further point of criticism levelled against the functionalist explanation of institutional change is that the explanation is *institution-free* or, pushed to the extreme, argues that *institutions do not matter*. March and Olsen (1989), for instance, argue that functional theories explain institutional outcomes exclusively as a function of external functional demands to solve a particular collective action problem in which institutions do not matter. Thus Przeworski argues that institutions can be reduced to the functional needs they fulfil (Przeworski 2004) and the functionalist conception of institution as a self-enforcing agreement/equilibrium (Riker 1980; Schotter 1981; Calvert 1992) focuses on the stability that arises from mutually understood actor preferences and optimizing behaviour (Crawford and Ostrom 1995: 582). In other words, stable patterns of behaviour are treated as institutions. However, as we have seen, many agreements on institutional solutions are by no means 'self-formulating, self-determining, or self-enforcing' (Ostrom 1980: 11), such as in prisoners' dilemma situations, but need institutional rules to ensure their observation. Finally, even a parsimonious functionalist explanation of the change of a given institutional rule at t2 takes into account the existing formal institutional rule of t1 as an important parameter for the strategic interaction of actors in the process of reshaping the rule. The specification of the institutional parameters plays an important role in explaining an outcome of institutional change (Sjöblom 1993: 398).

Efficiency Orientation of Institutions vs. Intended Inefficiency of Institutional Rules

It has further been criticized that an efficiency-oriented functionalist approach to institutional change is more appropriate to explain market institutions than political institutions. We cannot expect market-like competition processes in the formation of political institutional rules for the reasons stated above,[34] and

---

[33] The distributional aspect and power aspect in the process of institutional change will be further elaborated in the discussion of the distributive variant of rational institutionalist theory in the next section.

[34] i.e. the difference between the production of political rules that are more finite and the production of consumer goods; the simultaneity of production and consumption of political rules; the existence of few producers and many consumers; and the non-interchangeability of actors to which rules are relating (Knight 1995).

therefore we must expect less efficient outcomes than in markets. Moreover, if composite actors, such as states, are engaged in rule-making it has to be specified whose interest it exactly is that is being maximized in the evaluation of efficiency. But even if this could be identified, this explanation of institutional change based on the existence of incentives to create more efficient institutions 'implies the relative quick and frequent change of institutions' (Mantzavinos 2001: 95). However, as Heiner (1990) argues, institutions serve to offer some orientation in a complex world, therefore are not changed so quickly (Mantzavinos 2001: 95).

In a more principled way it may be argued that institutions sometimes may be purposefully 'inefficient' because they are meant to achieve other than efficiency goals, such as the redistribution of power[35] or the protection of minorities. Finally, while institutional rules seek to save transaction costs in the solution of collective action problems, institutional rules sometimes also purposefully *increase* the transaction costs of institutional change (as by increasing the necessary quorum of a decision) (Knight 1995) to guarantee the stability of an institutional rule. Thus, constitutions have been defined as examples of 'institutional stickiness by design' as amendment processes require very large majorities in order to render change difficult (Moe 1990). In a similar argument historical institutionalists claim that established institutional rules resist change in spite of their revealed inefficiency and continue to develop along established paths because of the sunk costs linked to them and the coordination mechanisms which have evolved around particular institutional rules (Pierson 1996).

Unintended Consequences of Institutions

As we have seen, the functionalist argument explains an institutional change in terms of its desired effects. There is no doubt that the establishing of many institutional rules is initially driven precisely by such objectives to fulfil a particular task. However, institutions in their daily operation over a longer period of time while fulfilling these objectives may also have unintended consequences, that is institutional rules may lead to very different outcomes than originally envisaged by the designers of these rules (Alston, Eggertsson, and North 1996). One important reason is, as Bartolini (2005) argues, that institutional rules are set up as a result of collective decision by a relatively small circle of actors with the authority and power to design the institutions

---

[35] It may not be the increase of the economic welfare which is at the centre of actors changing institutions but it may be the maximization of the own power of an actor, as compared to the other actors, i.e. their relative power (Grieco 1988; Krasner 1988).

who are seeking to achieve functional goals in the light of their interests. After being established, however, in most cases, these institutions are applied by many actors who never participated in the original design and, very likely share not the same interests. Therefore, a simple deriving of the functioning of an institution from the original motives at the moment of their creation may be doubtful (Bartolini 2005).

Instead of the *coincidence of actors designing and actors applying an institutional rule* as assumed by most functionalist theories, we are faced with a *disjunction* of actors designing and actors implementing an institutional rule. And this has important implications for institutional change. Kay links this argument to the unintended effects of institutions and emphasizes that the particular structure of these effects needs to be analysed more systematically, differentiating between those who have adopted the rule and those who are affected in distinctive ways by an institutional rule. In a first step, consequences—thus Kay—should be classified according to the dimensions of 'intended' or 'non-intended', as well as 'recognized' and 'unrecognized'. A functional analysis should raise the question by whom the consequences were intended and by whom they were recognized (Kay 2003: 7–8). Distributional impacts may be differentiated according to their impact on two different groups: those who are designing the rules that are to be explained, and those who benefit from those rules, that is for whom they are in some sense 'functional'. The question of intention arises only for the first group; the question of recognition may arise for both (Kay 2003: 7–8). The effects may be unintended by the designing actors, but recognized by those who benefit from them or are disadvantaged by them. The losers then might function as agents of institutional change.

Strict (perfect information) functionalists would argue that an institutional rule would, by definition, not produce unintended consequences when adequate enforcement mechanisms have been provided for in the design stage. These mechanisms allow to monitor compliance and punish non-compliance (Koremenos 2005).[36] The possibilities to alter the valid institutional rule would thus be restricted. If still non-intended effects were identified, this would be because the enforcement mechanisms did not work and were not correctly designed (Cortell and Peterson 2001: 772).

While Bartolini (2005) and Kay (2003) point to different groups of actors affected by institutional rules, other authors, in particular Pierson, focus on the relevant time perspective in question. While an institutional design may meet the objectives within a relatively short time span, over a longer period of

---

[36] Personal communication.

time it is much more likely that institutional rules will produce consequences that were not anticipated by the original group of designers. This draws the attention to the need of looking at different phases in the development of an institutional rule and to investigate the particular links between the different phases.

3.3.7. Scope Conditions

It is unlikely that one theory can claim to account for institutional change under each and every circumstance, that is to hold universally. Rather, each theory[37] has a selective grasp on reality, a selectivity which is grounded in its assumptions. So, under which conditions would the functionalist theory, based on assumptions of actors' intentionality and a deliberate process of calculation, be most successful in accounting for institutional change?

Scope conditions derived from the most important assumptions of strict functionalist theories are that actors must be able to identify the costs and benefits of an institutional rule. This holds for the benefits linked to a particular solution to a collective action problem, as well as for the transaction costs of changing the rule and of enforcing the old and potentially new rule. Self-imposed institutional rules are most likely to be adopted when the potential benefits of collective action are high and the transaction costs of developing, negotiating, monitoring, and enforcing the political contract are low (Heckathorn and Maser 1987; Taylor and Singleton 1993; Lubell et al. 2002; Lake 2004). These conditions are by no means always given. Sometimes it is not clear what exactly the costs and benefits are and how they distribute across actors. In other words, if costs and benefits of an institutional rule are unknown and the transaction costs involved in the shaping of the rule and the maintenance of the rule are unclear as well, then the functional explanatory approach is less likely to provide a powerful explanation of institutional change. Moreover, the hypotheses derived from the strict functionalist theory hold more explanatory power, if the change in external conditions is incisive and clear-cut, when actors set out from new external conditions to negotiate a set of new institutional rules or to renegotiate the old rules. In conclusion, functional theory lends itself to the formulation of propositions that can be empirically assessed, if the motives of the actors

---

[37] I distinguish between a general framework listing all relevant variables for a particular outcome to be explained; a theory producing a set of logically linked general hypotheses (if—then statements) concerning outcomes; and a model which specifies a set of independent and dependent variables in propositions that can be submitted to empirical confirmation (see, among others Ostrom 1999).

for introducing a change have been defined *ex ante*, and an exogenous event is identified which leads you to expect a change in the cost–benefit relationship of the existing institutional rule in dealing with a problem of collective action. Functionalist theories, on the other hand, that release the strict assumption of actors' perfect information and emphasize actors' needs to learn from changed circumstances, contribute to a widening of the scope of application of functional theory. The iterative learning processes allow for an incremental change of institutional rules, if they do not lead to satisfactory results in the first instance.

While efficiency-oriented functional theories emphasize the overall increase of benefits that derive from an institutional rule to all involved actors, they neglect the *distributive* impact linked to a specific rule and the power dimension in the shaping of the rule. We now turn to a variant of rational choice institutionalism which emphasizes these aspects in the explanation of institutional change.

3.4. DISTRIBUTIONAL RATIONAL CHOICE INSTITUTIONALISM

Distributional rational choice institutionalism emphasizes the distributional implications of institutions as an outcome of a power-oriented bargaining process (Knight 1992). This theory—as opposed to the functionalist theory—does not only compare the overall outcomes produced by an institution with the outcomes produced if there were no institution, but makes assumptions about the social context in which the interaction takes place and relates them to the pay-offs of the interaction. The argument is that institutions have different distributional consequences for the involved actors and that institutional rules are compared under this perspective (Knight 1995: 100). Unlike the functional approach, it does not stress the shared concern with achieving joint gains or efficiency through cooperation, but emphasizes political conflict and strategic bargaining among actors. In addition, it explicitly relaxes the assumption of symmetry of power of actors made in some versions of functionalist theory.

Given multiple possibilities of cooperation to deal with a collective action problem, the selection of an institutional rule to achieve this goal is often contested. Each possible institutional solution '...resolves the strategic problem inherent in a situation in which there are a number of ways of doing something.... The task is to establish a common way of doing it' (Knight 1995: 96). Choosing a particular one is conflict prone because distinct rules frequently imply different distributions of benefits among participants (Snidal 1996: 125). In other words, institutions lock-in a particular division of the joint gains (Lake 2004: 3). Why and how do actors arrive at one of these institutional rules? The answer is power. Thus, focusing on the distributive dimension linked to institutional rules, '...power needs to be given pride of place' (Krasner 1991).

Asymmetries in resource ownership explain the result of a bargaining process over an institution. Resource ownership affects the willingness of rational self-interested actors to accept the bargaining demands of other actors. Here the asymmetries of resource ownership serve as an *ex ante* measure of the bargaining power of the actors in a social interaction (Knight 1995: 108). The most important resources available are 'those available to the actors in the event that bargaining is either lengthy and costly or ultimately unsuccessful. For any particular bargaining interaction, many factors may determine the availability of these resources. We can think of these as the existing resources that an actor might retain after the effort to achieve a bargain breaks down. Or we might think of them as the other options available to the actors if they are left to achieve a bargaining with some other party' (Knight 1995: 108). If an actor disposes of fallback positions in case of bargaining failure, this has implications for his attitudes towards risk (and time preference) during the bargaining process. 'There is a positive relationship between ownership of resources and risk acceptance' (Knight 1992, 1995: 109) and a negative relationship between a lack of ownership and risk aversion. Or as Elster puts it, if an institutional rule is to be imposed by those who stand to benefit most from it, they need leverage over those who prefer another institutional rule. 'Often, the leverage is that those who have the most to gain also have the least to lose.... For the weak, law and order is very important, even if it is heavily biased against them. Without law and order—in the state of nature—they would not survive. The strong also prefer law and order to the state of nature, and they naturally prefer law and order biased in their favour over law and order favouring the weak. Nevertheless, they are strong, they could survive in the state of nature. There is less stake for the strong, which is another way of saying that they have more bargaining power, which they can use to impose their preferred equilibrium' (Elster 1989*a*, 1989*b*: 111–12). Accordingly, asymmetries in resource ownership explain the result of a negotiation over an institutional rule. Resource ownership will affect the willingness of actors to accept the bargaining demands of other actors. The asymmetries of available resources serve as an empirical *ex ante* measure of the bargaining power of the actors in the negotiation of institutional rules (Knight 1995: 108). According to the distributive rationalist view, therefore, the institutional outcome will reflect the asymmetric resources of the actors who have been engaged in the bargaining process.

Incorporating distributional effects into the bargaining of institutional rules renders the process much more difficult. It will be more lengthy to reach an agreement (Knight 1992).[38] The longer a distributional bargain is expected to be valid, the harder actors will negotiate over the distribution of gains and the more difficult cooperation will be (Fearon 1998). In so far as an institutional rule, such as a unanimity rule in voting, produces an outcome that is different from the likely outcome of a simple majority rule, the losers under a particular rule, in the above case, the majority, will seek to *change* the existing rule (Riker 1980: 444–5). Whether they succeed in doing so depends on the support they can muster in the negotiation process. Since institutions give strategic advantages to those who control them, any attempt to change them must surmount considerable resistance (Sened 1991: 398) and will generate conflicts between the involved actors (Carey 2000: 746).

Following this theoretical argument, what are the factors that set into motion a process of change of institutional rules? It could result from a breaking apart of the dominant change-resisting coalition (Tsebelis 1990); this would have to be traced to a change of the preferences of the most powerful actor(s), and a change in the balance of power between the involved actors (Lake 2004: 4). It could also result from a change in the bargaining power of the actors due to a change in their resources or fallback positions (Knight 1992), possibly caused by technological change in the environment. All these factors setting off a process of change of institutional rules are external to the explanatory model (Rittberger 2003a).

Taking distributional implications for the bargaining process and institutional outcomes into account directs the attention to distinctive distributive implications. If, for instance, the distributive implications are relatively evenly divided, actors tend to choose institutions that rely on reciprocity (Mitchell and Keilbach 2001: 892). A case in point would be a rotating chair in a decision-making body. Since all know that they will chair at one point in time, they are willing to accept the chair of another actor for a limited period. Since the chair rotates, each chair will be moderate in her behaviour since she has to fear retaliation for excessive behaviour once the chair has passed on (Sugden 1986; Farrell and Héritier 2004). Other situations may be of asymmetric distributive impact in the sense that 'downstream actors' may be the victims of 'upstream actors' (Mitchell and Keilbach 2001: 891). This

---

[38] De facto, however, most issues mix efficiency (wealth increasing) issues with distributive issues (Snidal 1996: 125).

would hold for institutional rules defining a sequence of decision-making; actors deciding first have an advantage over actors deciding later. For obvious reasons in asymmetric situations of power institutional solutions are faced with severe enforcement problems (Mitchell and Keilbach 2001: 916). We submit that

H: Power-induced institutional change with distributive implications
'Given a change of preference of a powerful actor or a change of power balance between actors, an existing institutional rule may be subject to renegotiation in order to alter the rule in such a way as to reflect the (changed) preferences of the powerful actor or the changed power balance.'

3.4.1. Mediating Effect of Institutions

One might object that institutional outcomes are not a *one-to-one reflection* of the relative bargaining power of the involved designing actors. Formal rules in place at t1 matter in how power affects institutional change and, therefore, the outcome at t2. To give an example: if an institutional rule on how the votes of the members of a polity are weighted is decided on the basis of a majority vote, the outcome will be different from when this decision would be taken on the basis of a unanimity rule. In other words, preferences and power do not immediately translate into outcomes but are mediated by the existing formal institutional rules. These rules may either enhance or detract from the advantages of the most powerful (Snidal 1996: 127). As Snidal has formulated: institutional rules at t1 'drive a wedge between power and outcomes' (Snidal 1996: 127). Davis (2004) for instance has shown that the institutional structure of a negotiation process, that is the agenda setting rules and the procedural rules governing the negotiation, influence the outcomes. Thus a particular institutional rule, such as a widely defined agenda, may support the credibility of a linkage strategy across multiple issue areas. As a result, the bargaining process will offer more possibilities of give and take through issue linkages and package deals across multiple issue areas, and enable redistributive outcomes. This would be more difficult if the formal decision-making rule would limit the discussion to *one* issue area on the agenda (Davis 2004: 153–4). Similarly, the definition of the *decision sequence*, whether it will be a separate decision on each issue or a single decision on *all* issues, is likely to make a significant difference as to how power translates into outcomes. In other words, the broadening of the scope of actors and interests can provide the impetus for change and the attenuation of power (Davis 2004: 154, 167). Or in general terms, actors dissatisfied with the status quo must *broaden* the scope of the institutional issues discussed, using the linkage of give and take to convince the losers to support a particular rule by compensating them in another issue area (Mitchell and Keilbach 2001: 892). We may therefore expect that

H: Distributive, power-based bargaining of institutional change mediated by institutions
'The institutional rules governing the bargaining process make a difference with respect to the outcome, i.e. the changed institutional rule.'
'A wider scope of decision-making issues and simultaneous voting on all issues will lead to more redistributive outcomes of the negotiation process than voting on single issues sequentially.'

An institutional separation of different modes of negotiations, that is integrative and defensive bargaining to influence negotiation outcomes, was proposed by Scharpf (1991, 1997). In a first phase, negotiators discuss possible institutional solutions which are beneficial to all and establish a general formula of fair treatment; in a second phase, taking into account the general formula of fair treatment, they bargain over outcomes with distributive implications. 'Expanding the pie' (Raiffa 1982) or problem-solving oriented and value-creating negotiations (Lax and Sebenius 1986) take place during the initial search for and identification of possible solutions which are in the common interest (Walton and McKersie 1991).[39] Status quo oriented bargaining follows in which all actors seek to get as much of the enlarged pie as possible for themselves. While bargaining is related to manipulative tactics, misrepresentation of preferences, threats and firm commitments ('I cannot change my position') and a win or lose attitude and finally compensation offers and trading of gains, problem-solving involves the sharing of information, the communication of true preferences, a joint search for common interests and a win-win attitude (Fisher and Ury 1981).[40]

Integrative bargaining as opposed to defensive bargaining may to some extent be influenced by institutional measures, such as a separation of different phases of negotiation or the definition of the agenda of items. But whether integrative or defensive bargaining prevails also depends on the particular *problem type* at stake. One relevant distinction is between complex decision-making areas on the one side and simple issues on the other; another more analytic distinction relates to the redistributive or distributive nature of issues;

---

[39] This discussion links up with the sociological institutionalist argument about arguing and bargaining. If arguing prevails the power of the better argument comes to bear. The measure more likely to improve the welfare of all concerned is at stake whereas under a self-interested bargaining process the aim is to defend and improve an actor's own status-quo position (Risse 2000; Checkel 2001a).

[40] As Scharpf points out, the honest problem solver in a bargaining process is at a risk that he reveals his true preferences that subsequently may be exploited in the defensive bargaining process (Scharpf 1997).

yet another refers to the question whether a problem of collective action invites free-riding (a prisoners' dilemma problem) or whether it constitutes a coordination problem from the solution of which all gain. Thus, when institutional rules are complex, and fraught with uncertainty, it is more likely that problem-solving will prevail. Actors will first seek to find out what the institutional status quo is and what possible changes imply and what may be beneficial solutions for all concerned, before they proceed to defensive bargaining. If issues are redistributive in nature and the proposed changes clearly reveal who is to gain and who is to lose, defensive bargaining will prevail. Or, in the case of a prisoners' dilemma problem, all might agree to contribute in principle, but then decide to defect during implementation. If by contrast a coordination problem is at issue from the solution of which all stand to win, agreement will be easy.

Therefore, additionally to the existing institutional rules governing the negotiation process, distinguishing between problem types and their likely link to negotiation outcomes would lead us to the claims:

H: *Problem type, institutional rules and integrative vs. defensive bargaining*
'If redistributive issues are at stake, the process of institutional change will be characterized by defensive bargaining. The outcome will reflect the asymmetry of power of the involved actors.'
'If in a first, institutionally separate stage of negotiation, actors focus on problem-solving, they may identify institutional solutions beneficial to all; the developing of such solutions may have an impact on the second stage of defensive bargaining because the space of feasible options has been extended.'

In these refined power-based distributive bargaining explanations of institutional change, the factors triggering off a process of change are—as described above—an altered power base, changed preferences of key actors, etc., in other words, they are *exogenous* to the model. There are, however, theoretical arguments building on this strand of theory that seek to *endogenize* the factors of institutional change.

3.4.2. Endogenizing Institutional Change

The distributional power–based institutionalist explanation identifies altered preferences of the involved actors or an increase of power of particular actors or actor coalitions as the source of institutional change. The reasons why these preferences have changed and why some actors have gained in power is not explained by the model accounting for institutional change.

Another distributive power-based institutionalist approach developed by Farrell and Héritier (2003, 2004, forthcoming) proposes an *formal/informal/formal dynamics* of institutional change based on an *endogenous* explanation. Starting out from the assumption of formal institutional rules as incomplete contracts,[41] we argue against an explanation of institutional change according to which all institutional features are fixed at the point of design reflecting fully the desires of the designing actors, such as functionalism argues.[42] Assuming, moreover, limited information and actors' desire to maximize their institutional power, we contend that in the course of their daily application these rules are subject to renegotiation, giving rise to informal rules that govern the application of the incomplete formal rules (see also Stacey and Rittberger 2003). Informal rules are defined as rules that are usually not written down, may not be subject to formal sanctioning in case of non-compliance (without the 'Or Else'—Crawford and Ostrom 1995) and are usually not subject to third-party dispute resolution. They are 'created, communicated, and enforced outside of officially sanctioned channels' (Helmke and Levitsky 2004). The informal rules emerging in the daily application of the formal rule may be of a mere efficiency-increasing nature, that is all are better off due to their application, or they may be of a distributive nature, that is affect the decision-making power of the involved actors.[43]

We argue that these informal rules emerging in the daily application of ambiguous formal rules are a result of bargaining that reflects the relative power of the involved actors. Two factors determine the relative power of

[41] Since actors' rationality is bounded, actors are unable to design institutional rules (contracts) taking into account every relevant contingency. Decisions are time-consuming and costly, therefore actors make mistakes and complete contracts cannot be settled. Therefore actors design incomplete contracts 'that do not implement an *ex ante* designed complete set of . . . behavioural rules that will *ex post* solve all coordination problems. They rather design decision-making devices that *ex post* will state the required behaviour by contractors to ensure the possible cost-efficient coordination and to guarantee the enforcement of mutual commitments' (Brousseau and Fares 2000: 10). Hayek argues that rules always only focus on certain aspects of concrete action and provide for a general scheme that then has to be adapted to specific situations. 'They will often merely determine or limit the range of possibilities within which the choice is made' (Hayek 1967: 56).

[42] Or, alternatively, where these rules have somehow escaped the control of its creators (unintended effects).

[43] Informal institutions specify, modify, or even supersede formal rules. Rules may be accommodating, complementary, substitutive, or competing with existing formal institutions (Lauth 2000; Helmke and Levitsky 2004: 728). By accommodating themselves to and complementing the formal rules, they contribute to the specification and better functioning of the latter. But informal rules may also tend to substitute existing formal rules by making them obsolescent, or by competing with the formal rules allowing actors to choose between the formal rule and the new informal rule. They thereby may have implications for the existing formal institutions, effectively modifying, or in extreme cases effectively replacing, or undercutting them (Helmke and Levitsky 2004).

the actors in negotiating the informal rules: the actors' formal institutional positions in the decision-making process at t1. The extant formal institutional rules grant general competences to actors, and have a substantial effect on actors' ability to credibly threaten specific kinds of action. Thus, the unanimity rule, giving the right of veto to every single decision-making participant, invites the emergence of informal institutions to avoid a deadlock situation (Héritier 1999; Goodin 2000). The second factor determining the outcome of the negotiations of the specific informal rules filling out the original formal rules is the available fallback position in case of the failure of negotiations. The better the fallback position, expressed in a longer time horizon of the actor and a lesser vulnerability towards failure, the more powerful the actor is, the more likely she will be able to shape the outcome of the negotiations. Thus, some actors take a longer view than others. Shorter time horizons may make actors vulnerable to pressure; other actors may be willing to delay decisions for long periods, or to threaten such delay, if this serves their particular interests. And some actors may be less sensitive to failure in that they are less affected by failure to reach agreement on a specific item of decision-making than others because of differences in the intensity of preferences. These actors will be better able to make credible threats with regard to this item (or items) of legislation, in order to enhance their overall position in the legislative process (Elster 1989*a*, 1989*b*; Knight 1995). The two factors are likely to have important—and differential—impact on the ability of actors to decisively shape terms of interaction within a particular institutional rule in a sense which is favourable to them. Over time, a basic modus vivendi is likely to be hammered out, consisting of informal rules which provide a basic structure to interactions under the institutional rule between actors by coordinating expectations, which will reflect the differential power of actors to make credible threats that other actors must take account of. When informal institutions have arisen, these are likely to structure the decision-making process under the existing institutional rule and constitute a first phase of institutional change.

But informal rules which emerge in the specification and renegotiation of an existing formal institutional rule in a second time may also affect the next bargaining round in the revision of the *formal* rules and lead to a formalization of the 'interstitial'[44] institutional change that has occurred (Farrell and Héritier 2006). They change the status quo by having de facto changed the rule content. In a subsequent round of rule revision, the designing actors will have to take this de facto rule change, the new status quo, into consideration. We argue

---

[44] Interstitial is derived from the Latin 'interstare', indicating the period *between* two formal rule revisions.

that formalization will happen when all actors agree that the informal rule should be formalized because it is beneficial to all; alternatively all actors may agree to abolish the informal rule that has been bargained interstitially. However, when actors diverge in their views and unanimity cannot be expected, actors who are affected by the rule as implementing actors, but do not have a formal say in the institutional design of the rule (arena A) may still exert significant pressure on whether or not to formalize the rule. This may happen if these affected actors have competences in a linked arena (arena B) which they may use to credibly threaten a veto (linked-arena veto) to exert pressure on the arena A where the rule change occurs. They will use the powers in arena B as a lever to press for a formalization of informal rules that are beneficial to them in arena A.

The distinction between the particular functions of *actors as designers*, from those who are *affected and involved as implementors* of the rule, is important in this context. It indicates that on some categories of actors the changed formal rules are simply *imposed*. They have no direct negotiating power in influencing the design of institutions, nor can they walk away from the institutional rule if they do not like the outcome, as Moe (2005) rightly emphasizes.

This explanation of institutional change is *endogenous* because the elements of explaining the source of institutional change are included in the model: that is in the assumptions of a given ambiguity of a formal institutional rule (incomplete contract) and actors' wishes to strengthen their institutional power. The factors explaining the outcome of the rebargained institutional rule are the given formal institutional decision-making rule and the power of the actors defined as their fallback position in case of a failure of negotiations. If the capabilities of the involved actors uniquely derive from their formal institutional position, no exogenous factors are used in order to explain the institutional outcome. To be true, it is rare that the capabilities of an actor in negotiating institutional change uniquely depend on his or her formal institutional position. Often the fallback position of actors negotiating a change also depends on exogenous factors, such as material wealth, size, and political importance of an actor, for example a member state in the EU.

To the extent mentioned, our explanation of institutional change would be mainly endogenous. The above theoretical consideration let us hypothesize that:

H: 'Institutional change through a formal/informal/formal dynamic'
'Formal rules at t1 that are ambiguous give rise to informal rules that further develop the formal rules. These informal rules will reflect the bargaining power of actors, as determined by formal institutions and the fallback position of the negotiating actors reflected in different time horizons and a different sensitivity to failure.'

And

'The outcome of the formal negotiations at t2 will reflect informal bargained institutions if all designing actors agree to accept the informal change or if the implementing/affected actors can exert pressure through a linked-arena veto.'

Another distributive bargaining approach to institutional change developing an *endogenous* explanation of institutional change *across levels* is Jupille's 'procedural politics', or everyday politics with respect to rules. He argues that ambiguous higher-level institutional rules offer a basis for choosing strategically among different pertinent lower-level institutional rules. Actors will seek to ensure the usage of institutional rules that maximize their political (and policy) influence. Given available institutional alternatives they have incentives of potential influence gains and will use these strategic opportunities. They therefore engage in 'procedural politics' by forming coalitions that seek to take influence on the criteria that govern institutional selection with predictable effects on rules themselves, but also the contents of public policy. In case of bargaining gridlock, the conflicting actors turn to third-party dispute resolution to issue an authoritative decision about which rule to use.

In a second stage, *procedural politics* also may have an impact on long-run changes in higher-order rules, that is constitutions, that is across levels of decision-making. Why would procedural politics feed back into higher-order rule revision? Jupille argues that the selection of such procedural rules and, particularly, the conflicts over the selection of a specific lower-order rule are costly with respect to time spent in procedural conflicts that are diverting resources from the efficient pursuit of substantive outcomes.[45] Procedural politics may serve as an indicator of the incompleteness of the higher-order contract. As a result, a revision of the most ambiguous macroinstitutional rules that were the reasons for procedural politics is likely, leading to higher-order institutional change in the course of which the loopholes in the higher-order rules are filled. Jupille therefore proposes that as the frequency of procedural political disputes increases, the likelihood of higher-order institutional change also increases (Jupille 2004*a*, 2004*b*). This constitutes an *endogenous, multilevel* explanation of institutional change within the framework of the extant institutional rules (Jupille 2004*a*, 2004*b*) *linking* different phases of institutional change. We may therefore expect that:

[45] These 'influence costs' (Milgrom and Roberts 1990), Jupille argues, represent deadweight losses to actors. As these deadweight costs increase, so do the costs of leaving the higher-order institutional rule unamended.

H: Procedural politics

'Given a choice between different lower-order procedural rules, actors will seek to employ the rule that maximizes their influence. The relative bargaining power of an actor will determine the outcome.'

'In case of stalemate between the bargaining actors, third party-dispute resolution indicates the rule to be employed.'

'A high frequency of procedural politics over lower-order rule level 'feeds back' into higher-order institutional change by providing information about gaps in the prevailing constitutional contract and by raising the opportunity costs of leaving the treaty unamended.'

The two theories of endogenous institutional change focusing on the formal/informal/formal dynamic and procedural politics, focus on the links between different phases of institutional change, that is longer-term sequences. In both cases, the explanation of longer-term institutional change is not a story of punctuated formal redesigns starting with *ex ante* defined change of preferences,[46] followed by a bargaining process over formal institutional change which leads to a reform of the institutional rules marking the end of the causal chain (Moravcsik 1993, 1998). Starting then with a new bargaining round which is fed by a new round of changed preferences of the involved actors, leading to revised formal institutional rules, in which '...each successive grand bargain is pushed by new set of social and economic pressures' (Caporaso 2006: 4) reflected in changed preferences.

Rather, the two endogenous theories of institutional change focus on longer-term institutional change that are based on the feedback effects of the created institutional rules: ambiguous formal rules giving rise to informal rules at t1, the informal rules possibly giving rise to a revision to the formal rules at t2. In a subsequent sequence t3 the remaining ambiguities of the formal rules give again rise to the development of informal rules. These subsequently may be swept up in a formal treaty revision at t4 etc. Under procedural politics the conflict about selecting among a number of possible lower-order rules leads to a conflict and bargained solution over the 'proper rule' and subsequently, possibly, to an intentional revision of the higher-order rules. Both views of endogenous institutional change focuses on the impact of institutions on institutional change and back to institutions. These longer-term views of institutional change clearly differ from the punctuated equilibrium view of longer-term institutional change where a longer period of institutional stability is followed by crisis and a redefining of existing institutions.

---

[46] These preferences are derived from national and transnational pressures that are processed in domestic political processes (Moravcsik 1993, 1998).

It implies an incremental view of 'bounded' institutional change (Caporaso forthcoming).

3.4.3. Structural Perspective: Levels/Arenas and Types of Actors

From the *level/arena perspective*, the distributive power–based bargaining explanation of *endogenous* institutional change looks also at decision-making *across different levels or arenas* of institutional rules and focuses on the link between higher-order and lower-order rules. It is the ambiguous higher-order rules which give rise to informal lower-order rules or the possibility of choosing among different lower-level rules which may then feed back into a revision of the higher-order rules in order to incorporate or eliminate the institutional developments which have emerged between the formal rule revisions.

Moreover, establishing links between arenas of bargaining may serve an actor as a 'tying your hands' mechanism in one arena that may increase his leverage in negotiating institutional change in another arena. Being committed to a particular position in an issue of institutional change at the national institutional rule-making level may help avoid making concessions in the bargaining of institutional change at the international level. And vice versa, commitments made at the international bargaining table, may strengthen your bargaining position domestically (Putnam 1988; Moravcsik 1998). We may, therefore, expect that:

H: Bargaining institutional change across levels/arenas
'Having an actor's hands tied in one arena improves his bargaining position in shaping the outcomes in another arena.'

The *type of actors perspective* draws the attention to the fact that both *designing actors and implementing/affected actors* are engaged in rule change. In the theories of punctuated equilibria of formal changes, it is uniquely the designing actors that bring the change about. The endogenous theories, however, focusing on designing and implementing actors at different levels point out that it is precisely the divergent preferences of the different types of actors[47] that in the daily application of the formal rules may give rise to informal rules and may exert indirect pressure on the negotiation process in the latter's subsequent formalization or non-formalization.

---

[47] Lindner and Rittberger underline the usefulness of this distinction arguing that, when the preferences of the institutional-design coalition is driven by conflicting (ideational) concerns, the resulting institutional rules are likely to be open to interpretation and subject to contestation by the institutional enacting-coalition (Rittberger 2003: 14).

*Summary of Hypotheses Derived from Rational Distributive
Bargaining Theories (see Table 3.2)*

H: Power-induced institutional change with distributive implications
'Given a change of preference of a powerful actor or a change of power balance between
actors, an existing institutional rule may be subject to renegotiation in order to alter
the rule in such a way as to reflect the (changed) preferences of the powerful actor or
the changed power balance.'

H: Distributive, power-based bargaining of institutional change mediated by institutions
'The institutional rules governing the bargaining process make a difference with
respect to the outcome, i.e. the changed institutional rule.'
'A wider scope of decision-making issues and simultaneous voting on all issues will
lead to more redistributive outcomes of the negotiation process than voting on single
issues sequentially.'

H: Problem type, institutional rules and integrative vs. defensive bargaining
'If redistributive issues are at stake, the process of institutional change will be characterized by defensive bargaining. The outcome will reflect the asymmetry of power of
the involved actors.'
'If in a first, institutionally separate stage of negotiation, actors focus on problem-
solving, they may identify institutional solutions beneficial to all; the developing of
such solutions may have an impact on the second stage of defensive bargaining because
the space of feasible options has been extended.'

H: Institutional change through a formal/informal/formal dynamic
'Formal rules at t1 that are ambiguous give rise to informal rules that further develop
the formal rules. These informal rules will reflect the bargaining power of actors, as
determined by formal institutions and the fallback position of the negotiating actors
reflected in different time horizons and a different sensitivity to failure.'

And

'The outcome of the formal negotiations at t2 will reflect the bargained informal
institutions if all designing actors agree to accept the informal change or if the imple-
menting/affected actors can exert pressure through a linked-arena veto.'

H: Procedural politics
'Given a choice between different lower-order procedural rules, actors will seek to
employ the rule that maximizes their influence. The relative bargaining power of an
actor will determine the outcome.'
'In case of stalemate between the bargaining actors, third party-dispute resolution
indicates the rule to be employed.'
'A high frequency of procedural politics over lower-order rule level "feeds back"
into higher-order institutional change by providing information about gaps in the

Table 3.2. Distributive bargaining theories of institutional change: process and structural perspectives

Perspective	Process: causal mechanism	Source of change: exogenous/ endogenous	Links in time	Structural: level(s)/ arenas	Structural: types of actors
Distribut. bargaining theory	Bargaining	Exogenous	None; punctuated equilibria	One and multiple	Designing actors
Instit. mediated distr. bargaining theory	Bargaining	Exogenous	None; punctuated equilibria	One and multiple	Designing actors
Interaction between ambiguous formal and informal rules	Bargaining	Endogenous	Link between interstitial change and subsequent formaliz. of interstitial changes	Two	Designing and implement. actors
Procedural politics	Bargaining	Endogenous	Link between interstitial and subsequent formaliz. of interstitial change	Two	Designing and implement. actors

prevailing constitutional contract and by raising the opportunity costs of leaving the treaty unamended.'

H: Bargaining institutional change across levels/arenas
'Having an actor's hands tied in one arena improves his bargaining position in shaping the outcomes in another arena.'

and

H: Bargaining leverage through arena-linking
'Actor A, using a formal veto in one arena X, can create a leverage in another linked arena Y in which actor A has no formal vote.'

3.4.4. Critique of Distributional Bargaining Theory

The distributive bargaining-oriented theory of institutional change has been subject to criticism for a variety of reasons, most importantly because of the lack of attention to

— the transformative power of institutional rules;
— institutional 'stickiness';
— the unclear nature of the costs and benefits of institutional rules;
— the transformation of rules through interpretation and socialization processes instead of bargaining.

The critique evoking the *transformative power of institutional rules* argues that institutional changes are not a mere epiphenomenon of the power balance at the moment of creation and the moment of application of these rules. If institutions are forged out of political struggles and their particular shape reflects the prevailing balance of power among the designing actors and implementing (or affected) actors, then, as a logical consequence, they should change either in response to changes in the balance of power among those actors, or in response to changes in the preferences of the most powerful actors. Institutions understood as simple *epiphenomena* of power and cooperation as an expression of actors' interests should be subject to change by simple 'political fiat' (Lohmann 2003: 7).

However, this very often is not the case. As pointed out above, once an institutional rule has emerged from a political struggle, it may, in interaction with other institutional rules, exert a transformative impact on subsequent bargaining processes and their outcomes. Thus, as we have seen, the existing formal institutional rules, for example qualified majority rule with a specific formal structure of the agenda and sequence of decision-making (Davis 2004) may attenuate and modify the raw impact of power and render the 'give and take' among winners and losers more complicated, thereby making a difference with respect to the distributive outcomes. This means that the translating back of institutional rules into a particular power constellation is not straightforward but more complicated. It also means that the abolishing of an institutional rule is more difficult. As Snidal put it, outcomes cannot be predicted simply by understanding states' power (and interests) without references to the institutions that connect them. These institutional rules may enhance or detract from the advantages of the most powerful. That does not mean that power does not matter but rather that *how* it matters depends on the existing institutional rules (Snidal 1996: 127).

Stinchcombe argued that the factors responsible for the genesis of an institution may not be the same as those that sustain it over time (Stinchcombe 1968). Here the distinction between institutional rules as rules of behaviour and institutions as organizations—as two different elements of institutions— (Greif 2006) becomes relevant. The organization part of institutions, consisting of persons, buildings and resources, that have been set up in order to ensure the implementation of an institutional rule, are likely to develop goals of their own that may make the abolishing of the institutional rule difficult once it does not reflect the preferences of the designing actors any longer.

A related argument against a simple one-to-one relationship between power-based bargaining in the process of shaping an institutional rule and its outcomes is presented by *historical institutionalism* similarly pointing out that existing institutional rules may very likely not have been created by the political groups that *now* benefit from those institutions. Although at their point of creation their substance may have reflected the balance of power among the creators of the rule, over time the institutional rule may undergo a change that shifts the balance of costs and benefits (Thelen 2003: 216). The question is, of course, what are the underlying mechanisms of transformation to which the institutional rule is subject once it has been created. The answer may lie precisely in these processes of endogenous institutional change based on functionalist and distributive power-based institutional theory discussed in the last sections, that is: the endogenous institutional change based on a positive reinforcement of existing rules in the light of marginally changed external circumstances (quasi-parameters) (Greif and Laitin 2004), or the dynamic linked to the interaction between ambiguous formal rules, emerging informal rules and their subsequent formalization (Farrell and Héritier 2003), or procedural politics (Jupille 2005), that is the conflict over the selection of one among several possible lower-order rules subsequently leading to a filling of the loopholes in the formal revision of higher-order rules (procedural politics/Jupille 2004*a*).

The path-dependency argument of historical institutionalists (Mahoney 2000; Pierson 2000*b*) adds to the critique by emphasizing that the distributive bargaining approach of institutional change underestimates the *institutional inertia or stickiness* of formal institutions or the difficulty to leave a

certain path of institutional rule development once embarked on.[48] As both
Mahoney (2000) and Pierson (2000*b*) argue, a path-dependent institutional
development is characterized by the combination of some contingency at the
beginning, a 'critical juncture' and some degree of determinism in the ensuing
path-dependent process. Institutional changes depend on initial conditions
(i.e. early events are more important than later events), non-ergodicity (i.e.
contingent events do not necessarily cancel out), and inertia (i.e. once in
motion, processes tend to stay in motion until an equilibrium or final outcome
is reached) (Mahoney 2000: 1). Institutions tend to be stable because of large
set-up costs, learning and coordination effects as well as adaptive expectations
(Pierson 2000*b*) which generate increasing returns of existing institutional
rules. Their persistence is likely once an institutional development triggered
by a contingent event has developed along a particular path of institutional
attributes. The initial choice gets 'locked in'. It is difficult to change the institutional rule even if a competing one seems to be more efficient, because all the
relevant actors have adjusted to accommodate the prevailing pattern and alternatives become increasingly difficult to realize. The various mechanisms of
reproduction of a particular set of institutions, however, as Mahoney argues,
may be explained by using functionalist, power based and legitimation arguments (Mahoney 2000).[49] Accordingly, from the view of path dependency,
institutional change is expected to occur when institutions show *decreasing*
returns, that is absent coordinating and learning effects; or alternatively if
there are low fixed costs for setting up a new institution; where there is relative
certainty concerning the prospective effects of institutional reform, and where
the institutional provisions for change are permissive (simple majority rule)
(Pierson 1993, 2000*a*, 2000*b*).

The relatively stark contrast between institutional creation at critical junctures and institutional stability and instability proposed by some path-
dependency approaches is criticized by Thelen (2003), Immergut (2005),
Streeck and Thelen (2005), and Crouch and Farrell (2004). While increasing
returns and the mechanism linked to them, as described by Pierson and
Mahoney, do explain stability, they do not account for (path dependent)
change. However, institutions frequently change slowly 'by the cumulative
effect of ongoing but often subtle changes in institutional arrangements

---

[48] As Mahoney put it 'any path dependent study minimally entails the analysis of sequences
in which initial contingent events set in motion institutional patterns or event chains that have
deterministic properties' (2000: 1).

[49] Thus Mahoney adds to the versions of path dependence coming out of economics and
focusing on only one particular set of mechanisms behind increasing returns—utilitarian cost–
benefit analysis a wider range of mechanisms including power, and legitimation mechanisms
that contribute to the persistence of institutional arrangements (Mahoney 2000).

that persist over long stretches of time...' (Thelen 2003: 210). By adjusting to changed external social, political, and economic conditions, institutions evolve in ways that are not predictable, but follow a particular pattern (Thelen 2003). Or as Crouch and Farrell put it 'path-dependent development trajectories interact with exogenously changing environments' (Crouch and Farrell 2004: 6) and successfully 'escape from path dependency' (Crouch and Farrell 2004: 12) by viewing actors as positively benefiting from the interaction with the external environment by an 'entrepreneurial discovery of concealed, unacknowledged, or surprising potentialities of the available institutional repertoire' (Crouch and Farrell 2004: 33).

Thelen (2003) proposes a theory of *political constructionism* that, on the one hand, underlines the influence of prior political arrangements, rules, leaders, ideas, practices, and attitudes (Orren and Skowronek 2000), on the other hand, focuses on the ongoing political contestation, definition, and redefinition of these established structures (Thelen 2003). Critical junctures or turning points in institutional development should not be accounted for through external events, but endogenously on the basis of given historical structures and the limits they set for actors as they respond to new opportunities and challenges in their political and economic environment (Thelen 2003; Streeck and Thelen 2005). Importantly, political constructionists stress tensions among the various institutions emerging out of distinct political conflicts and different ordering principles and '...stresses dissonance and incongruity in the ordering principles around which a society's institutions are organized' (Orren and Skowronek 1994: 320–2; Thelen 2003).[50]

---

[50] Along a similar vein of argument Lieberman stresses the plurality and variety of orders (institutions and ideas) and the tensions among them as a source of change. While each order in itself is seen to be coherent, the various orders that prevail are not coherent, '...their lack of fit constitutes the motor of change.... There is no reason to presume, ...that the ideological and institutional currents that prevail at any given time or place are necessarily connected with each other in any coherent or functional way' (Lieberman 2002: 702). This is because political arrangements are rarely the products of a coherent vision of politics. 'New policies, institutional arrangements, or ideological paradigms, thus do not replace the old but are layered atop prior patterns...' (Lieberman 2002: 702). 'There may be instances in which ideological and institutional patterns "fit" together and cumulate into something that looks like an equilibrium.... At other times, however, they will collide and chafe, creating an ungainly configuration of political circumstances that has no clear resolution, presenting actors with contradictory and multidirectional imperatives and opportunities' (Lieberman 2002: 702). Building on Thelen's argument Lieberman goes on to argue that institutional change is caused by a mismatch between the governing institutions (legislature, judiciary, executive, and administrative agencies), the organizational environment (political parties, NGOs, etc.) as well as the ideological and cultural repertoires that legitimate and structure political discourse, therefore, can bring change about (Lieberman 2002: 702). Each of the different components produce different incentives and opportunities of action. They point into substantially different directions, 'especially if they subject the same set of actors to conflicting pressures that pose acute dilemmas and make conventional moves untenable' (Lieberman 2002: 703).

The problem with this argument is that such frictions between different elements of order that pull into different directions and set conflicting incentives for individual actors are always present, but do not necessarily lead to institutional change. Once an institutional transformation has been identified, it may always be traced to some friction between the different components of the political order. However, it is very difficult to formulate *ex ante* general claims on under which conditions such friction does indeed lead to institutional change and under which conditions it does not.

Streeck and Thelen (2005) outline different mechanisms of gradual institutional change. Starting out from Schickler's argument (Schickler 1999) they propose an empirical inventory of modes of gradual transformative change (Streeck and Thelen 2005: 2): displacement, layering, drift, conversion, and exhaustion. Under 'displacement'—which presupposes the above described coexistence of different institutional arrangements—the traditional rule is pushed to the side and replaced by a new rule (Streeck and Thelen 2005: 20). 'Layering' consists of the renegotiation of some elements of a given set of institutions while not touching others (Schickler 1999). Schickler argues that institutions develop through a layering of new institutions on top of pre-existing structures (Schickler 1999: 13, see also Héritier 2001). Developing a similar argument, Lanzara talks about institutional 'bricolage' which consist of a recombination and reshuffling of existing institutional components, allowing to protect sunk costs, but also allowing for partial exploration (Lanzara 1998; Crouch and Farrell 2004: 20).[51] To go for entirely new institutional solutions would require a building of new coalitions and at the same time would evoke too much political opposition if they would entirely replace existing institutions (Thelen 2003). Because some rules may be locked in by the power of the constituencies that have created them, new ones have to be built around 'the existing institutions rather than dismantling the old' (Schickler 1999: 13). Thus, as opposed to what path dependency claims, these partial innovations do not push the development of institutional rules along the same track as suggested by the increasing returns arguments of the path-dependence approach (Thelen 2003). 'Drift' denotes the lack of the active maintenance of institutions. If this does not happen, in reaction to a changing political and economic environment, the institution starts to 'drift' (Streeck and Thelen 2005: 24) and changes due to a lack of adjustment to changing external conditions. 'Conversion', still another mode of incremental change, describes how an institution designed for one set of goals is incrementally

---

[51] Bricolage may present a solution between excessive stability of path dependence, or a 'success trap' that derives from institution-specific capabilities, i.e. a 'competence trap'. The exploration of other possibilities becomes unlikely and rigidity ensues. There is no switch over from exploitation (increasing returns) to exploration (trying out new things) (Lanzara 1998).

turned towards other goals because of new requirements of the environment or the pressure of a political, previously more marginal, group who had lost in the last political conflict and is seeking to reorient the institution (Thelen 2003; Streeck and Thelen 2005).

All these modes of gradual change pointed out in critique of models claiming a stark contrast between institutional stability and institutional change as proposed by a strict notion of path-dependent development (in turn criticizing the distributive bargaining approach of institutional change for neglecting institutional stickiness), offer differentiated and insightful, but *ex post* empirical descriptions of institutional transformations. They do not lend themselves to the formulation of general *ex ante* claims about which mode of transformation is likely to come to bear under which particular context conditions. By contrast, the endogenous models of institutional change based on the formal–informal–formal mechanism of institutional change (Farrell and Héritier 2003, 2004, 2006) as well as the mechanism of 'procedural politics' (Jupille 2005) produce such general claims that may be subject to disconfirmation.

Another point of criticism addressed to the distributive bargaining approach of institutional change points to the fact that an institutional rule may *not be clear-cut* with respect to the involved *costs and benefits*. As we have seen, according to the distributive bargaining approach, institutions are a by-product of strategic conflict over substantive outcomes, and actors produce institutions in order to seek distributional advantages for themselves (Knight 1995: 108). However, sometimes it is difficult to attribute clear policy outcomes to a particular institutional rule. Thus an institutional rule may prescribe that actors should meet at least once per a specified period of time. This rule is unlikely to have distributional implications for the involved decision-maker in the sense that one is clearly advantaged over the other (Cortell and Peterson 2001: 772). Gourevitch (1999) has suggested that in moments of institutional design actors are choosing behind a 'veil of ignorance' (Rawls 1971) about future distributional benefits and therefore that principles and norms are likely to matter more than distributional outcomes (Lake 2004: 4–5). It would be different in cases where an institutional rule would establish a clear relationship of super- or subordination of one actor vis-à-vis the other because clear institutional gains or losses would be involved. To the extent that redistributive bargaining theories of institutional change distinguish between rule changes that are beneficial for all actors involved in the decision-making process and those that are clearly redistributive, they take this criticism into account.

A further critique addressed to the distributive bargaining (and the functionalist efficiency oriented) theories of institutional change comes from sociological institutionalism. It is argued that the most important source of institutional change is a process of *socialization into changing sets of values and ideas*. The behavioural assumption is that actors shape and comply with institutions not as a result of cost–benefit calculations, as rational institutionalism submits, but because they think that following particular norms of behaviour and societal values is the legitimate or 'right' thing to do. Behaviour is determined by 'rules of appropriateness' (March and Olsen 1989, 1998).[52] Without denying that actions may be purposive[53] this approach maintains that individuals tend to follow 'scripts' or 'templates' given to them by the institutions in which they are acting. They create or socially construct the actors' identities, belongings, definitions of reality, and shared meanings (Rothstein 1996: 147). On this view institutions include duties, social obligations, and norms (Powell and DiMaggio 1991). They reflect a shared understanding of what actors consider to be legitimate, efficient, or modern (DiMaggio and Powell 1991) and embody shared cultural understanding of the way the world works (Zucker 1983; Meyer and Rowan 1991; Scott 1995; Greif 2002). Certain ways of action are taken for granted as the 'right' way to do things (Scott and Meyer 1994; Radaelli and Schmidt 2005). Such institutions are quite stable, given that it is difficult to change normative or ideological investments (North 1990a, 1990b).

Along a similar vein, Risse and Wiener (1999) argue that a polity (such as the European Union) consists of a system of principles, rules, and procedures which might have socializing effects on actors exposed to these norms. '... Actors internalize the norms which then influence how they see themselves and what they perceive as their interests' (Risse and Wiener 1999: 778). Or as Wendt argues: 'As actors become socialized to norms, they make them part of their identity, and that identity in turn creates a collective interest in norms as ends in themselves. The result is internalized self-restraint: actors follow norms not because it is in their self-interest, but because it is the right

---

[52] There has been a very lively academic debate about the relative importance of explanations based on behaviour following rules of appropriateness as opposed to rules of consequentiality. Thus, Sjöblom criticizes that in sociological institutionalism, as developed by March and Olsen, rules of appropriateness are underspecified. Appropriate for whom? At what level? What if there is a conflict between rules? (Sjöblom 1993: 402). When March and Olsen argue that what is appropriate for a particular person in a particular situation is defined by political and social institutions and transmitted through socialization (March and Olsen 1989), it is not clear what that means for concrete behaviour. 'Suppose that we meet a poor bureaucrat with a large and hungry family in a corrupt country. His answers to the four questions: What kind of situation is this? Bribe will be offered; Who am I: a poor family father; how appropriate are different actions in this situation: to feed the family; do what is most appropriate: take the bribe' (Sjöblom 1993: 402).

[53] Goldmann points out that sociological institutionalism claims to include rational choice approaches; to act as a utility maximizer may be one template among others (Goldmann 2005).

thing to do in their society (Wendt 2001: 1025).[54] Such institutions change in an integrative process.'[55] As March and Olsen argue, 'the will of the people is discovered through deliberation by reasoning citizens and rulers seeking to find the general welfare within a context of shared social values' (March and Olsen 1987: 118).

New institutions are adopted because they are understood to be legitimate in the light of changing existing practices, roles, or responsibilities (March and Olsen 1987; Radaelli and Schmidt 2005). Thus a change would occur when a 'prevailing "script" is replaced or superseded by another'. Fligstein has explained changes in corporate institutional rules as a response to changes in dominant ideas about 'the "modern" or rational way to conduct business' (Fligstein 1997). As a result, the dimensions of conflict and strategy among actors as a source of change disappear from this view because the scripts, by definition, are shared normative persuasions. But could it not precisely be changes in power relations that create opportunities for new scripts to become dominant? And, moreover, as Immergut points out, if 'institutions socialize actors and thus endogenize preferences . . ., then it is difficult to explain why these actors would suddenly prefer a new set of institutions'; '. . . a convincing

---

[54] The socialization explanation of institutional change has been challenged on methodological grounds, for instance by Lichbach. He argues that, first of all it is difficult to ascertain empirically that norms exist. Cultures as communities of norms have poorly defined boundaries. Norms are also contested between individuals, within individuals, among groups, between individuals and society, between groups and society. In view of this, how can we empirically establish that a norm exists? Norms are also incomplete and are in a process of change; moreover norms may sometimes only be weakly held. Second, norms are not directly observable, they are derived from artefacts. Insiders may observe norms differently from outsiders (this is illustrated by the diverging interpretation of the famous Balinese cockfight—Geertz 1980). Norms may also be self-fulfilling prophecies: following norms reinforces norms; at the same time the violation of a norm does not necessarily question this norm, i.e. norm is not dependent on being complied with. Third, norms can be a source of conflict, cooperation, stability, change, etc. Thus a norm may promote conflicts, i.e. the norm is to engage in conflict. Lichbach goes on to argue that, from an analytical viewpoint, norms are a difficult concept to deal with because a norm is tied to action. You can always explain an action with some norm, e.g. people vote because it is their duty to vote. If norms are both empirical regularities of behaviour *and* prescriptions of behaviour they have no analytical significance, but are just another name for behaviour. Moreover, norms need not be followed to be a norm. Therefore, outcomes cannot be used to refute an existing norm (Lichbach 2003).

   To make an analytical argument about a socialization and learning process, the mechanism of learning (norms) needs to be isolated, otherwise the argument would be that the norms fulfil the purposes of the culture or community. Norms or rules of appropriateness by themselves cannot explain action, they do not determine behaviour. An actor is not only a homo sociologicus, an oversocialized man (Dahrendorf 1977; Lichbach 2003).

[55] March and Olsen distinguish between an aggregative process and an integrative political process. In an aggregative process the will of the people is identified through electoral campaigns and bargaining among rational and self-interested citizens within given institutional majority rules (March and Olsen 1987).

account of institutional change must contain within itself its own negation . . . '
(Immergut 2005: 290).

To specify the conditions under which learning and socialization into new
institutional rules occur Checkel (2001*a*, 2001*b*) and Risse (2000) propose a
number of factors. Thus successful socialization or learning may take place
if only a limited number of persons are involved, under conditions of insulation, non-hierarchical decision-making structures, and under conditions of
uncertainty regarding the 'right' problem solution (Checkel 2001*a*). It also
is more likely to prevail when the persuadee has few prior, ingrained beliefs
that are inconsistent with the persuader's message; when the persuader is
an authoritative member of the in-group to which the persuadee belongs
or wants to belong; when the persuader does not lecture or demand, but
instead acts out principles of serious deliberative argument and finally when
the persuader–persuadee interaction occurs in less politicized and more insulated environments (Joergensen, Kock, and Roerbech 1998 cited in Checkel
2001*c*: 222).[56] Under such conditions—they argue—processes of persuasion
or learning are more likely to take place.[57] The advantage of this argument over
the simple socialization argument which does not specify conditions under
which socialization occurs, is that the explanatory variable (the particular
conditions) is clearly independent from what is to be explained, the extent
of socialization into a particular norm representing a particular institutional
rule.

Further scope conditions under which deliberation/persuasion/arguing as
opposed to bargaining is more likely to occur are outlined by Goodin.

---

[56] Moravcsik points out that all of these hypotheses could be linked with a rational choice
approach as well. First, in novel situations the generation of information is more costly, second
Bayesian learning is based on prior experience as a measure of the extent to which an actor
is willing to accept disconfirming evidence and that actors are more likely to update beliefs
when prior evidence and experience point in the same direction. Third, that a persuader with
the same goals as the persuadee or who is powerful is more likely to be successful. Fourth, the
emphasis that actors are more likely to update beliefs and policies when the persuader has similar
preferences or a long experience of exchanges, or when it is linked with a wish to gain access to
a group. Equally, rational choice theorists would argue that argumentative persuasion is more
likely when the persuader offers payments and points to incentives to comply. Under rationalist
theories of signalling and commitment it is 'not the *form* (original emphasis) of deliberative
argument that matters, but the extent to which those arguments signal the truth of substantive
claims. . . . These can either demonstrate the proven investment of the persuader in the veracity
of arguments about consequences, or the willingness of the persuader to strategically coerce, or
induce compliance' (Moravcsik 2001: 234).

[57] Schimmelfennig distinguishes between manipulative and argumentative persuasion.
Rhetorical action consists in the strategic use of arguments and builds on this manipulative,
instrumental, understanding of persuasion. Argumentative persuasion, by contrast, involves
changing attitudes about cause and effect in the absence of overt coercion (Schimmelfennig
2001).

According to his argument, deliberation (he uses the term 'discourse') pre-supposes the absence of conflicts of interests between the involved parties (Goodin 2004: 8). Since most political decisions consist of a mixed-motive game of strategy or, worse, a game '...of pure competition, in which one person's gains are the other's losses. It is a massive leap of faith to suppose that all parties to a conversation-cum-deliberation share the same view of the "purpose" of the discussion, of "what it is about"' (Goodin 2004: 10). He sees the most favourable conditions for deliberation and socializing effects in the 'caucus room' which is characterized by candour. 'Members can speak freely, knowing that what is said in the caucus room stays in the caucus room. There deliberation can achieve "authenticity" without "deception"....' (Goodin 2004: 19). The caucus condition meets the general condition of insulation and confidentiality as specified by Checkel (2001*a*, 2001*b*) and Risse (2000; Risse and Wiener 1999) as a general condition favouring deliberation. In contrast, Goodin goes on to argue, the next stage, the parliamentarian debate, is a public arena where one's case is put. 'Each party sets out the most coherent and persuasive justification it can, for its preferred position. Arguments are registered and responded to, but nobody is expected to change his or her mind' (Goodin 2004: 20).[58] Concern for the common good is shown and participation is open to all Members of the Parliament (MEPs). Under the conditions of the election process, the next stage, there are again features of openness and considerations of the common good are frequently invoked, even if it may be in only a strategic sense (Goodin 2004: 22). Other elements of the deliberative process such as coherent rational arguments are clearly less present. Respect for opposing groups, their interests and arguments is likely to suffer (Goodin 2004: 20). In the bargaining stage the actors come with fixed preferences and firm demands.

Fligstein (1997), but also Finnemore and Sikkink (1998) specify conditions, too, under which persuasion and learning to initiate institutional change are more likely to unfold: they expect the existence of entrepreneurs to be crucial,

---

[58] The parliamentary debate shows some elements of deliberation as defined by Steiner et al.: (*a*) open participation: every competent actor should be free to take part in the discussion; (*b*) justification of assertions and validity of claims: assertions should be introduced and critically assessed through exchange of information and reasons; the tighter the link between premises and conclusions, the more coherent the justification, the more will it contribute to deliberation; (*c*) consideration of the common good: sense of empathy, other-directedness or solidarity that induces the participants to consider the well-being of others and of the entire community; those arguing on the basis of self-interest must demonstrate that it is compatible with or contributes to the common good; (*d*) respect: participants should acknowledge the needs and rights of other social groups and respect their demands as long as they can be considered as justified and show respect towards counter-arguments; (*e*) aim at a rationally motivated consensus or at least mutually acceptable compromise; authentic preferences should be stated (Steiner et al. 2004).

entrepreneurs who actively promote specific social institutions in the process of persuasion and learning. Gradually the new institutional rules are internalized by political actors and affect their identities and interests (Fligstein 1997; Finnemore and Sikkink 1998). One question that emerges is, of course, where this entrepreneur promoting the transformation of social rules comes from? Is she an *exogenous* factor which is parachuted into the explanation of institutional change? Or is the entrepreneur a constitutive element of the formal institutional arrangements within which the transformation occurs? The same question arises when Finnemore and Sikkink argue that there are different stages in the process of socialization into changed institutional rules; the passage from one to the next is critically helped by supporting infrastructure and a critical mass of actors supporting the new institution (Finnemore and Sikkink 1998). Focusing on these conditions allows them to empirically validate their hypotheses.

A critique against the distributive-bargaining based, formal–informal– formal dynamic theory of institutional change developed by Farrell and Héritier, from the sociological institutionalist perspective (Olsen 2003; Sverdrup 2005)[59] is that the informal rules which arise in the daily application of a formal rule, do not present an outcome of a bargaining process, but are an outcome of arguing and deliberation and a socialization into particular social norms of how to handle decision situations. Püttner (2003) as well as Joerges and Neyer (1997) have argued along a similar vein, when they submit that the particular relevance of informal communication among political actors[60] is their ability to routinize and 'communize' the process of interpretation of constitutional norms at the intergovernmental level (Joerges and Neyer 1997). Püttner distinguishes three different modes of informal communication that constitute a discussion: deliberative discussions, information exchange, and informal bargaining (Püttner 2003: 115). He aims to assess the relative importance of the different dimensions and to relate them to the particular institutional setting and content of discussions under which they are likely to occur, thus defining scope conditions under which one or the

[59] J. P. Olsen personal communication at an ARENA workshop in Oslo 2003; Sverdrup personal communication at a workshop at the European University Institute, May 2005.

[60] In this particular case member-state representatives in comitology committees. This process may lead to a shared normative framework changing existing national traditions because the advocates of the different positions in the ongoing dialogue have to explain their own understandings and can challenge the views of their counterparts. They call this form of informal mediation 'deliberative intergovernmentalism'. There has been much discussion about whether processes of deliberation in small groups lead to a convergence of preferences or rather a polarization of preferences (Sunstein 2000); and, more than that, over whether it is desirable to achieve such a convergence of preferences or whether under many circumstances it may not be better to retain different preferences and strike a compromise fair to all.

other comes to bear. Following Habermas (1987) he argues that arguing and deliberation is about truth seeking. Actors are prepared to retreat from their initial strategic motivation if the discourse persuades them to do so. Arguing can make a difference because it refers to a particular set of shared values of rationality and impartiality (Püttner 2003: 116). Exchange of information does affect the preferences of the actors involved; finally hard bargaining 'in which negotiators are not interested in talking to each other in the sense of persuading their counterparts implying that the preferences of the latter ones are wrong or inadequate' (Püttner 2003: 117). As Checkel (2001*a*) and Risse (2000), Püttner argues that arguing is more likely to occur in a closed setting under conditions of confidentiality without being subject to public scrutiny (Püttner 2003: 117).

And, finally, different from Farrell and Héritier's endogenous explanation of institutional change, based on power and bargaining, Stone Sweet and Sandholtz (1997) have developed a theory of endogenous institutional change which also starts from rule ambiguity, but focuses on dispute resolution in the conflict over rule interpretation as the driving motor of institutional change. They argue that, within a given structure of institutional rules, 'actions trigger disputes since it is impossible to cover every possible contingency by the rules encompassed in the normative structure. To support their cases, actors employ arguments which are grounded in *analogies with some prior case* (legal precedents, A.H.). The outcomes of these arguments lead to a modification of a particular rule' (Sandholtz and Stone Sweet 2004: 240). The causal mechanism driving institutional change, analogical reasoning is 'the process through which people reason and learn about a new situation (the *target* analogue) by relating it to a more familiar situation (the *source* analogue) that can be viewed as structurally parallel' (Sandholtz and Stone Sweet 2004: 240). It is prevalent in novel and unfamiliar situations.

Against the background of these various elements of critique of the distributive-bargaining based theory of institutional change what are the particular scope conditions under which the explanatory power of this theory in its different variants is particularly high?

3.4.5. Scope Conditions

Some scope conditions may be derived from the underlying assumptions. One restrictive assumption is that the negotiating actors are relatively independent from existing institutional and policy entanglements, and can pursue their goals of institutional change relatively freely in the bargaining process. However, as we have seen, the modified distributional bargaining-oriented approach of institutional *change*, as opposed to institutional *design*, takes into account the existing institutional structure at t1 in order to account for institutional outcomes at t2. This means that the institutional rules, given at t1 are a factor in the explanation of institutional outcomes as well. It also means that the transforming aspect of institutions may be taken into account in that given institutional rules at t1 can correct the one-to-one impact of power onto institutional outcomes at t2.

An important scope condition of the applicability of this approach is the possibility to clearly delimit costs and benefits of an institutional rule. Hence these theories will best explain institutional change when the empirical conditions are such that there are clear differences in both the distributional consequences of rules and clear differences in the distribution of power of the negotiating actors.

Another boundary condition of a distributive bargaining explanation, as compared to a functional explanation of institutional change, is given with the very nature of the issue at stake. Thus Lake argues that security issues, as an instance of a public good accessible to all and subject to non-rival consumption, generally lack strong distributional implications, 'thus tend to be influenced more strongly by efficiency rather than distributional considerations' (Lake 2004: 8). The same holds for areas of decision-making where there is a lot of uncertainty with respect to the distributive implications of a rule.

4

Empirical Cases

4.1. METHODOLOGY

It is the aim of the empirical part of the book to investigate the patterns of long-term institutional change which are typical for a number of important institutional rules governing the decision-making process in the European Union.[1] I will try to account for the change of these institutional rules over time in the light of the 'thin' rational choice institutionalist theories presented and discussed in Chapter 3. If it were to be shown that they do not satisfactorily explain the change of the institutional rule, I will turn to the theories criticizing the rational institutionalist theories to discuss alternative explanations. I start from the assumption that it is unlikely that only one theory is able to explain different types of changes of a particular institutional rule over the entire long period of time. Rather it is likely that under different scope conditions, as specified in the third chapter, different theories will hold more or less explanatory power.

Therefore, the de facto development of the five institutional rules in question will be carefully scrutinized in the light of the theoretical explanations outlined in the third chapter, in order to assess which theory offers the most plausible explanation for the institutional change which has occurred in a particular period of time, or whether several factors derived from different theories interact with each other in explaining the outcome (Mayntz 2002). Different theoretical explanations may also be linked over time in accounting for different stages of development. The explanatory approach employed here is, therefore, to look at the variation on the dependent variable, that is the institutional change in a particular stage, and to account for it as far as possible on the basis of one theory; if this theory reaches its limits, I seek for further theoretical explanations to account for 'the rest' of the change and discuss possible interactions between different theories. This is not done in the sense

---

[1] I use European Union (EU), the present formal name of the polity when talking in general. When analysing previous stages I use the then valid formal name, e.g. European Economic Community (EEC).

of a strict hypothesis testing, but as an attempt to conduct an empirical plausibility probe of the hypotheses developed in Chapter 3.

In accounting for institutional change, the dependent variable or explanandum is the altered institutional rule at t2 as compared to t1. This means that institutions figure both on the side of the independent and dependent variables.[2] I claim that existing institutional rules, at least in part, give rise to changed institutional rules. Having institutions on both sides of the equation makes the argument vulnerable to tautology. Two arguments may be made in order to meet this critique. First, institutional rules at t1, on the side of the independent variable, may be different from the institutions to be accounted for on the side of dependent variable at t2. Thus, a macro-institutional rule, such a particular treaty provision may be explaining why the application of a particular lower-order institutional rule is excluded. If institutions at t1 account for the altering of institutions at t2, we offer an *endogenous* explanation of institutional change. However, second, it must be allowed that not only endogenous, that is institutional arguments, are presented to account for the change of institutional rules at t2, but exogenous factors are employed, as well. The causal process invoked to account for the process leading from the independent to the dependent variable frequently includes an element of *exogeneity.* Thus, an actor's bargaining power not only depends on the existing formal institutional rules, but may also derive from an increase in power accruing from some external factor, for example material wealth.[3] There are very few, purely endogenous explanations of institutional change. As Caporaso puts it so well: pushing the 'institutions account for institutions' argument too far would amount to 'autistic institutions', non-responsive to their external environment; and, conversely, pushing the exogeneity argument too far by claiming that institutions respond exclusively to external 'demand' factors (Przeworski 2004) would amount to the statement that 'institutions do not matter' (Caporaso 2007). In short, the theories discussed in the following in order to account for institutional change build on both, that is endogenous institutional processes and exogenously driven change of existing institutions.

The five empirical cases, instances of important decision-making rules in the European Union, have been chosen from three analytically relevant angles: (*a*) rules that have undergone a *drastic change* over the last decades

---

[2] The argument made is one of theories of institutions and institutionalist theory (Diermeier and Krehbiel 2003). Diermeier and Krehbiel distinguish between theories of institutions in which institutions are the explanandum and institutionalist theories in which institutions are the explanans accounting for policy outcomes.

[3] The suggested causal mechanism may include intermediate variables of non-institutional nature (Gerring 2005: 166)

(the Parliament's role in legislation; the Parliament's investiture of the Commission) and rules that have *changed little* (the rules governing comitology; the composition of the Commission); (*b*) rules that were *initially designed* (the Parliament's role in legislation; the composition of the Commission) and rules that *developed 'out of nothing'* (the Parliament's right of investing the Commission; the rules governing the Presidency of the Council); and (*c*) rules that are clear-cut in their *distributional implications* as regards actors' power (Composition of the Commission; the Parliament's role in legislation; the Parliament's role in investing the Commission) and rules that address coordination problems (rules governing the Presidency of the Council). The 'process' perspective and 'structural' perspective discussed in the theoretical part will be applied in the explanation of all empirical cases. The process perspective focuses on the causal mechanisms driving change and their triggers (exogenous or endogenous) and the sequence or links between different types of changes; the structural perspective focuses on the levels/arenas across which change plays out and the types of actors focus on designing actors and implementing/affected actors.

The time periods under scrutiny will follow the most obvious mode of periodization mostly delimited by the formal (higher-order) rule revisions. In other words, the transformation of institutional rules are followed and accounted for within the framework of periodical formal changes.

The empirical data which are used in the analysis of the cases are based on three different sources: (*a*) data collected in interviews conducted with decision-makers in the European Union, (*b*) data collected from archival material, and (*c*) data drawn from secondary analysis of existing primary empirical research.

4.2. INSTITUTIONAL RULE ONE: THE EUROPEAN PARLIAMENT'S ROLE IN LEGISLATION

This case of institutional change investigates the change of the rules governing the Parliament's role in legislation.[4] In a period of almost fifty years, the institutional rule initially giving the Parliament a merely consultative role in legislation changed into a rule that established the Parliament as a co-equal legislator with the Council of Ministers under the co-decision procedure. The period under analysis will be divided into a number of shorter periods delimited by the formal institutional changes brought about under

---

[4] See also the general literature on the European Parliament, such as Scully 1997; Maurer 1999, 2003; Corbett 2000; Kreppel 2000; Shackleton 2000; Hix 2001.

treaty revisions, that is the formal redefinition of the higher-order rules. Five different successive periods will be distinguished:

1. from the consultation right under the EEC (1957) to the cooperation right under the Single European Act (SEA) (1986);
2. from the cooperation right under the SEA (1986) to the co-decision right under the Maastricht Treaty (TEU) (1992);
3. from the co-decision right under the TEU (1992) to the expanded codecision right under the Amsterdam Treaty (1997);
4. from the co-decision right under the Amsterdam Treaty (1997) to the further expanded co-decision right under the Nice Treaty (2001);
5. from the Nice Treaty (2001) to the changes under the Constitutional Treaty (2004).

In each period, I start out from the formal status quo rule, that is the rule defining the role of the Parliament in legislation, trace the empirical changes that the rule underwent in the defined period and ask the question: how can this change or absence of change be explained? What is the underlying process that brought the change about and how can it be theoretically grasped? Is the process triggered by exogenous or endogenous factors and how do different phases of change link? Does institutional change extend across different levels and which actor categories (designing or implementing/affected actors) are crucial for the outcome of the process of change?

4.2.1. From the European Economic Treaty to the Single European Act

The first period under study starts out from the right of the Parliament to be consulted as laid down in the original treaties (1957) and ends with the Parliament's right to cooperation in the legislative process as introduced under the SEA (1986). Under the Treaty of the EEC and the Euratom Treaties of 1957, the Parliament only had a limited, *consultative* role in the adoption of Community legislation. The legislative power was entirely in the hands of the Council of Ministers.[5] In twenty-two articles of the EEC Treaty, and in eleven articles in the Euratom Treaty, the Council was obliged to consult the Parliament before the adoption of legislative proposals. In being consulted, the

---

[5] Under the European Coal and Steel Community Treaty, the Parliament held a right of control over the High Authority (Commission), but had not formal role in legislation. As one parliamentarian official put it: 'Council...treated Parliament with complete disdain and disregard. Each new Council President would hardly turn up in Parliament' (Interview EP Official, Dec. 2004, quoted in Boucher (2006).

Parliament was *not* subject to a deadline formulated by the Council by which it had to formulate its opinion[6] (Corbett, Jacobs, and Shackleton 2000: 176).

The Parliament, as Corbett, Jacobs, and Shackleton (2000) describe it, very quickly set out to press for an extension of the consultation procedure and demanded an application to a wider range of problems, urging that it should be consulted in all 'important problems'. The Council obliged in 1960 by extending consultations to more issues and adding the possibility of 'voluntary consultations'. In a further step in 1964, the consultations were expanded beyond 'important problems' without specifying the limits. By the mid-1970s, Council consulted Parliament on every legislative proposal (except those of purely technical or temporary nature) (Corbett, Jacobs, and Shackleton 2000: 177).[7] Moreover, in several letters in 1969 and 1970, the Council committed itself to inform the Parliament about the reasons if it should not take the Parliament's opinion into account when adopting legislation. First this applied only to legislation with financial implications, then to all 'important questions' (Corbett, Jacobs, and Shackleton 2000: 178).

Following the first enlargement of the Community in 1973 with Denmark, the United Kingdom and Ireland joining, the Paris Summit of Heads of governments called for a reinforcement of the powers of control of the Parliament and an improvement of relations with the Parliament. As a result, the Council committed itself to consult the Parliament on Commission proposals prior to examining the latter's legislative draft, provided that the Parliament's opinion be issued within an appropriate period of time (Corbett, Jacobs, and Shackleton 2000: 178). The Commission, too, stated its willingness to consult Parliament on all proposals (except minor technical ones); and—if agreeing with the Parliament's amendments—to incorporate them into its draft; to present the Commission's position on all amendments in the Parliament; and to inform Parliament of the proposal sent to the Council. The Council and the Commission also agreed that Parliament should be re-consulted when important changes were envisaged on a draft (Corbett, Jacobs, and Shackleton 2000: 178).

The first direct democratic election of the members of Parliament (MEPs) in 1979 strengthened the Parliament[8] the bearer of direct democratic

---

[6] By comparison, such a deadline was provided for in the case of the consultation of the Economic and Social Committee in legislation.

[7] Moreover, in 1968, the Council began to consult the Parliament on non-legislative texts, e.g. Council resolutions and Commission memoranda laying down guidelines, timetables, and commitments for forthcoming legislation. The Parliament could adopt a resolution on these texts (Corbett, Jacobs, and Shackleton 2000: 177).

[8] 'The direct election didn't make any great change, certainly not immediately. It was a slow evolution. Parliament dragged new power out of the consultation process... and built itself up in the new treaties' (Interview diplomate, August 2004; quoted in Boucher 2006).

legitimation, in its endeavours to strengthen its own position vis-à-vis the Council and the Commission. After the elections it set up a subcommittee for 'institutional problems' in the Political Affairs Committee to 'investigate' the relations between the Parliament and the Council and the Parliament and the Commission. This subcommittee proposed a number of institutional reforms, all within the context of the existing treaty.[9] One set of issues discussed the relations between the Parliament and the Council. The upshot of the resolution on the report submitted by the eight rapporteurs was that the goal of the Parliament was to share in the exercise of powers 'attributed by the treaties to the other institutions, by means of joint agreements with them' (Corbett 1998: 132). Joint agreements should be formed between the Parliament and the Council, and the Parliament and the Commission, allowing the Parliament to share in the power that formally was not granted under the treaties.

Regarding the Parliament's role in legislation, the most important demand made was that the Commission should consult the Parliament on all drafts of legislation before making a formal proposal to the Council; that the Commission should alter its proposal following the amendments made by the Parliament; and should withdraw its proposal if rejected by the Parliament; the Council (after the Luxembourg compromise) should return to majority decisions, for dealing with a Council that decides on the basis of QMV is easier for the Parliament than dealing with a Council deciding on the basis of unanimity; moreover, that the Council should formalize and honour commitments made to the Parliament regarding the consultation process and, in particular, provide sufficient information to the Parliament and re-consult the Parliament after the amendment of texts. Finally, the Parliament demanded that the conciliation procedure (employed in budget matters) should be extended to all proposals that Parliament deems important. The response of the Commission (1981) was predominantly positive except when it came to incorporating the Parliament's amendments as they stood and to automatically withdraw its own proposal if rejected by the Parliament (Corbett 1998: 133).

The Council, by contrast, made minimal concessions and only promised to regularly inform the Parliament (Corbett 1998: 134). It committed itself to fully inform the Parliament of the reasons that led it to adopt its common position in writing. However, as Corbett reports, the first such justification

---

[9] Dealing with the right of legislative initiative, the appointment of a new Commission, the relations between the Parliament and national parliaments, the role of the Parliament in European Political Cooperation, the relations between the Parliament and the Economic and Social Committee, the relations between Parliament and the European Council, the role of the Parliament in the negotiation and ratification of treaties of accession and of other treaties and agreements between the European Community and third countries (Corbett 1998: 131–2).

merely referred to the preambles of the draft directives (Corbett, Jacobs, and Shackleton 2000: 201).[10] It appears that eventually, the explanations provided by Council improved with the latter presenting the Council's viewpoint on the substantive issues of draft legislation and pointing out where Council disagrees with the Commission draft (Corbett, Jacobs, and Shackleton 2000: 202).

In 1981, two member states, notorious for their supportive attitude towards the Parliament, Germany and Italy, took an initiative (the so-called Genscher–Colombo initiative) to relaunch the impetus of European integration alongside with an institutional reform that accommodated many of the proposals of the Parliament. This initiative prepared the ground for the Stuttgart Solemn Declaration (1983). The initiative proposed the creation of a European Union.[11] Germany and Italy could not agree whether to engage in a revision of the treaty, nor did a working party of foreign ministers reach an agreement (Corbett 1998: 135). In a meeting of foreign ministers and the Parliament's Enlarged Bureau, the Council refused to accept the Parliament's suggestion to establish 'a contact group' of MEPs and permanent representatives to involve Parliament in on-going legislative discussions. In response, the Parliament reasserted its institutional demands, proposed to develop an 'inter-institutional agreement' and insisted on the establishing of a contact group. Finally, the debate came to a conclusion in the 1983 Stuttgart Solemn Declaration of the European Council. The Declaration met some of the Parliament's demands albeit in a 'considerably watered-down' form (Corbett 1998: 137). The Commission promised that it would consult the Parliament more frequently on draft legislation, but insisted that it would not automatically accept the Parliament's amendments (Corbett 1998: 137). Member states declared that 'the application of the decision-making procedures laid down in the treaties of Paris and Rome is of vital importance in order to improve the EC's capacity to act' (Corbett 1998: 139). Disappointingly to the Parliament, its demand to be reconsulted and the provision of information was not mentioned in the Solemn Declaration (Corbett 1998: 139).[12]

In sum, the Parliament from the very beginning pressed for a change in the application of the consultation rule, particularly with regard to the scope of its application and was quite successful in achieving this aim informally.

---

[10] The Parliament expected that the Council should at least react to each of Parliament's amendments (Corbett, Jacobs, and Shackleton 2000: 202).

[11] Independently from the Genscher–Colombo initiative, the Parliament had also developed a plan to create a political union (Beach 2005: 36).

[12] While the Commission was willing to extend the conciliation procedure to other non-budgetary issues, the Council—lacking the support of Denmark—was not. However, Council accepted to interpret the legislation 'with appreciable financial implications' more flexibly (Corbett 1998: 140).

However, when it came to the formalization of these informal institutional gains which would have implied a formal shift of power in its own favour, it had only limited success. In spite of the support of two member states launching an initiative favourable to its institutional interests (the Genscher–Colombo initiative), the Stuttgart Solemn Declaration of the Council of Ministers remained far behind the hopes of the Parliament.

Recognizing the limits of a strategy of *institutional self-promotion by simply advocating the expansion of its institutional rights* within the existing formal rules, the Parliament changed gears and exerted stronger political pressure. It increasingly started using a strategy of delaying its opinion on a legislative item. The *absence* of a time limit set for the Parliament to deliver its opinion on legislative drafts served as a lever. By delaying the legislative process, the Parliament could underline its demands for a more extensive interpretation of its formal rights. These changed institutional rules, although informal, according to the Parliament should be stated in an exchange of letters, or in an 'interinstitutional agreement' between two bodies, that would subsequently guide the interaction of the two players in the legislative consultation process (Corbett, Jacobs, and Shackleton 2000: 176).

The Parliament had yet another—albeit indirect—means through which it could exert pressure in order to achieve an extension of its legislative consultation rights: by using its budgetary powers. In 1975, a conciliation procedure had been introduced in order to reduce conflicts between Council and Parliament that emerged in the context of the new budgetary powers of the Parliament. The budgetary rules created in the 1970s had been vaguely formulated, thus providing distinct incentives and opportunity structures for the actors that operated under them: the Parliament consistently challenged them (Rittberger 2003a, 2003b, 2005). The prevailing practice that had developed under its budgetary powers was that the Parliament could prevent the implementation of legislation with budgetary implications. The Council was therefore willing to negotiate and agree on a mechanism to reduce such a risk (Joint Declaration of March 1975—Corbett, Jacobs, and Shackleton 2000: 181).[13] The Parliament considered the Joint Declaration[14] as an encouraging step of reform in the right direction accomplished within the existing treaty

[13] Whether such a joint declaration is legally binding has not yet been tested, though the European Court of Justice (ECJ) has referred to their existence (Corbett, Jacobs, and Shackleton 2000: 182). The Parliament could threaten not to vote for the necessary credits in the following year's budget. This, however, was only a credible threat if the Parliament was totally opposed to the proposal which was rare. According to Corbett, Jacobs, and Shackleton (2000), the Council had, therefore, little incentives to make major concessions to Parliament in the conciliation procedure (Corbett, Jacobs, and Shackleton 2000: 182).

[14] And the Lunst Westertorp procedure under which the Council had agreed to involve Parliament more closely in discussion on international agreements with third countries.

rules (Corbett 1998: 131). In the 1980s, it therefore set out to widen the scope of application of the conciliation rule, as it had done for the consultation rule, to all 'important' Community acts and laid this down in its Rules of Procedure. Due to reservations from Denmark, the Council refused to agree to the Second Joint Declaration proposed by the Commission, however, was willing to apply the notion of legislation with 'appreciable financial implications' in a flexible way, allowing for more conciliation.[15] Hence, due to these only minor concessions of the Council, Corbett concludes that '...the great hope of the Parliament to develop its legislative powers by the extension and improvement of the conciliation procedure was dashed' (Corbett 1998: 140).

In applying delay as a means of pressing for an extension of its consultation rights, the Parliament ran into a conflict with the Council. To settle these conflicts the parties turned to the ECJ which ruled in the famous Isoglucose case of 1980: Parliament had debated the draft of the Isoglucose decision in plenary. It had not taken a final vote on the resolution as a whole but had referred the text back to the responsible committee. This obviously delayed its opinion and draw out the decision-making process. The Parliament blamed the Council for not having requested the urgency procedure provided for by the internal rules of the Parliament, nor asked for an extraordinary session of Parliament (Corbett 1998: 119). One of the new internal rules of the Parliament provided that it could decide to postpone the final vote on the Commission's proposal until the latter had taken a position on its amendments. If the Commission refused to accept the amendments, Parliament could refer the matter back to committee for reconsideration. If by contrast the Commission took the Parliament's amendments into account, the latter would take a final vote in plenary (Corbett 1998: 119). These amendments would then be incorporated into a revised proposal that the Council could change by unanimity only (Corbett, Jacobs, and Shackleton 2000: 180). In the Isoglucose case, the Council, because of the delay, moved ahead and adopted the Isoglucose Directive. Parliament challenged the decision before the ECJ. The Court annulled the Directive because Parliament had not given its opinion. The Court, referring to the direct election of the Parliament, argued that through the consultation of the Parliament '...the people should take part in the exercise of power through the intermediary of the representative assembly' (quoted in Corbett, Jacobs, and Shackleton 2000: 179). The Isoglucose ruling gave Parliament an important instrument to underline its institutional demands in the cooperation with the Council and the Commission. Corbett, Jacobs, and Shackleton

---

[15] Moreover, several informal conciliations took place, such as on the first stage of the monetary union, among Council Presidency, Commission, and responsible parliamentarian rapporteurs and committee chairmen. 'Such flexibility contributed to a wide range of reasonably successful conciliations during the 1980s' (Corbett, Jacobs, and Shackleton 2000: 183).

stress, however, that Parliament was careful 'to avoid explicitly blocking decisions by withholding its opinion indefinitely, instead pleading a need to get
further information, to investigate the social consequences, to pursue discussions with other institutions or interested parties, to hold public hearings, or
to wait for related events' (Corbett, Jacobs, and Shackleton 2000: 180).

To draw an *interim theoretical conclusion*, how can these first institutional
gains of the Parliament in legislation between 1957 and 1983 be *theoretically*
explained? Why was the Parliament rather successful in extending the scope
of the application of the consultation rule, that is the 'Aim' dimension of
institutional rules according to Crawford and Ostrom (1995), but why did
it fail to realize the ambitious institutional reforms proposed in 1980? Five
processes of change emerge from the empirical description of this period from
1957 to 1983.

First, in the 1960s and early 1970s the Council and the Commission seem
to have voluntarily obliged with an extension of the scope of application of
the consultation rule, giving in to the constant institutional self-promotion
and demands of the Parliament. Since there is no evidence of an exertion of
political pressure of the Parliament in these years, it may be concluded that
the Council and the Commission made the concessions under the impression
of a *normative argument of democratic legitimation*. Throughout this period
the Parliament, in its attempts to strengthen its own institutional position
by extending the consultation rights, was supported by the general call for
a stronger democratic legitimation of European decision-making. It used
this 'resource' in arguing for why its own competences should be extended.
This argument corresponds to a *sociological institutionalist* argument of the
normative force of *appropriate rules of democratic legitimation* that are to
be followed in European legislation. However, if this normative force would
have been the prevailing factor, the Parliament since its first direct election
in 1979, should have much faster become a full colegislator alongside with
the Council. Instead it had to fight for it for another twelve years against
the resistance of some member states and in part also of the Commission
until the full co-legislative power was introduced under the Maastricht Treaty
(1992).

Secondly, this development was supported by an exogenous event of a
round of enlargement with new members supporting the power of the Parliament, and two new ambitious tasks: the project of the completion of the
internal market and monetary union programme that had been put on the
agenda (Genscher–Colombo initiative; Dooge Report). These exogenous factors favoured a reconsideration of the existing institutional rule governing the
role of the Parliament in legislation. Accordingly, a widening of the policymaking scope of the European Community should be linked to a strengthening of
the role of the Parliament in the legislative process. However, there was no

willingness on the part of the majority of member states to formalize these demands under the Stuttgart Declaration. This explanation corresponds to an *exogenous functional interpretation and liberal intergovernmentalist explanation* of the causes of institutional change (Moravcsik 1998).

Formal progress being modest, the Parliament, thirdly, started to link its extensive interpretation of the existing right of consultation to a *threat to delay* the delivery of its opinion on a legislative draft. Thus, the Parliament implicitly[16] bargained for a more extensive interpretation of the existing formal rule of consultation, leading to new informal rules that indeed guaranteed a more extensive scope of application (the 'Aim' dimension—Crawford and Ostrom 1995) of the rule. Corbett (1998) calls the Parliament's strategy a policy of reform *within* treaties. The Council and the Commission accepted it because the Parliament could threaten to withhold its opinion. Thus Corbett, Jacobs, and Shackleton (2000) emphasize that urgency strengthened the bargaining position of the Parliament. This explanation confirms Farrell and Héritier's theory (2003, 2004, forthcoming) of *endogenous institutional change based on power-based bargaining* between formal treaty revisions.[17] The Parliament underlined its pressure by linking its demands for an extension of its consultation rights with its existing general budgetary powers, that is preventing the implementation of legislation with budgetary implications. It used a *linked-arena veto*.

Fourth, as we have seen, this strategy of the Parliament gave rise to a conflict with the Council which—disregarding the consultation right of the Parliament—proceeded with legislation. The conflict was solved by a third party whose interpretation of the institutional rule henceforth guided the application of the rule.[18] This is the mechanism of change theoretically captured by Stone Sweet in his theory of *institutional change driven by the settling of a rule conflict through the authoritative decision by a third party* (Stone Sweet 1999).[19]

---

[16] For a distinction between implicit and explicit (around the table) bargaining, see Sebenius (1992).

[17] Here the comparison with the Economic and Social Affairs Committee is instructive whose delivery of an opinion on a legislative draft was subject to a deadline and hence did not lend itself to a delaying strategy to reinforce bargaining power.

[18] Another Court ruling in 1995, however, imposed on the Parliament the duty of loyal cooperation (Corbett, Jacobs, and Shackleton 2000: 180).

[19] The argument put forward by the Parliament in the Isoglucose case that the Council had not observed the Parliament's self-defined rules of decision-making in cases of urgency is interesting in itself. The Council, of course, rejected to act according to the rules of procedure unilaterally defined by the Parliament. Westlake in his analysis concludes: 'If consultation enables Parliament to influence legislation this can only be done obliquely, through dealing and thanks to a series of undertakings by the other institutions and an open/ended Court ruling. Indeed, Parliament's legislative influence under the consultation procedure is better described as an ingenious response to its lack of true legislative powers' (Westlake 1994: 135).

To resume the *empirical account* after the Stuttgart Declaration (1983), it appears that, in spite of some success, the institutional grounds gained by the Parliament in legislation had remained limited. As Corbett argues, the mere delaying power and the absence of a direct veto-power of the Parliament resulted in only limited institutional change. The ignoring of its institutional reform proposals by the Council and the only scarce response to the Parliament's legislative amendments[20] '... led to a radicalization of attitudes' (Corbett 1998: 142).

So far the treaty revision avenue had not been considered a viable option, hence all efforts of the Parliament had centred on a *within-treaty* change. By 1981, however, a treaty revision had become a major objective. The integration process had stalled despite the introduction of the European Monetary System (EMS). The Genscher–Colombo initiative (1981), as we have seen, calling for a deepening of the Community in the light of economic recession, however, had met with resistance in some member states (Moravcsik 1991: 145). In this situation, Altiero Spinelli, an independent member of the Parliament, gained a wide cross-partisan support of MEPs (the Crocodile Club)[21] for a project of treaty revision (Corbett 1998: 142–4). The group proposed that the Parliament should assume responsibility 'for debating and voting reforms which would be submitted for approval to the constitutional bodies of the member states in order to avoid immediate burial in a Council working party' (Corbett 1998: 145). The Crocodile Resolution was adopted with a large majority in the plenary in 1981 (Corbett 1998: 145).

In a first step towards implementation, the Parliament's Committee on Institutional affairs issued a list of far-reaching institutional reforms aiming at strengthening the power of supranational organizations (Corbett 1998: 148).[22] Spinelli and his group in a draft treaty called for 'a Union capable of dealing more effectively with the internal and external problems facing Europe ...' (Corbett 1998: 149), most importantly economic and social policy and foreign and security policy. This would require a strengthening of the Commission, an increased use of QMV in the Council, and the joint legislation by the Council and the Parliament (Corbett 1998: 151). The Parliament, in 1984, adopted the proposal for treaty reform (DTEU) with a large consensus[23] (Corbett 1998: 153–4).

---

[20] As well as the experience of the rejection of the 1980 budget.

[21] The group opposed to the Crocodile group, the Kangaroo group, argued for a liberalization of the European markets as a means to 'relaunch Europe'.

[22] The Committee also organized a series of hearings with presidents of other organizations, social partners, and academics.

[23] Of the Socialist, EPP, Liberal, and Communist groups, a majority support of the Conservatives and the abstention of EPD (Gaullists) (Corbett 1998: 153–4).

By taking this step, the Parliament was crucial in putting a treaty reform on the agenda. As pointed out above, the Genscher–Colombo initiative had also advocated far-reaching institutional reforms under the roof of a 'Political Union', but could not agree whether this should be *within* the treaties or in a revised treaty.[24] The Commission rejected the idea of establishing a new treaty, but called for amendments of the existing treaties, and strongly welcomed the endeavour for a relaunch of the Community (McAllister 1997; Beach 2005: 41). It also proposed to introduce a cooperation procedure for the legislative process. Member states in the 'Solemn Declaration on European Union' (1983) had emphasized the need of cooperation in additional policy areas and the urgency of an institutional reform, in particular the application of QMV in the areas provided for in the treaty, mainly in internal market questions. Instead of invoking the unilateral veto member states should abstain from decision-making in order to reduce the danger of a stalled decision-process (Rittberger 2005: 145). The French government was particularly supportive (Corbett 1998: 177). A committee of personal representatives of heads of governments (Dooge Committee)[25] was established to discuss a possible reform of the legislative process (Gazzo 1995: 123–47). It came up with two different conclusions: the more ambitious position supported the extension of the use of QMV and wider institutional reforms in an IGC; the more modest position (UK, Denmark, and Greece) called for only minor changes and no convening of an IGC, but an informal agreement on a wider use of QMV (Beach 2005: 37). The Dooge Report confirmed the Parliament's view of the need for a new treaty, but made only little explicit reference to the Parliament's draft. Corbett points out that in substance there were many similar proposals, that is an extension of QMV, the strengthening of the Commission, the Parliament appointing the Commission and co-decision by the Parliament (Gazzo 1985: 123–47; Corbett 1998: 181–2). A more critical view (Beach 2005) assesses the Parliament's goals to have been '...so far outside of any realistic zone of acceptable agreements' (Beach 2005: 45) that the Parliament had little impact (Beach 2005: 59). According to Beach, governments only 'paid lip service to the DTEU ... with the Dooge report stating that the negotiations for a draft for a European Union treaty should be guided by the spirit and the method of the draft treaty voted by the European Parliament' (Gazzo 1985: 144). In his view, the DTEU was 'in reality politely but resolutely shelved by governments prior to the IGC, and there is little evidence that it had any significant impact whatsoever in the negotiations' (Beach 2005: 59).

---

[24] Mitterrand supported the draft treaty of the Parliament (Gazzo 1985: 96–7).
[25] Under the chair of the Irish Senator Dooge.

While the Dooge Committee was at work to prepare institutional reforms, Delors had become President of the Commission. He had consulted with all national governments to develop a 'big idea' to revive the integration process (Moravcsik 1998: 362). The idea enjoying most support from the ten member states was the Single Market project (Armstrong and Bulmer 1998: 21).[26] As a result, the Brussels Summit of the European Council asked the Commission to develop a programme for the Single Market (McAllister 1997: 172).

The establishing of a Single Market was to be facilitated by decision-making rules that guaranteed greater efficiency. The newly elected Parliament (1984) called for the convening of an IGC which should base its work on the DTEU developed by the Parliament. It also requested a procedure in which the Parliament would be included in the agreement on a new treaty text[27] (Corbett 1998: 183). The final decision on the Dooge report and a possible IGC was scheduled for the Milan Summit (Corbett 1998: 184–5). The Commission under Delors actively promoted the idea of an IGC. Delors in a series of talks emphasized that the completion of the Internal Market was necessarily linked to an institutional reform, most importantly the introduction of majority voting (Dinan 1999: 143). Germany, Italy (which held the Presidency), and France were in favour of convening an IGC, the UK was opposed. However, the UK with Margaret Thatcher pursuing liberal economic perspectives was keen to achieve the completion of the internal market (Rittberger 2005: 147).[28] In exchange Britain offered to support a more frequent use of QMV and to limit the use of a national veto on the basis of an informal agreement, however, *without* an explicit treaty reform. '...The proposed change did not and should not require a formal revision of the treaty but could be achieved more "pragmatically" within the existing framework and by employing "soft law" instruments such a "gentlemen's agreements"' (de Ruyt 1989: 57).

The Parliament, in the meantime, had been actively mustering support for the realization of its institutional reforms[29] by developing its relationships

---

[26] France strongly supported monetary union. Germany and Italy, by contrast, preferred a strengthening of foreign policy cooperation (Moravcsik 1998: 315–16).

[27] Different from the original Spinelli plan, the Parliament 'accepted' that the draft had to be decided in a procedure involving negotiation among the member states and sought to secure a role for itself in this process (Corbett 1998: 183).

[28] The internal market programme and institutional reform became closely linked: the Commission White Paper of Commissioner Lord Cockfield had proposed the passage of 297 items of legislation necessary to harmonize national legislations on internal market matters, for which a more speedy decision-making procedure was needed (Rittberger 2005: 149).

[29] It also held an 'institutional debate' (April 1985) in which it incorporated the Dooge report into its own draft and restated that the Treaty should be ratified even if not all member states supported it (Corbett 1998: 209).

with national parliaments.[30] The Committee on Institutional Affairs had visited all national capitals. All of them, except the Danish parliament, were in favour of widening the scope of European policies and of strengthening the role of the European Parliament through the introduction of a legislative co-decision procedure (Corbett 1998: 193–4). Corbett concludes that 'in at least some countries, the tactic of going behind the government's back to speak directly to national parliaments, parties, and interest groups may have increased the pressure on the government to take a favourable attitude' (Corbett 1998: 202) to convening an IGC and thereby created a political momentum for a treaty reform.

At the Milan summit it was to be decided whether to go for a new treaty on a European Union or to stick with the existing treaty. In the run-up to the Summit, the Italian Presidency conducted many bilateral talks and put forward a proposal referring to the Dooge report, the Stuttgart Declaration, and the draft treaty of the Parliament (Corbett 1998: 211). The outcome of the summit talks first converged around an informal agreement proposed by the UK not to convene an IGC (Moravcsik 1998: 363; Budden 2002: 77), a view that was opposed by Germany, Italy, and France. The Commission restated that the completion of the Internal Market required a reform of institutional rules and proposed more specifically that all single market measures should be decided under QMV and that the powers of the Parliament should be strengthened (Beach 2005: 53). Due to these conflicting views the decision-making process stalled. Surprisingly to all, the Italian Presidency called for a vote[31] that resulted in a majority in favour of convening an IGC (Armstrong and Bulmer 1998: 363; Corbett 1998: 218; Beach 2005: 38; Rittberger 2005: 148).

Once it had been decided to engage in a treaty reform, the question remained as to the role of Parliament in this reform. There was no institutional rule to go by since previous treaty reforms had been negotiated *within* the Council and then approved by an IGC (Beach 2005: 46–7).[32] In its proposal of the DTEU the Parliament had sought to circumvent member states adopting a treaty reform on the basis of unanimity (Corbett 1998: 170) asking national parliaments to institute the procedure for the adoption of the draft treaty in accordance with their respective constitutions and approved by governments (Corbett 1998: 153; Beach 2005: 58–9), in short, *not* to use the relevant treaty

---

[30] That would have to ratify a revised treaty.

[31] The UK, Denmark, and Greece which had not opted for an IGC considered the calling of a vote on this question 'a coup d'état' (de Ruyt 1989).

[32] Art. 236 (now Art. 48) did not specify the role of the Commission in an IGC, except that its opinion could be stated prior to the IGC. Yet in 1985 the Commission acted as if it had the same right of initiative in the IGC as it had in everyday policymaking, and no member state objected (Budden 2002: 90).

article which lays down a procedure for the revision of the existing treaty. This was '...both because it felt that this article was inapplicable to such a project and because it disliked the procedure laid down by Art. 236' (Corbett 1998: 170). The Parliament argued that Article 236 requiring the consent of all member states[33] did not hold because the creation of a new treaty was at stake, not a mere revision of the existing treaty. Hence, the DTEU of the Parliament provided that the treaty was to come into effect when it was ratified, by only a majority of member states representing two-thirds of the Union's population (Art. 82 DTEU cited in Beach 2005: 43). Moreover, the Parliament's Committee for Institutional Affairs requested that the Parliament should be an equal partner in the IGC (Corbett 1998: 219) since it was the only 'legitimate representative of all the citizens of Europe' (Gazzo 1985: 35) and therefore should have a seat at the IGC (Beach 2005: 47) and decide jointly with the IGC on the new treaty (Corbett 1998: 222). While Corbett describes the reactions of member states to these demands as 'divided' (Corbett 1998: 222), Beach concludes that the reaction to the demand fell 'on deaf ears' and that the Parliament 'was clearly an unwanted guest in the 1985 IGC' (Beach 2005: 47) because its position was much too extreme (Beach 2005: 47).[34] At the end of the day, the Conference conceded to take account of the draft treaty proposed by the Parliament, and of further proposals made by the Parliament, as well as to 'submit' the results of the IGC work to the Parliament (Budden 2002: 91). But what did 'submit' mean? The Committee on Institutional Affairs interpreted it as meaning that the Parliament should be able to make amendments on the outcome of the IGC, which would in turn be resubmitted to the IGC and, if necessary, to a conciliation procedure. However, the President of the IGC stated that 'submit' meant to merely 'inform' the Parliament so that it could give its opinion and that there would certainly be 'no second reading' in the IGC (Corbett 1998: 223). Parliament continued to press its point, but to no avail although it was supported by Italy's declaration that it would only ratify a new Treaty if it were accepted by the Parliament (Corbett 1998: 223).

If we consider the change of institutional rules governing the Parliament's role in legislation between the Stuttgart Solemn Declaration (1983) and the eve of the IGC on the SEA (1985), several aspects are striking from a *theoretical* perspective of institutional change.

[33] Since the treaties have created a new legal order limiting the sovereignty of member states, the treaties—according to the dominant legal opinion—can only be amended under the procedure prescribed under Art. 236.

[34] The Parliament's role in the revision of the treaty was reduced 'to fighting for its views outside of the negotiating room prior to and during the IGC despite repeated attempts to carve a role for itself' (Beach 2005: 48).

First, discontent with the progress of an exclusive 'within-treaty' strategy at the legislative level, the Parliament pressed for more ambitious changes at the *higher-order rule* or constitutional level. From a *link* perspective a stage of purely within-rules changes was followed by changes linking the two levels of lower-order and higher-order rules. The higher-order institutional changes that the Parliament pursued, were twofold. It sought to alter the higher-order rules in such a way as to increase its competences in legislation, that is the lower-order rule-making. In order to achieve this, it attempted to change the meta-rules, as well, that is the rules determining how to revise the higher-order rules, proposing a role for itself in the designing of higher-order rules. But what gave the Parliament leverage to put such a proposal into practice? It sought to form an alliance with the national parliaments who would have to confirm the revised treaty, in order to put pressure on governments opposing an increase of parliamentarian competences. Additionally, it applied a strategy of linking its delaying powers in the legislative arena to the issues at the IGC level (Farrell and Héritier 2006). Or as Beach describes the strategy: to '... exploit discretion in the exercise of their formal powers in daily policymaking by linking outcomes they could control in daily policy to IGC outcomes, for example by threatening to withhold an opinion or proposal of an issue in order to force governments to grant them greater power in the IGC' (Beach 2005: 44). These explanations follow the pattern of the *distributive bargaining theory of endogenous institutional change*. Yet, as we have seen by the outcome, the leverage applied by the Parliament was not very strong and it did not obtain what it wished as measured by its institutional role in the IGC.

But the Parliament certainly played a key role in setting a treaty reform on the agenda. By mobilizing national parliaments and trying to form an *alliance with them as potential veto-players* in the treaty confirmation, it developed a political momentum for reform.[35] This was a strategic step to gain some leverage in a decision-making process, that is treaty reform, in which the Parliament did not have an established formal role.

Secondly, a strong pressure for institutional reform of the higher-order rules certainly derived from the Single Market project, an exogenous factor, confirming *a functionalist theory of institutional design*. Making the rules more effective in order to deal with this demanding new task was a driving force behind the willingness to schedule an IGC and to reform the treaty. In the ensuing bargaining process a trade-off was established between the actor with a high preference for completing the internal market on the one hand (UK),

---

[35] Six of ten national parliaments took a very favourable attitude to the Parliament's draft Treaty. 'Two even calling on their governments to ratify it as such' (Corbett 1998: 251).

and those favouring both the Single Market *and* institutional reforms (Germany, Italy).

Finally, in trying to gain a role in the treaty revision process, the Parliament invoked its role as the sole directly legitimized political actor. But to no avail; its role in the treaty reform remained the role of an outsider. Hence, a *normative socialization* impact cannot be identified.

Returning to the *empirical account* of the negotiations of institutional reforms during the IGC, it emerges that the Parliament only had an indirect influence. It received all the documents tabled and closely followed the negotiations. In three plenary debates it discussed the different positions. Moreover, there was a meeting between a delegation of the Parliament and the IGC (Gazzo 1986: 8). In substance it would have liked to see its draft (DTEU) to serve as a basis for the negotiations, however, that was not the case, although relevant parts were included in the different dossiers (Corbett 1998: 223).

In the governments' negotiations three positions emerged which formed the basis for a compromise: the granting of full co-legislative powers to the Parliament in a co-decision procedure was supported by Germany and Italy; the introduction of a new cooperation procedure was favoured by a majority of member states and the Commission; and the maintaining of consultation was proposed by a minority of member states (Beach 2005: 55). In order to form a compromise Germany proposed three different 'baskets' of distinctive legislative competences of the Parliament (consultation, cooperation, and joint legislative action). While the 'basked-idea' as such was welcomed by governments, there were many reservations regarding particular aspects of the German proposal. The Commission, too, saw its own competences at danger and proposed an alternative: an extended consultation procedure and a conciliation procedure that would apply to all major items of legislation but would only be triggered by a joint agreement of Council and Parliament, the final decision remaining with the Council; it also proposed a new cooperation procedure based on QMV and joint legislative action in limited areas. Italy submitted a proposal based on the Dooge report and the DTEU of the Parliament (de Ruyt 1989: 80), France supported a combination of the German and Commission proposal (Corbett 1998: 244). The UK, stressing the need of efficient decision-making, did not object in principle to a strengthening of the Parliament's power as long as the Council would keep the last word in the legislative process (Rittberger 2005).[36] The Luxembourg Presidency, based on a Commission proposal, suggested the introduction of a Council

---

[36] Thatcher was willing to accept a moderate increase in the powers of the European Assembly if the ultimate decision was guaranteed to the Council of Ministers (Rittberger 2005: 160).

'common position' and a second parliamentarian reading to link the extent of QMV with enhanced parliamentary participation. Thus the Parliament would gain considerably in formal influence, but at the same time the Council's prerogatives would be protected (Rittberger 2005: 166).[37] On the basis of this proposal the negotiators came to an agreement.

The agreement provided that the new *legislative cooperation procedure* should apply in nine articles, that the Parliament could amend the draft in second reading, amendments that the Commission could or could not pass on to the Council. The European Council charged the foreign ministers to specify the procedure that should be observed if the Parliament should reject the Council's common position in second reading (Corbett 1998: 245–6). The Parliament urged the foreign ministers to provide that cooperation should apply to all acts requiring QMV, but without success. However, due to the support of Italy, the foreign ministers did agree that all parliamentarian amendments during second reading should be submitted to the Council, even if not approved by the Commission. More important still, they provided that the parliamentarian amendments which were not taken up by the Commission could only be adopted by unanimous vote in the Council (Budden 1994: 365; Corbett 1998: 245–6). This gave the Parliament 'an additional lever over the Council: if the EP decided to reject the Council's common position, the Council could only overturn the rejection by unanimity... "This minor change would alter the balance within the EC's decision-making system. If the EP had one ally among the ministers ... the Council—having to decide within a three-month deadline—might come under considerable parliamentary leverage over such decisions"' (Budden 1994: 366 quoted in Rittberger 2005: 170–1; Tsebelis 1995). Still, the Parliament in the light of its initial high ambitions as formulated in the DTEU found the outcome 'unacceptable' (Gazzo 1986: 105; Corbett 1998: 245). It threatened to reject the 1986 budget, censure the Commission, and/or to withhold its opinion on the IGC. However, member states did not consider these threats to be credible (Armstrong and Bulmer 1998; Budden 2002; Beach 2005: 59). At the end of the day, most MEPs—although disappointed—decided to accept the package (Corbett 1998: 248) and did not further encourage non-ratification by national parliaments (Corbett 1998: 249). However, the Parliament also announced its determination to 'exploit to the very limit the possibilities offered by the SEA' (Corbett 1998: 248).

---

[37] This solution allowed the British and German governments—both under strong domestic pressure—to face their domestic audiences: 'for the British government, it was crucial that the Council kept the last word (even though it needed unanimity to change amendments by the Commission and EP) while for the German government it was important to present the domestic audience with an outcome that represented a qualitative improvement for the EP, even though falling short of co-decision' (Rittberger 2005: 169–70).

To sum up, the outcome of the institutional change of the SEA (1986) provided that under the cooperation procedure the Commission proposes a legislative draft, the Parliament states its opinion and the Council takes a decision, the common position. Then follows a second reading in which the Parliament can approve, reject, or propose amendments. If these amendments are supported by the Commission and incorporated into the revised proposal, the Council can only modify the draft by unanimity, but can adopt it by majority. Hence, amendments not supported by the Commission, require unanimity of the Council (Corbett, Jacobs, and Shackleton 2000: 187). In the case of a high priority issue of the Council, a Commission–Parliament alliance can exert considerable pressure. The Council must decide within a relatively short deadline (three months) whether to accept or amend a proposal or drop it entirely. One member state in Council can strengthen the Parliament's position if it threatens to reject the proposal if the Parliament's amendments are not taken into account, therefore increases the Parliament's bargaining power (Corbett, Jacobs, and Shackleton 2000: 187).

A theoretical interpretation of the negotiations over the rule governing the Parliament's role leads to the following conclusions: *redistributive bargaining theoretical explanations* of institutional change goes some way in accounting for the outcome. As Rittberger argues, the heads of government were well aware of the fact that empowering the Parliament in legislation would impinge on the Council's powers (Rittberger 2005: 163).[38] In the final stages of the IGC bargaining clearly prevailed in the interactions between the national delegations. Threats to delay or entirely jeopardize the adoption of the SEA, mostly by the Italian government, were formulated. Budden argues that the 'maximalist rejection group' sought to 'raise the negotiations' common denominator with threats to reject the whole process if it did not go far enough' (1994: 326 quoted in Rittberger 2005: 170–1).

Even though some states, particularly Germany, were '... rhetorically eager to lament the democratic deficit, (they, A.H.) did not try particularly hard to convince recalcitrant governments of the desirablity and appropriateness of their "quest" to empower the Parliament' (Rittberger 2005: 165), neither did France (Rittberger 2005). Hence it cannot have been the *power of normative democratic convictions* that were the driving force of the change of the institutional rule. Rather were these arguments used strategically 'to justify and realize their own preferences regarding the powers of the EP' (Rittberger 2005: 165).[39]

---

[38] So was the Commission which repeatedly sought to ensure that the rule change would not cut too much into its prerogatives.

[39] 'Proponents of the federal state legitimating belief ... exercise social pressure on recalcitrant states with the aim of shaming them into acquiescing to the EP's empowerment.

Theoretical Summary: From Consultation to Cooperation

Which are the main factors explaining why the Parliament obtained that its rights in legislation were extended from consultation to cooperation? It was shown that the Parliament managed to exploit given treaty provisions to the fullest and gain some institutional territory by exerting political pressure through delaying the decision-making process and applying a linked-arena veto based on its budgetary powers. This strategy of the Parliament is reflected in the distributive, power-based bargaining theory of endogenous institutional change as formulated in:

H: Institutional change through a formal/informal/formal dynamic
'Formal rules at t1 that are ambiguous give rise to informal rules that further develop the formal rules. These informal rules will reflect the bargaining power of actors, as determined by formal institutions and the fallback position of the negotiating actors reflected in different time horizons and a different sensitivity to failure.'

And

'The outcome of the formal negotiations at t2 will reflect informal institutions bargained if all designing actors agree to accept the informal change or if the implementing/affected actors can exert pressure through a linked-arena veto.'

Additonally, another pattern of institutional change emerged: The Parliament's practice of delaying an opinion gave rise to a conflict with the Council that, in turn, led to a third-party dispute resolution by the ECJ the outcome of which was in favour of the Parliament (Isoglucose case). This reflects the argument that a *development of institutional rules may occur through the settlement of a rule-conflict by a third-party dispute resolution* that subsequently becomes an authoritative reference point for further rule development (Stone Sweet 1999).

Would the Parliament have been able to exploit existing formal rules to the same extent if it were not the only directly democratically legitimized body in European decision-making? Referring to its direct democratic legitimation— and linking up with national parliaments as co-equal bearers of democratic legitimation, very likely helped the Parliament to advance its institutional objectives. This reflects the argument of *sociological institutionalism* that a *change of institutional rule comes about through the force of normative ideas,* that is democratic legitimation. But bearing in mind the relatively modest results the Parliament obtained as measured by its initial objectives (DTEU), it is evident that the power of direct democratic legitimation was by no

Recalcitrant member states will downplay the outcomes, question their relevance or reinterpret them to their advantage in the light of domestic opposition (Rittberger 2005: 162–3).

means a sufficient condition. Rather, the actors at whose costs the Parliament was to gain powers (the member states and the Commission), were very reluctant to share competencies and mustered considerable opposition. Therefore, the Parliament had to fight for the strengthening of its legislative powers by using political pressure, forming coalitions with individual member state governments and possible veto-actors in the treaty confirmation process.

Another important set of factors triggering and accelerating institutional change were the *exogenous demands* set by enlargement and the planned completion of the internal market and monetary union. This points to the importance of a *functionalist redesign and a power-based redistributive bargaining argument*. The new external challenges altered the cost–benefit calculations regarding existing institutional rules and increased actors' willingness to redesign the existing institutions. The fact that Britain was willing to change the legislative decision-making rules in exchange for the single market programme is a case in point. What emerges, too, is that the functional considerations and the democratic legitimation argument were closely linked. The pooling of competences at the supranational level that was necessary for the completion of the internal market implied a loss of sovereignty at the national level that was to be compensated by an increase of democratic legitimation at the European level, that is by strengthening the Parliament.

This is reflected in the claim of:

H: Functionalist transaction cost–based hypothesis
'If, due to an external event, the benefits of rule A have decreased, the rule will be changed, if the gains of the proposed altered rule B including the transaction costs will be higher.'

And bearing in mind the shift of competences linked to the proposed change of rule and the ensuing power-based bargaining process:

H: Problem type, institutional rules, and integrative vs. defensive bargaining
'If redistributive issues are at stake, the process of institutional change will be characterized by defensive bargaining. The outcome will reflect the asymmetry of power of the involved actors.'

From a *structural perspective* it was shown that the *multilevel aspect in changing institutional rules* played an important role in accelerating institutional change. The Parliament tired of the only modest success obtained at the level of intra-treaty changes, shifted its ambitious goals of institutional change to the higher-order level *and* the meta-rules defining how to change the revision of higher-order rules.

H: Shifting levels/arenas to accelerate institutional change
'Given a choice between different levels/arenas of decision-making, an actor, by opting out of one arena and shifting the decision to another, may improve his prospects of obtaining an institutional change according to his preferences.'

As was shown, the Parliament was successful in setting the agenda for a treaty revision by constantly reiterating its requests for a treaty revision. In this it was supported by the new functional exigencies of the Single Market project. It totally failed, however, in seeking to change the meta-rules calling for a change of the entire treaty revision process going far beyond a possible zone of agreement in the negotiation process of governments (Beach 2005).

This points to the *types of actors* perspective: The Parliament as a mere 'implementing actor' of higher-order rules proposed a change of the meta-rules about how to change the higher-order rules to gain access to the circle of 'designing actors'.

What are the typical *links between different types of institutional change and different explanations of institutional change* that emerge from the empirical account from consultation to cooperation? Four types of typical links may be distinguished. One link consists of (*a*) a functional institutional redesign of a formal institutional rule as a response to an external demand that is followed (*b*) by a further development of this formal rule in the course of its application leading to the emergence of an informal rule. If this informal rule guiding application provokes a conflict between the involved actors due to an ensuing shift in power, (*c*) a third-party dispute resolution mechanism may ensue that decides on the rightfulness of the rule in question and its further applicability. The first explanation is based on a functionalist design argument with an exogenous cause of institutional change; the second on an endogenous distributive power-based bargaining argument of a formal–informal–formal dynamic and the third on an analogy-based endogenous conflict solution and rule development theory. Thus, the empirical material shows that in a first instance the Parliament built on an endogenous type of change, seeking to extensively use the existing formal rule based on power-based distributive bargaining mechanisms, supported by the 'resource' of democratic legitimation, and leading to a third-party dispute resolution. When the limits of within-treaty changes were reached—due to the limited bargaining power of the Parliament—it established (*d*) a link between the lower-order and higher-order level hoping to obtain more important institutional changes. But here, the Parliament's bargaining power was even more limited. More limited because the Parliament had to apply a delaying strategy across levels, from daily Community policymaking (refusing budgetary means, delaying its opinion in legislative consultation) in order to exert pressure on the higher-order rule makers, or alternatively form an alliance with a formal veto-player among the higher-order rule-makers (national parliaments or individual member state governments).

4.2.2. From the Single European Act to the Maastricht Treaty

With the SEA the Parliament had gained the competence to cooperate in the legislative procedure; with the adoption of the Maastricht Treaty six years later it obtained the power to codecide in the legislative process. How can this institutional change be accounted for? Discontent as it was with the outcome of the SEA, the Parliament soon made another attempt to obtain a reform of the existing treaty in its favour. In a resolution of 1989 it called for the convening of an IGC to establish a Political Union of a 'federal type' (European Parliament 1990) extending among other things the Parliament's powers alongside to the EMU IGC. This request was supported by Italy and Belgium (Corbett 1993). At the same time, Germany, supported by France, Italy, and the Benelux countries expressed a strong interest in a Political Union IGC, too (Moravcsik 1998; Beach 2005: 104). France was convinced by Germany,[40] and in return expected support in the ratification of the monetary agreement (EMU). In a joint letter, Kohl and Mitterrand proposed to convene a second IGC on a Political Union dealing with institutional questions to be held in parallel to the conference on economic and monetary union. Britain was originally opposed, but then agreed to convene another IGC (Moravcsik 1998). The Commission, which initially had only focused on its highest priority, the EMU, eventually supported the call for a Political Union as well.[41] As a result the European Council of June 1990 agreed to organize a second IGC.

Once the decision had been taken to convene another IGC, all member states, the Parliament, and the Commission presented an opinion about a treaty of the European Union. By presenting its opinion first, the *Parliament*

[40] Which was under pressure from its own parliament to strengthen the European Parliament (Moravcsik 1998).
[41] According to Ross, the idea of a Political Union caught '...Delors without time to do a great deal of preparation. Given this limited timing, the Commission could not play its crucial agenda setting role, making the IGC a chaotic affair largely governed by member states' (Ross 1995: 197).

tried to set the agenda.[42] It called for the introduction of a co-decision procedure. If after two readings, Parliament and Council failed to agree, a conciliation committee (consisting of twelve members of the Parliament, twelve
members of the Council and members of the Commission) would work out
a compromise. The agreement should then be submitted to both Council
and Parliament to be confirmed. It also announced not to confirm any treaty
that did not grant enough power to the Parliament (Jean Pierre Cot, head of
Socialist Group) (Ross 1995: 98). The *Commission* shared '... the table with
a huge amount of similar papers from the member states' (Ross 1995: 97). It
supported a strengthening of the competences of the Parliament, however, not
at its own costs (Ross 1995: 98). In its original opinion (March 1991), it did
not opt for co-decision, but the expansion of the cooperation procedure to all
areas of QMV. It then changed its position[43] and supported co-decision, linked
to a conciliation procedure under which, in case of failure, the Commission
would present a new proposal (Ross 1995: 98).

The governments in favour of strengthening the Parliament's competences
in legislation were the Benelux, Germany, Italy, to a lesser extent Spain and
Greece. The UK, Denmark, France, Portugal, and Ireland were opposed. More
specifically, Germany and Italy (and with some reservations Spain)[44] supported co-decision; Belgium and Greece proposed the possibility of rejection
by different majorities. Belgium supported an extension of the cooperation
procedure to all legislative matters under QMV (Belgian memorandum II.1).
Italy fully endorsed co-decision (Italian Parliament resolution 21.3.1990).[45]
The Netherlands first advocated an extension of the cooperation procedure, then in 1990 switched and supported co-decision and—like the Italian
government—threatened not to ratify the treaty if the Parliament's powers
would not be significantly extended (Dutch memorandum Oct. 26, 1990,
point 2.2.). France, the UK, Ireland, Portugal, and Sweden wanted to maintain the cooperation procedure and opposed co-decision (Moravcsik 1998:
390).

Again, as under the SEA IGC, the Parliament sought to influence the meta-
institutional rule of IGC decision-making and proposed that the IGC should
include representatives of the Parliament, the Council, and the Commission.
However, the attempt was not successful. As in the 1985 IGC, the Parliament

---

[42] Report Martin I March 1990 and Report Martin II in July 1990.

[43] According to Ross 'the Parliament's stridency bolstered Commission commitment, since
the Commission needed the Parliament to pressure member states on other matters' (Ross 1995:
98).

[44] Spain proposed to limit the scope of codecision (Ibanez 1992).

[45] Prime Minister Andreotti repeatedly stated that Italy would ratify a modification of the
Treaties only after agreement by the Parliament.

was not present at the bargaining table (Beach 2005: 83).[46] Another attempt
was made to influence the IGC agenda and its outcome. In an unprecedented
act, the Parliament convoked the national parliaments in European Assizes,[47]
to muster support for its claims. The assizes adopted with a large majority
all the main proposals made by the Parliament in its reports (Martin I and
Martin II) and declared that the Parliament must play an equal part with
the Council in the legislative and budgetary functions of the Union (Jacobs,
Corbett, and Shackleton 1995: 304). '...Never before has a major international negotiation been preceded by a conference of the very parliaments that
would later have to ratify the outcome of the negotiations' (Corbett 1993: 30).
Moreover, it proposed a number of 'inter-institutional conferences' between
the member states, the Parliament, and the Commission. The discussions on
institutional questions offered the Parliament a possibility to directly discuss
with ministers participating in the IGC. Additionally, the Parliament visited all
national governments to build support for its proposals (Corbett 1993: 33).

To what extent were these efforts reflected in the outcome of the IGC? Corbett argues that in the Political Union IGC as opposed to the EMU IGC (Dyson
and Featherstone 1999), the Parliament, by formulating precise and detailed
proposals, provided important points of reference for the negotiations and
that '...in the compromises that emerged..., it obtained a far from negligible
proportion of its aspirations' (Corbett 1998: 342). It was most influential in
matters that regarded its own powers (Beach 2005: 105). More specifically, the
European Council in Rome (Rome II) and the presidential report declared
that the legislative role of the Parliament should be strengthened by extending
the cooperation procedure to all areas of QMV and by considering to develop
a co-decision procedure for acts of legislative nature (Corbett 1993: 30).

The formal negotiations lasted one year extending through three presidencies[48] (Corbett 1993: 30). The Luxembourg Presidency in its non-paper
(April 1991) proposed that co-decision should be applied in environmental
and research policy, in developmental cooperation and in economic and social
cohesion policy. The conciliation committee should include twelve members
of the Council and the Parliament respectively, plus the Commission without a
vote and without the right to withdraw its proposal. If conciliation should fail,
the Council could adopt its own draft and this text would become law unless

---

[46] According to Beach the Parliament '...was clearly an unwelcome guest in the IGC' (Beach 2005: 83).

[47] Two-thirds of its members from national parliaments, one-third from the European Parliament.

[48] There were twelve ministerial sessions on political union. Between the sessions work was
carried out in weekly meetings of personal representatives of the ministers (Corbett 1993: 30).
On the importance of the pre-decision making role of the permanent representatives in treaty
revisions see Reh (forthcoming).

rejected by the Parliament (ECE, Conf. Intergouv. Union politique, Fiche n.12, 7.11.1991).

The Dutch Presidency rewrote the draft, departing strongly from the Luxembourgish draft which had already been agreed on as a basis for further negotiations, thereby antagonizing the other delegations (Beach 2005: 110). The text was rejected and the IGC went back to the Luxembourg text submitting modifications on an item by item basis, including a broader application of the co-decision procedure to all areas of cooperation. As a concession to the British, the reference to the federal nature of the treaty was dropped, in return the UK accepted more competences of the Parliament (Corbett 1993: 56). According to Beach neither the Luxembourgish nor the Dutch draft utilized the Parliament's proposals as sources in their texts because the 'EP's position was far from the centre of gravity of the debates' (Beach 2005: 105). The Parliament in a resolution (November 1991) threatened to reject the treaty unless significant changes regarding its own powers were introduced (Agence Europe No. 5615, 23.11.91, 3–4). However, it is doubtful whether '...governments perceived this "threat" as credible...', as under then Article 236 of the EC Treaty (now Article 48 EU) the EP has no right of assent over the final treaty' (Beach 2005: 105).

In the last stage of negotiations, governments initially opposed to co-decision, such as Denmark and Ireland, switched to accepting codecison in limited areas. So did France and Spain. Portugal[49] and the UK sustained their opposition. Germany linked the outcome of the Political Union IGC to the outcome of the EMU IGC. In the face of domestic resistance to EMU, the government established a link between EMU and more democracy, Kohl supporting the Dutch Presidency in thrashing out a compromise with the UK. Under this compromise the latter was willing to accept co-decision, if limited in scope (Corbett 1993: 56; Ross 1995: 148).[50] The Dutch Prime Minister in bilateral talks took key players aside to extract their positions. All governments were finally satisfied because they won in some domestically important issue area. The UK obtained an opting out clause both on EMU and social policy; Germany and Italy secured increased powers for the Parliament; the

---

[49] Portugal arguably made its support dependent on compensation in cohesion funds. Moreover, Portugal being the next Presidency of the Council did not want to take over the IGC negotiations from the Dutch.

[50] At the European Council at Nordwijik a deal emerged between the British and the French to limit German desires for increased parliamentary power. 'The Germans were willing to allow this because the British seemed to be moving towards a more general treaty deal' (Ross 1995: 148). In the Group of Permanent Representatives no change of positions was noted from the ministerial meeting. But the Commission rejected the provision allowing the Council to modify the parliamentarian amendments at QMV (Group of Permanent Rep. Compte rendu 17.4.1991).

Mediterranean countries obtained increased funds for social cohesion and the French and German commitment to a beginning of common defence policy.

The result was that co-decision was accepted in fifteen issue areas. Under the provisions the Commission could withdraw proposed legislation in the conciliation committee. However, while the Council in other procedures can only amend a Commission proposal by unanimity, under co-decision the Council can adopt Parliament's previous amendments, even if rejected by the Commission, using QMV during conciliation (Beach 2005: 111). In the following meeting of the Group of Permanent Representatives a majority of member states (Belgium, Denmark, Ireland, The Netherlands, and the UK) agreed with the amendments proposed by the Commission seeking to re-establish its rights. Germany and Spain were opposed (GPR, Compte rendu 17.5.1991.)

In its final text the co-decision procedure provides for two readings instead of one. Until second reading the procedure is identical to the cooperation procedure, that is a Commission proposal is followed by the Parliament's first reading and opinion, after which the Council states its common position and Parliament's second reading, approving, amending, or rejecting the common position. If the Parliament rejects the common position by majority of members, the legislation falls (unlike in the cooperation procedure where Council could still adopt the text if it were unanimous) (Corbett, Jacobs, and Shackleton 2000: 188). If the Parliament approves the common position, it is adopted (without needing any further confirmation by Council as is required under the cooperation procedure). If Parliament amends the common position, it returns to Council. If the Council accepts each amendment, the text is adopted. If not, it is referred to the Conciliation committee. The Committee, also attended by the Commission, has six to eight weeks during which to negotiate a compromise text based on the common position of the Council and the second reading amendments voted by Parliament. If there is an agreement the text has to be confirmed by the plenaries of the Council and the Parliament. If the Conciliation Committee fails to reach an agreement, the Council can reintroduce its common position and submit it to a third reading in Parliament.

Thus, the Council in the areas of co-decision now had to share competences with the Parliament, but was still keeping the last say in case of a failure of conciliation. The Commission lost power: under the cooperation procedure it was critical for the Parliament to win the support of the Commission for its amendments. Only if accepted by the Commission are they incorporated into the revised proposal and can only be taken out or modified by the Council on the basis of unanimity. Under the co-decision procedure, the Commission '... does express its views on the Parliament's second reading amendments, but whether or not the Commission is favourable to them, as soon as it emerges that the Council cannot accept all of the Parliament's amendments, attention turns to the conciliation committee negotiations where Council (...) and Parliament are free to reach an agreement on individual amendments independently of the opinion of the Commission' (Corbett, Jacobs, and Shackleton 2000: 189–90).

In sum, the Parliament was quite successful in obtaining the extension of its own power in legislation, that is the introduction of a co-decision procedure in certain issue areas, including most internal market issues, public health issues, consumer protection, educational and cultural measures, issues of equivalence of diplomas and qualification, the free movement of workers, the framework programme for research, and the guidelines for trans-European networks. Among all institutional objectives,[51] it is fair to say, that this was the Parliament's prime objective. From Maastricht on, co-decision existed alongside consultation and cooperation.

Theoretical Summary: From the Single European Act to the Maastricht Treaty

So what, in a nutshell, are the prime factors that helped the Parliament obtain this competence of co-legislator? The most salient factor is the *multilevel strategy* used by the Parliament.

H: *Shifting levels/arenas to accelerate institutional change*
'Given a choice between different levels/arenas of decision-making, an actor, by opting out of one arena and shifting the decision to another, may improve his prospects of obtaining an institutional change according to his preferences.'

Immediately after the SEA, the Parliament set out to seek a revision of the macro-institutional rules although it does not have a formal role in this decision procedure. In a first step, in the usual act of self-promotion, it emphatically called for institutional changes in its own favour and defined desirable institutional objectives. In order to increase the prospects of their realization, it then very systematically developed a strategy of pressure and alliance-building with some member states and the national parliaments to take influence on the decision-making of the 'designing actors', that is member

---

[51] The Parliament also sought to reach an extension of its budgetary powers, and a right of formal confirmation of the Commission President. In the first instance it did not achieve its objective, in the second it did obtain a right of consultation and was successful in achieving the adjustment of the terms of mandate for the Commission and the Parliament. The Parliament also asked for a limited right of initiative, but the Commission rejected these demands (Beach 2005: 106).

states. By forming alliances with national parliaments which have to confirm the revised treaty it sought to exert pressure for its own cause. As an
outside actor, not being part of the designing actors, it therefore strove to
indirectly influence the *negotiation process* among the designing actors. Since
the negotiating actors had divergent preferences regarding the institutional
rule in question, that is the role of the Parliament in legislation, and given
unanimity rule, the Parliament was able to have some clout on the decision-
making outcome. This explanation corresponds to a *distributive power-based
bargaining explanation* on which the Parliament sought to take influence by
indirectly establishing a *linked-arena veto*.

However, it has also been argued that the creation of co-decision was very
much owed to German leadership in the negotiations. And the motives behind
the German support for co-decision may be seen in the typical link between
a *functional and a democratic legitimation argument*, already pointed out for
the explanation of the cooperation procedure. Widening the tasks of the
European Community should be linked with a change in institutional rules
to increase efficiency in decision-making. At the same time, this expansion of
tasks should go hand in hand with a strengthening of democratic legitimacy
in European policy-making by strengthening the power of the Parliament.
Thus, an *exogenous event*, monetary union, accelerated institutional change
and played an important role. Similarly, considerations of future enlargement
were of some importance although not considered as urgent yet. Hence a
functionalist explanation of why the institutional redesign came about is able
to throw some light on the causes of institutional change. The distributive
bargaining argument explains how the change came about.

H: Functionalist transaction cost based hypothesis
'If, due to an external event, the benefits of rule A have decreased, the rule will be
changed, if the gains of the proposed altered rule B including the transaction costs will
be higher.'

In short, the type of institutional change prevailing in this period is a negotiation process in the context of the IGC, in which the Parliament indirectly
(through the support of some member states and the alliance with national
parliaments) sought to gain some clout. A *close link* between two modes of
changes may be seen in the *exogenous functional trigger* of a new policy task
(EMU) and the ensuing *power-based distributive negotiations* in the course of
which a deal was struck between actors setting high stakes on the EMU and
actors pressing for increased parliamentary power in legislation. A compromise was thrashed out based on compensation across different policy areas
EMU, cohesion and co-decision. Here, indirectly, democratic legitimation

(and pressure from some national parliaments such as in the German parliament) came to play a role in the bargaining process.

By contrast, a *within-treaty, power-based bargaining process producing informal rules* cannot be identified in this period. One reason may be that soon after
the adoption of the SEA it was clear that there would be another IGC. The SEA
stated that member states and the Commission could submit proposals for a
treaty revision of 1991–2. So the Parliament immediately set out to realize its
institutional objectives at the higher-order rule level, in other words used a
cross-level strategy. But, as in the case of the SEA, in could not gain access to
the circle of 'designing actors'.

The empirical account also shows that the existence of the cooperation
procedure did help the Parliament to improve its position because the second
reading gave Parliament a chance to react to the Council's position. 'The habit
of two readings gave the impression of a classic bicameral legislative procedure ... and helped pave the way towards full co-decision' (Corbett, Jacobs,
and Shackleton 2000: 187). From there it was only a small step to a role of
almost equal co-decision-maker. Still, one has to bear in mind the resistance
deployed from specific national governments as well as the Commission in
order to prevent the quasi-automaticity of this development.

4.2.3. From the Maastricht Treaty to the Amsterdam Treaty

Under the Maastricht Treaty (1992) the scope of co-decision was limited.
Under the Amsterdam Treaty (1997) it was considerably extended. What are
the factors and processes that led to this extension of the scope of application
of the co-decision procedure? The introduction of the co-decision procedure
was followed by a series of institutional battles between the Parliament and
the Council over how co-decision should be applied (Farrell and Héritier
2003).[52] This was by no means self-evident. Ambiguities in the treaty text led
Parliament and Council to adopt differing interpretations. While the Parliament maintained that co-decision effectively gave it equality with Council in
the process of debating and deciding legislation, the Council initially acted
as before and would merely indicate those items of legislation that it was
prepared to accept or reject, on a 'take it or leave it' basis. The Parliament
threatened to block or slow down legislation in order to increase its negotiating power. After a series of hard-fought legislative battles, the Council
gradually accepted that it did indeed need to negotiate with the Parliament

---

[52] The informal institutional changes described in this section are discussed at greater length
in Farrell and Héritier (2003, 2004, forthcoming).

over legislative items that came under the co-decision procedure (Corbett, Jacobs, and Shackleton 2000).

More specifically, in the first years Parliament withheld its approval from particular items of legislation in order to strengthen its institutional position vis-à-vis Council; this was the case in the battle over comitology, where the Parliament wished to share authority with the Council over matters of implementation (Corbett, Jacobs, and Shackleton 2000; Hix 2002; Bergström 2005; Farrell and Héritier forthcoming) in the decision on open voice telephony directive. Gradually, the Council, Parliament and Commission began to create a system of regular meetings, which would allow them to negotiate over legislative matters subject to co-decision (Shackleton 2000). These meetings over time assumed semi-recognized status as 'trialogues'[53] were introduced during first reading. They include few figures from the Parliament, Council (and Commission)[54] seeking to reach a compromise on politically contentious matters. They greatly increase the efficiency of decision-making, because they drastically shorten the decision-making process and enable both sides to speak more frankly and to explain more in detail what the underlying reasons are for the positions that they adopted (Interview with Council official, Oct. 2001).[55] As Corbett, Jacobs, and Shackleton (2000) put it: 'The sheer volume of co-decision procedures .... means that both institutions have an important interest in *not* allowing all disagreements to spill over into the conciliation process. As a result there will be much more intense contact between the institutions earlier in the procedure' (Corbett, Jacobs, and Shackleton 2000: 191, emphasis added).

The trialogues lead to 'early agreements' on certain codecision dossiers. Under early agreements, the Parliament and Council seek to reach agreement on a proposed piece of legislation *before* the Council adopts a formal common position, or the Parliament provides its official opinion. This 'fast track legislation' places a premium on informal negotiations between the respective representatives of Parliament and Council that seek to reach agreement before they invoke the formal machineries of Parliament–Council negotiations. The Parliament clearly derives some very significant advantages from early agreements. It can use early agreements strategically to affect deliberations within the Council itself; for the negotiations between the Parliament and Presidency take place before the Council has adopted a formal common position. In the words of an official from the Parliament, 'this institutional innovation

---

[53] The original trialogues, of a different type, take place after the second reading, but before the Conciliation Committee's meeting, in order to hammer out compromises over issues of dispute (Rasmussen 2006).

[54] Trialogues usually include members of COREPER I, the Council Presidency, the rapporteur(s) from the Parliament, and possibly a member of the responsible DG of the Commission.

[55] Interview with Council Official B Oct. 2001.

has ... served to generate a variety of procedural norms and shared beliefs about how the parties should behave which can only be described as "rules of engagement". By the end of the Maastricht era, they had become so self-evident that no one contested them'.[56]

Originally, the early agreements were intended for non-controversial dossiers, where there was little likelihood of substantial disagreement between Parliament and Council, and thus, little need for formal negotiations. However, it has increasingly been expanded to non-technical and politically salient dossiers with some degree of urgency.[57] The outcomes of the trialogues, the early agreements, are not formally binding; neither Council nor Parliament is obliged to adhere to agreements reached in these meetings. However, because Council and Parliament engage with each other repeatedly in the legislative process, it is usually in their interest to make agreements stick; otherwise the defaulting party is likely to lose credibility, and to be punished in future interactions. These trialogues and the early agreements have increasingly gained overt recognition as 'fast track legislation' and as such a vital part of the legislative process, amounting to more than a third of all legislative items in the period 2003–4 (EP Activity Report 2004). Between August 2000 and July 2001, 29 per cent of the 66 co-decision dossiers were concluded at first reading, 41 per cent at second reading, while 30 per cent went to conciliation (European Parliament 2001); between 2001 and 2002, 26 per cent of 73 co-decision dossiers were decided at first reading, 51 per cent at second reading, and 23 per cent went to conciliation (European Parliament 2001–2). From 2002 to 2003, 27 per cent of 87 co-decision items were concluded at first reading, 56 per cent at second reading, and 17 per cent went to conciliation (European Parliament 2002–3). The corresponding figures for 2003–4 are 39, 46, and 15 per cent (EP Activity Report 1999–2004: 13).

However, there are problems associated with the process. Most obviously, there is the problem of transparency. Trialogues conduct important business on an informal and relatively secretive basis, at the expense of more visible parts of the co-decision procedure. It is often difficult for others within the Parliament, let alone outsiders, to have any idea of what exactly is going on in a specific brief. And, when it works successfully, the Parliament and Council do little more than sign off on an early-agreement deal that has already been negotiated among a small group of actors. They are not open to public

---

[56] Interview with Official of the Parliament Nov. 2000.

[57] Thus, e.g. the conclusions of the Lisbon European Council stated the need for the EU to make rapid steps towards improving its approach towards information technology, and laid down hard deadlines by which legislation had to be adopted. This led to the use of the early agreement procedure in areas such as 'the unbundling of the local loop' in telecommunications, an area of policy that was highly technical, but that was also highly controversial.

scrutiny, leading to criticisms that the Parliament is failing in its responsibility to provide democratic accountability. This lack of accountability poses clear risks for Parliament's democratic legitimacy. If Parliament does not take steps to redress the balance, it will mean that open and public debate in committee and plenary with the full participation of all political groups and members would tend to be reduced in importance by informal negotiations taking place elsewhere.[58]

While the Parliament is unhappy with the lack of transparency, it also sees trialogues and early agreements as providing it with opportunities to increase its influence over the legislative process. The Council had a strong interest in ensuring that discussions with Parliament began at an early stage, and were conducted reasonably smoothly. This was especially so as the Council was relatively understaffed, and had difficulty in dealing with a large volume of contentious legislation. Trialogues and the ensuing early agreements after first reading provided the Council with an important means of limiting its own workload to manageable proportions.

On the Parliament's side the power of the rapporteurs and shadow-rapporteurs of large political groups is greatly increased while the chairs of committees and the MEPs from small political groups[59] suffer from a relative loss of influence. On the Council's side, the Presidency clearly has gained in influence. COREPER may be sidelined by the successful attempts of the Presidency to dominate the policymaking process in the thrashing out of early agreements. The latter offers a unique possibility to realize its policy agenda within six months. Who appears to be losing are the national ministers from non-Presidency parties, and national parliaments (Farrell and Héritier 2004).[60]

In sum, there have been fears that the Parliament may be drawn too much into the kinds of secretive bargaining that better characterize inter-state

---

[58] See the Vice-President's discussion document on 'Improving the functioning of the code-cision procedure,' available at www.statewatch.org/news/2001/mar/codecision.pdf.

[59] Members of small parties have traditionally relied on their ability to propose formal amendments at committee stage as a means of influencing legislation. Now, they are finding themselves increasingly marginalized, as larger parties and the Council reach pre-arranged informal deals, which the large parties push through by voting down amendments in committee.

[60] Early agreement also has consequences for democracy at the national level. Each member state now has a specialized committee in its national-level Parliament dealing with European Union legislation although the effective power of these committees varies substantially from country to country. However, when legislation is brought through under early agreement provisions, it is difficult for these committees to exercise oversight; decisions are typically taken before the member states have even had the chance to reach a consensus on a common position, let alone to defend their negotiating strategies vis-à-vis their respective domestic parliaments. Efficiency is enhanced at the expense of accountability (Caporaso 2003).

negotiations than democratic debate. It has sought to respond to these pressures by opening a new round of bargaining with the Council, suggesting that it will not participate in the informal trialogues unless the Council agrees to come to parliamentary committee meetings, to discuss dossiers, and thus transfer some of the negotiation process to a more formal and publicly accessible environment. These contacts, according to Corbett, Jacobs, and Shackleton (2000: 206), have increased. Presidents-in-office of the various specialized Councils would come to the responsible parliamentary committees to discuss parliamentary amendments to legislative proposals Corbett, Jacobs, and Shackleton (2000: 206).[61]

However, the Council has indicated its continued unwillingness so to do because COREPER hesitates to reveal member states' positions in the bargaining process in a public forum (interviews Council October 2001;[62] and EP March 2001), and it is by no means clear that Parliament can credibly deliver on its threat of non-cooperation—many key power brokers within the Parliament actually benefit from current arrangements.[63] Nor is it clear that Parliament will not be prepared to sacrifice openness for increased power over the longer term.

Early agreements were not the only informal institutional rule emerging from the practical application of the new formal co-decision rule. Hix describes how in the application of the conciliation provision of the Maastricht Treaty the long-time chair of the Environment Committee, Ken Collins, in the negotiation of environmental legislation repeatedly introduced new amendments at the stage of conciliation, 'to use them as bargaining chips or to change the dimensionality of negotiations. Collins pointed out there was nothing in the treaty to prevent this interpretation of the rules' (Hix 2002: 276). Member states (and the Commission) objected to this practice, but had to take it into account during the conciliation bargaining process.

---

[61] Parliament also altered its Rules of Procedure accordingly: Council can come before its committees and comment on draft amendments on a proposal at first reading before the committee proceeds to its final vote (Rule 66); Council can come and present its common position to the committee responsible (Rule 76.2); and enter in a dialogue with the committee chair or rapporteur to look for possible compromise amendments at second reading (Corbett, Jacobs, and Shackleton 2000: 203).

[62] 'We have an old tradition ... that the Presidency does not reveal the individual position of national delegations ... It's fine to explain what the position of the Council is as long as you don't start pointing fingers at individual member states' (Interview Council Oct. 2001).

[63] The 'winners' under the institutional rule of early agreements in the Parliament argue that an overly formal approach would make it more difficult to reach a consensus (Interview rapporteur A, Oct. 2001). 'The rapporteur should be free ... to negotiate informally as much as possible with the Council, and not get bogged down in having formal scheduled meetings with some kind of preconciliation committee ... If you do that, the bureaucracies, the administrations of both the Parliament and the Council will get hold of this process and it will get gummed and glued up' (Interview Rapporteur A, Oct. 2001).

The most contested informal rule that emerged in the application of the co-decision procedure was the de facto elimination of the third reading by unilateral action of the Parliament. As we have seen, the provision of the Maastricht Treaty allowed the Council to reintroduce its common position in the case of a failure of the conciliation procedure unless an absolute majority of the Parliament could be mustered to reject it. This provision, from the very beginning, was a thorn in the Parliament's flesh because it felt that this introduced a bias in the relative power of the Council and the Parliament in the co-decision procedure. It, therefore, early on issued a new internal rule regarding the third reading to the effect that:

'1. Where no agreement is reached on a joint text within the Conciliation Committee, the President (of the EP) shall invite the Commission to withdraw its proposal, and invite the Council not to adopt under any circumstances a position pursuant to Art 189b(6) of the EC Treaty. Should the Council nonetheless confirm its common position, the President of the Council shall be invited to justify the decision before the Parliament in plenary sitting. The matter shall automatically be placed on the agenda of the last part-session to fall within six or, if extended, eight weeks of the confirmation by the Council ... 3. No amendments shall be tabled to the Council text. 4. The Council text as a whole shall be the subject to a single vote. Parliament shall vote on a motion to reject the Council text. If this motion receives the votes of a majority of the component Members of the Parliament, the (EP) President shall declare the proposed act not adopted' (Internal Rule of the EP, quoted after Hix 2002: 273).

When the Council for the first time reintroduced its common position, the Parliament proceeded to action. In an open conflict with the Council[64] it rejected in 1994 a proposal which the Council had reintroduced after a failed conciliation procedure, the proposal for a directive on voice telephony. Following the vote on the Open Telephony Directive the Council did not reintroduce its common position anymore but came to a compromise with the Parliament during the conciliation procedure (Corbett, Jacobs, and Shackleton 2000: 189; Hix 2002: 275). In another case on Financial Securities Regulation, when the Conciliation committee failed to reach an agreement on the legislative draft, Council—anticipating the rejection of the Parliament—decided not to reintroduce the common position (Corbett, Jacobs, and Shackleton 2000: 189).

To draw an interim *theoretical conclusion*, how can this development of new institutional rules, such as the early agreements or the tacit dropping of the third reading that emerged in the practical application of the co-decision procedure be accounted for? We have offered an *explanation of endogenous institutional change based on distributive bargaining theory* (Farrell and Héritier 2003, 2004, 2006). In this bargaining process the Parliament and the Council

---

[64] Concerning the right of controlling the implementation power of the Commission.

negotiated new informal rules guiding the daily application of the new co-decision rule. The outcome of the bargaining process was determined by the relative bargaining power of the two actors which was in turn in defined by (*a*) the existing formal rule (co-decision) and (*b*) the fallback position of the two actors, constituted by the time horizon and vulnerability towards a failure of the negotiation. We argue that the Parliament is winning out in the negotiation process because its time horizon is longer and its vulnerability in case of bargaining failure is smaller. The Council is frequently subject to time pressure because the Presidency wants to adopt its programme and the European Council imposes deadlines of legislative action on itself. By comparison, the Parliament is under less pressure to quickly adopt legislation. In the past it has frequently been observed to trade policy concessions against own institutional gains, that is by delaying or refusing the support to urgent policy matters, it obtained additional institutional power.[65]

There is also a *functionalist* element in the accounting for the Council's eagerness to engage in trialogues and early agreements: the workload which would arise for COREPER I if it would have to deal with numerous legislative items going all the way to conciliation, would be immense. These considerations of *functional efficiency* played an important role in developing the informal rule. What clearly emerges, too, is that the latter prevailed over norms of democratic legitimation. The Parliament, faced with the choice between gaining power in insulated trialogues and informal agreements on the one hand and a loss in its function as a democratic arena of debate on the other, decided in favour of the first. When seeking to partially remedy this loss of transparency by obliging Council to discuss its views on a legislative draft in the parliamentary committees it failed. It unilaterally stated corresponding rules of procedure which the Council mostly refused to go along with. But the Parliament's leadership also met resistance within its own ranks. Again, a *power-based distributive bargaining explanation* can account for this outcome.

Resuming the empirical account, the question arises: once the informal institutional rules guiding the application of co-decision had been established, what happened to them in the next treaty revision? The revision of the Maastricht Treaty was scheduled immediately after the end of the negotiations. Germany, Belgium, and Italy, in part due to the limited scope of co-decision introduced under Maastricht, had insisted on another IGC (Beach 2005: 114). The Parliament, once again, sought to formally gain access to the IGC. It argued that the IGC was 'being convened to prepare the Union for enlargement, and as the EP must approve of enlargement, the EP should therefore have a significant role in the IGC' (Lodge 1998: 486). It also insisted that as the only

---

[65] Such as in the extension of the consultation rights after 1957.

directly elected European political body, it should take part in the IGC to lend the process democratic legitimacy (Lodge 1998: 486). Both France and the UK were opposed to the Parliament taking part in the IGC while other member states supported the request. The final agreement was that the Parliament should take part in the work of the Reflection Group (Devuyst 1998: 618). The latter consisted of representatives from member states, two MEPs[66] and one member of the Commission. Moreover, there was an exchange of views between the Parliament President and ministers at the beginning of each IGC ministerial session; additionally, the Council Presidency organized a working meeting between IGC representatives and parliamentarian delegates. Thus the Parliament was closely associated with the IGC without being a formal party to the process (McDonagh 1998: 59).

The Reflection Group defined important aspects of the agenda of the upcoming IGC, but was not able to suggest solutions acceptable to all member states.[67] In the preparation of the IGC a Parliament White Paper demanded an extension of co-decision for all legislative matters, and the formalization of the possibility to come to an 'early agreement' at first reading; to drop the intention to reject a proposal at second reading; and to abolish the third reading (Committee on Institutional Affairs, Bourlanges/Martin report, 17.5.1995, Dury/Maij-Weggen report, 13.3.1996).[68] The Council Secretariat concurred in proposing the extension of 'early agreements'. The Commission did not make proposal to that effect. However, it was in favour of an extension of the co-decision procedure to twenty-three areas of decision-making and a general simplification of the procedure. It also proposed to drop the announcement of the intention to reject a proposal at second reading, to abolish the third reading and proposed to set time limits for the first reading.

While some member states (Italy and Germany) were in favour of extending co-decision to all legislative acts and to abolish the third reading, others (Belgium, Luxembourg, and Greece) proposed to link co-decision with QMV; others still (Austria, Ireland, the Netherlands, Portugal, Spain, Finland,

---

[66] The two parliamentarian delegates (E. Guigou and E. Brok) were said to have played a constructive part in the discussions of the Reflection Group (McDonagh 1998: 65; Maurer 2002: 420).

[67] In preparing the negotiations of the Amsterdam Treaty, the Parliament did not organize Assizes of the national parliaments to build support for its demands, arguably due to a lack of support from national parliaments. However, the two parlamentarian delegates in the Reflection group met the representatives of each parliament in order to collect information regarding their positions (EP Etat de la réflexion des parlements nationaux sur la CIG de 1996, 14.2.1996).

[68] The Parliament also proposed a revision of the Conciliation procedure which it considered to be too cumbersome, i.e. to bundle issues, simplify the decision-making rule and to give the Commission the power to propose a compromise between conflicting positions and put them to a vote (Views of the EP delegation to Conciliation Committee, 1996).

and France)[69] supported the extension of co-decision on a case-by-case basis. The UK was opposed to extending co-decision, arguing that the Parliament '...has shown a certain tendency to exercise them (their powers, A.H.) irresponsibly, endeavouring to force the Council to accept institutional changes not directly related to the legislation in question'.[70] The new incoming Labour government, however, was more favourable towards a further increase in the power of the Parliament (Devuyst 1998). Sweden and Denmark supported the strengthening of the Parliament in general terms.[71] In short: only the Parliament explicitly called for a formalization of early agreements; it also demanded, as did the Commission, Italy, Greece, and Germany, to abolish the third reading. All actors agreed to eliminate the declaration of intention of rejection during second reading. And regarding the extension of co-decision, member states held divergent views.

At the outset of the IGC negotiations in March 1996, the Italian Presidency listed different options of each topic under discussion to be commented on by delegations. On the basis of these comments the Presidency proposed possible compromises. At the European Council in Florence (June 1996) the Presidency drafted a progress report outlining the consensual goals: the reduction of legislative procedures to consultation, co-decision, and assent; the maintaining of cooperation for EMU and the Protocol on social policy; the extension of co-decision[72] and the simplification of co-decision. A majority of states wanted to keep the third reading. All delegations supported the possibility of coming to an agreement after first reading, only the Commission opposed the proposal.[73]

Real negotiations only started after the elections in the UK (Grunhage 2001: 19). The Irish and Dutch Presidencies introduced their draft texts very late before the summits, arguably to prevent that the proposals were 'examined too closely by the (national) experts before being entrusted to the Heads of State and Government' (Petite 1998: 3–4, quoted in Beach 2005: 129). This allowed the Presidency (and the Council Secretariat) and the Commission to have a negotiating advantage due to their technical knowledge (Beach 2005: 129). The Irish Presidency presented a draft which did not include specific

[69] France changed its position during negotiations.

[70] UK's July 1996 Note on quality of legislation; UK White Paper of 12.3.1996 on IGC: An association of nations.

[71] Moravcsik and Nicolaïdis explain the respective positions of member states by the strength of Social Democratic parties, the need of Germany and the Nordic states to demonstrate greater democratic legitimacy and the perceived connection of the Parliament with their own national parliaments (Moravcsik and Nicolaïdis 1999).

[72] The UK did not agree with this goal.

[73] All delegations agreed to abolish the phase of intention of rejection and there was a consensus not to give the Parliament a right of initiative.

compromises yet, but different options. 'It was difficult to move delegations from general support ... to specific agreement on detail.... Satisfactory agreement could only ... be reached on the basis of a package at the end of the process' (McDonagh 1998: 160). McDonagh argues that the tabling of specific compromises on the sensitive institutional question would not have been useful and that 'we were widely urged not to do so' (McDonagh 1998: 160). These sensitive institutional questions were deemed to be solvable only in the overall context of the final negotiations (McDonagh 1998: 107).[74] Interestingly, co-decision, except for the abolishing of the third reading, was not regarded as one of these delicate questions of the 'the institutional triangle', that is the extension of QMV, the reweighting of votes in the Council, and the number of Commissioners. The Irish Outline Draft Treaty proposed a general expansion of co-decision,[75] rather than on a case by case basis as well as the streamlining and speeding-up of the co-decision procedure (McDonagh 1998: 155; Beach 2005: 135); it also suggested the formalization of early agreements and that Council should adopt a modified Commission proposal by unanimity only. It supported the abolishing of the third reading. In its report the Presidency stated that the Parliament had threatened that it would reject any common position if the third reading would not be dropped (McDonagh 1998).

Regarding the thorny questions of the 'institutional triangle' as well as the abolishing of the third reading, little progress had been achieved yet. As one Commission observer in the group of permanent representatives complained: delegations only present their individual claims without compromising (CEC, note de dossier, CIG compte rendu 17.9.1996). At the end of 1996 the positions were almost identical to the very first meetings of the Reflection Group 28 months earlier.[76] Most of the sessions were simple 'tours de table', where member state delegates stated their positions without any notable changes. 'This was most evident at the foreign ministers level of the IGC, where ministers had locked-in mandates that prevented any real negotiation' (Dehousse 1999: 8–9 cited in Beach 2005: 132).

---

[74] A premature presentation of a proposal in textual form on which no consensus had emerged yet through the process of 'successive approximations' was considered to be a risky process (McDonagh 1998: 107).

[75] The idea of linking codecision with QMV was abandoned. Because member states could not agree on a reform of voting requirements which was shifted to the next IGC, the link between codecision and QMV was no longer feasible (Maurer 2002: 424).

[76] In November 1996 the Benelux, Germany, Austria, Finland, Italy, Greece, Sweden, and Ireland were in favour of extending co-decision to all legislative acts; Denmark, France, and Portugal supported the changing of cooperation to co-decision on a case by case basis. The UK opposed the extension of co-decision; a minority supported the abolishing of the third reading (I, D) (CEC Internal Note 23.4.1996).

The Irish Presidency included the possibility to approve the text amended by the Parliament at first reading, but incorporated the Commission's request that the Council should only unanimously adopt a modified Commission proposal (CEC Speaking note: Procédure de codécision, Nov. 1996). The Dutch Presidency confirmed this proposal and proposed the extension of co-decision to all legislative acts (Beach 2005: 135) as well as a simplification of the procedure including the abolishing of the third reading. In the group of permanent representatives most delegations were in favour of the proposal, however, a majority favoured the maintaining of the third reading (CEC, Note de dossier, Coreper 17 fevr.1997, 18.2.1997). Germany had consistently supported the proposal of abolition (Beach 2005: 142).

The final draft treaty submitted by the Dutch Presidency and formalized at the Amsterdam European Council provided for the extension of co-decision; the possibility to conclude at first reading; unanimity for the Council on amendments objected to by the Commission; and the abolishing of the third reading.[77] More specifically, the Amsterdam Treaty issued in August 1997 extended the field of application of co-decision from fifteen to thirty-eight areas (31 Treaty articles) including new areas such as transport, non-discrimination as well as some social policy and employment measures. Co-decision is now the normal legislative procedure covering more than half of Community legislation (Corbett, Jacobs, and Shackleton 2000: 191; Maurer 2003: 229). However, there are still areas, such as economic and monetary union, agriculture, fisheries, and fiscal harmonisation which are not subject to co-decision. Moreover, some co-decision areas (citizenship, freedom of movement for workers, measures concerning the self-employed, and cultural actions) require unanimity in Council (thereby indirectly reducing the influence of the Parliament) (Corbett, Jacobs, and Shackleton 2000: 191).[78] The Amsterdam Treaty in Article 251A (old 189A) included the provision that it is now possible to adopt a text at first reading if the Parliament does not propose any amendments or if the Council agrees with the Parliament's first reading amendments.[79]

---

[77] The Commission had 'warned member states (especially France)...that renouncing to drop the third reading would cause conflict with the Parliament' (CEC Internal note 23.4.1996, 17.6.1997).

[78] The Parliament did not reach one important objective: to increase its own budgetary powers by abolishing the distinction between compulsory and non-compulsory expenditures and treat all budget issues according to the procedure of non-compulsory expenses in which it has a formal say (Beach 2005: 137).

[79] The Treaty does not mention the obligation for the Council to vote at unanimity on the amendments with which the Commission did not agree. 'The Council, acting by qualified majority, after obtaining the opinion of the European Parliament, if it approves all the amendments contained in the European Parliament's opinion, may adopt the proposed act thus amended.' By

How can we *theoretically* account for this formalization of the informal practice that had emerged during the application of Art. 251A (old 189A) TEU? As Farrell and Héritier (2003, 2004, forthcoming) argue, the early agreements and adoption at first reading can clearly be seen as an unexpected informal institutional innovation—they were in no sense anticipated in the Maastricht provisions that introduced the co-decision procedure. Given the potential veto power of the Parliament over important items of legislation, the Council, and the member states had a considerable incentive to reach an appropriate modus operandi. Early agreements provided just this, and demonstrably eased transaction costs. As a consequence, member states were easily able to reach consensus on further formal treaty reforms that were intended to extend informal trialogues to other parts of the legislative process. The empirical evidence of the early agreement case supports an *endogenous bargaining argument of institutional change*. The Council and the Parliament, on the basis of an existing formal rule, bargained a new informal institutional rule guiding the application of co-decision. This new informal institutional rule fulfils *functional needs* of a speedier decision-making. In the subsequent round of formal treaty revision the informal rule was then formalized because it was *congruent with the wishes of all member states*.[80]

Another informal rule which had emerged in the application of the co-decision procedure, by contrast, was abolished because member states were in agreement on its undesirability. This is the case of the 'Ken Collins Amendment'. It shows that in *bargaining theoretical* terms, if all states are in favour of the rejection of an informal rule, the informal rule will not be formalized or will be formally out-ruled. In the Amsterdam negotiations member states were unanimous in trying to fill this 'loophole' and to prevent this exercise of discretion by MEPs by specifying the provisions governing the conciliation procedure. 'By specifying that conciliation negotiations are restricted to the EP and Council positions at second reading, the governments restricted any further EP interpretation of the rules to its advantage on this issue' (Hix 2002: 276).

The perhaps most interesting case of dealing with a newly developed informal institutional rule on the occasion of treaty revision is the case of the abolishing of the third reading. The informal rule 'imposed' by the Parliament by threatening to block legislation if the Council would use its right of reintroduction the common position after the failure of conciliation, bore

---

contrast, the adoption at second reading provides that the Council shall act unanimously on the amendments on which the Commission has delivered a negative opinion.

[80] A formal rule introduced under the Maastricht Treaty, i.e. the declaration of rejection during second reading, was entirely dropped because it was considered as unnecessary. All member states (and all organizational actors) agreed to abolish this possibility.

fruit. The Council did not make use of its right. In the negotiation of the Amsterdam Treaty, as we have seen, member states had mixed preferences as regards the formal abolishing of the third reading. A minority was in favour of abolishing, whereas a majority insisted on keeping it. Given these divergent preferences one would expect that member states would neither agree on formally dropping the third reading nor insist on its application. Yet, surprisingly, member states at the end of the negotiations accepted the abolition of the third reading.

This may be explained by the pressure that the Parliament, in an implicit bargaining process, applied across levels. It threatened that if the third reading was not abolished, it would reject any common position so confirmed (McDonagh 1998).[81] In other words, it threatened to block legislation in order to influence higher-order rule-making.[82] The Parliament had already previously made use of this strategy of a linked-arena veto in seeking to extend its consultations rights. An additional source of pressure resulted from its alliance with formal veto-players in the treaty revision, national parliaments. Italy and Belgium had committed themselves to not ratify the treaty if there were to be a negative vote from the Parliament (Etat de la réflexion des parlements nationaux sur la CIG de 1996, 14.2.1996).[83] In other words, it urged its 'allies' to use a linked-arena veto.

The destiny of the informal rule introduced in the case of the third reading shows that, given divergent preferences, member states are susceptible to pressure from other actors in linked arenas. The actor which gains from an informal rule, but does not have a formal role in treaty revisions, can exert pressure on formalizing this rule by using its veto power in other, linked, arena, in which she plays a role. Or as Corbett, Jacobs, and Shackleton observe: 'The right to say no whether at second reading or during conciliation, gives Parliament a bargaining position which it has hitherto lacked regarding Community legislation. . . . It can be no longer be accused of lacking teeth' (Corbett, Jacobs, and Shackleton 2000: 189). This distributive, power-based bargaining explanation for why the informal rule was formalized, seems plausible.

---

[81] In so doing it was supported by the Commission whose own institutional interest were also directed against the reintroduction of the common position of the Council since this possibility was impinging on the Commission's right of initiative.

[82] The Parliament also stated that if the results of the IGC were not satisfactory, it would reject the future enlargement of the Union (Maurer 2002: 420; Schiffauer 2004; Beach 2005).

[83] As opposed to 1990, no Assizes of national parliaments were organized by the Parliament to prepare the Amsterdam IGC despite of a call of the President of Parliament, Haensch, to that effect. Only the Belgian Parliament supported a proposal to hold another Assizes (Judge 1995). This was mainly due to the impression wrongly gained by the public from the final declaration of the Rome Assizes that the national parliaments would voluntary relinquish powers without demanding additional rights of control over their governments (Corbett 1998).

Would a *sociological institutionalist* argument emphasizing the *power of democratic legitimation* working in favour of the Parliament more plausibly account for the formalization of the informal rules increasing the competences of the Parliament? Prima facie, it seems convincing to argue that the Parliament obtained an equal position in the co-decision procedure through the abolishing of the third reading due to the fact that it is the only directly democratically legitimized body. Yet the empirical evidence of the political pressure that the Parliament needed to deploy in view of the resistance of most member states against this shift of power indicates that this cannot have been the only factor of influence. In the case of the abolishing of the Ken–Collins amendment the normative power of democratic legitimation argument would be flatly disconfirmed. Similarly, the case of the formalization of early agreements provides evidence for a *functionalist argument*: speedier legislation comes at the cost of a weakening democratic legitimation and less transparency and the Parliament has obviously been willing to 'pay this price' for more efficiency and power.

Theoretical Conclusion: From the Maastricht Treaty to the Amsterdam Treaty

The change of the institutional rules governing the legislative role of the Parliament between the Maastricht and Amsterdam treaties may first be accounted for by a power-based bargaining of informal institutional rules, that is early agreements, linked with a functionalist argument pointing to the need to adjust the existing rules to the large bulk of items in which the Parliament now played a role as a co-legislator. This change is reflected in the claim that:

H: *Institutional change through a formal/informal/formal dynamic*
'Formal rules at t1 that are ambiguous give rise to informal rules that further develop the formal rules. These informal rules will reflect the bargaining power of actors, as determined by formal institutions and the fallback position of the negotiating actors reflected in different time horizons and a different sensitivity to failure.'

The emergence of this informal rule begs the question of what follows, once the rule has been instituted. Is there a necessary *link* between informal rules and subsequent formalization? Under which conditions will they be formalized? It was argued that:

'The outcome of the formal negotiations at t2 will reflect informal institutions bargained if all designing actors agree to accept the informal change or if the implementing/affected actors can exert pressure through a linked-arena veto.'

In a first instance, a simple negotiation theoretical argument can explain why some informal rules were formalized and some were not. With *redistributive* issues at stake and given diverging member states' preferences, a more complicated, *multilevel, power-based bargaining argument* submits that the Parliament can apply a linked-arena veto. It uses its formal veto power in a linked arena, or forms an alliance with another veto player in a higher-order rule arena (e.g. national parliaments), to exert indirect pressure to obtain its preferred outcome.

An exogenous event, that is enlargement, causing a functionally motivated redesign did play a role in bringing about institutional change, as well.

H: Functionalist transaction cost–based argument
'If, due to an external event, the benefits of rule A have decreased, the rule will be changed, if the gains of the proposed altered rule B including the transaction costs will be higher.'

Another important exogenous events which had a clear impact on the negotiation process of the IGC was primarily the change of government in the UK. The coming into power of the Labour government clearly facilitated the agreement to widen the application of the co-decision procedure (McDonagh 1998: 184). This last explanation corresponds to a classical *liberal intergovernmental explanation* where a change of preference in a member state causes a change in the negotiation base for a change of an institutional rule.

From a *structural perspective* the process of change extended across levels: some informal rules were subsequently formalized at the *higher-order rule level,* pressure on the part of the Parliament was exerted through a *linked arena-veto.* The new informal rules guiding co-decision were developed jointly by *designing* and *implementing actors,* that is the Council and the Parliament. The formalization or non-formalization of these informal rules, however, were in the hands of the designing actors, member states, only.

4.2.4. From the Amsterdam Treaty to the Nice Treaty

In the period between the adoption of the Amsterdam Treaty and the adoption of the Nice Treaty the institutional rule governing the role of the Parliament in legislation was subject to another, however, only indirect formal change. At the very conclusion of the Amsterdam IGC, the next IGC was scheduled in order to resolve the delicate questions of the 'institutional triangle', that is the extension of QMV, the redefinition of number of Commissioners, and the reweighting of votes in the Council that so far had not been solved. Member states in June 1999 decided to let the Group of Permanent Representatives to do much of the preparatory work (Reh forthcoming) and to hold more informal discussions in the Council of Ministers (Beach 2005: 146).

In substance the Commission, going further than most member states (Dinan and Vanhoonacker 2000: 20), proposed to link QMV and co-decision in all legislative matters under the first pillar. The Parliament initially did not hold a unified view, but finally proposed that co-decision and QMV should be introduced for all legislative acts, that cooperation should be entirely abolished, and codecison should also be applied in police and judicial affairs (Jacobs 2000: 54). Member states had divergent preferences. While some governments only wanted to deal with the 'leftovers' from Amsterdam, others aimed for more extensive reforms to ensure that the institutional rules would work under conditions of an enlarged membership (Wessels 2001; Beach 2005). Regarding co-decision, one group (Belgium, Luxembourg, Greece, and Germany) proposed to apply co-decision in all areas subject to QMV, other governments (Finland, Italy, and Austria) opted for an extension of co-decision to new areas subject to QMV, and another two member states (UK and France) wished to extend co-decision only in exceptional cases; other countries (Denmark, The Netherlands, Finland, Spain, and Portugal), finally, supported an extension of co-decision on case by case basis (CEC Internal note 14.3.2000).

During negotiations, in a first period of exploration, the Finnish Presidency proposed to deal only with the 'institutional triangle' (European Council 1999 in Beach 2005: 147) and so did the Portuguese Presidency which drew up a list of twenty-five areas to be subject to QMV. All member states considered the extension of QMV in Council more important than a parallel extension of co-decision. The Parliament in its report stated that the large majority of delegations had not endorsed Parliament's call for an automatic link between QMV and co-decision and opted for maintaining the cooperation procedure under EMU. A majority supported the extension of co-decision on a case-by-case basis and the application of co-decision in new areas subject to QMV (Report of Portuguese Presidency 7.12.1999).

In the final negotiations under the French Presidency (Best et al. 2002; Dinan and Vanhoonacker 2000), each ministerial session was preceded by an exchange of views with the President of the European Parliament. The French Presidency discarded an IGC report that the European Council had accepted under the Portuguese Presidency and, rather than trying to step-by-step solve disagreements based on a single negotiating text bracketing sensitive questions and listing options in controversial areas, started anew with more principled questions (Gray and Stubb 2001; Beach 2005: 147). The most difficult issues, that is the 'institutional triangle', were shifted into the final Nice Summit 'where the French strategy appeared to be to put the heads of state and government under the gun ... to accept a compromise package, making them more prone to give in on national positions' (Beach 2005: 148). The negotiations on the reweighting of votes proved to be very difficult. With so many actors around the table it was difficult to engage in direct negotiations (beyond tour de table statements) giving rise to informal practices to thrash out compromises (Beach 2005: 164; Mateo Gonzalez 2004). Only by holding numerous confessionals could the French establish a linkage between the former and the composition of the Commission and present a proposal accepted by all but Belgium.[84] The outcome as regards co-decision was modest. It was not extended to all first pillar issues nor CAP as the Parliament had requested (Jacobs 2000: 55). QMV was introduced in only twenty-seven provisions, out of fifty initially proposed by the Commission.

Theoretical Conclusion: From the Amsterdam Treaty to the Nice Treaty

How can we account for the limited institutional gains in legislation that the Parliament obtained in this period? The most plausible answer is that the Parliament had already reached the formal status of co-legislator with the Council and a significant extension of the scope of the rule application ('Attribute' dimension—Crawford and Ostrom 1995) under the Maastricht and Amsterdam treaties. A second answer is that co-decision was linked to the contested question of QMV and there was little progress in the extension of QMV. This points to the importance of links between different decision-making rules, whereby the change in one rule implies a change in another rule. In this case the introduction of co-decision was linked to the introduction of QMV. QMV being such a vexed subject among member states where little progress was achieved, also meant that co-decision was not substantially extended.[85]

The pressure to renegotiate the rules was brought about by an exogenous event (enlargement) and a functional pressure to adjust the existing formal decision-making rules to the challenge of an enlarged European Union. Hence a functionalist redesign explanation seems plausible.

H: Functionalist transaction cost–based argument
'If, due to an external event, the benefits of rule A have decreased, the rule will be changed, if the gains of the proposed altered rule B including the transaction costs will be higher.'

---

[84] Which finally gave its acquiescence in exchange for a compensation in a completely different issue area.

[85] In bargaining terms the Parliament has less leverage when bargaining with a Council which has to apply the unanimity rule as opposed to a Council applying QMV. The Council can argue that it has 'its hands tied' by the unanimity rule, hence makes less concessions to parliamentarian demands.

The ensuing bargaining process to shape these institutional changes was complicated by the *zero-sum character of the 'institutional triangle issues'* to which the co-decision question was indirectly linked. This is reflected in the claim that

H: Problem type and integrative vs. defensive bargaining
'If redistributive issues are at stake the process of institutional change will be characterized by defensive bargaining. The outcome will reflect the asymmetry of power of the involved actors.'

The fact that these redistributive issues (in particular the extension of QMV question) could not be solved also implied an only moderate success in the area of co-decision.

These difficulties to come to an agreement when faced with redistributive issues points to a typical *link* between institutional changes. The bracketing of controversial institutional questions gives rise to the scheduling of another planned round of higher-order formal rule change. Here, however, given divergence of preferences in the face of redistributive issues, the negotiations are confronted with the same difficulties, resulting in another gridlock and a further shifting of the decision to a future intergovernmental bargaining round, triggering a process of continuous rule-change (see also Christiansen and Jorgensen 1999; Héritier 1999).

From the *structural perspective*, the institutional change in this phase plays entirely at the *higher-order level*. Only *designing actors* (i.e. member states) are engaged in the change of rules, the Parliament—except in a consultative role—not having formally gained access to the circle of actors redesigning the decision-making rules (Jacobs 2000: 58). Due to the constructive role the Parliament had played in the Amsterdam IGC, it was at least informally a more accepted partner in the Nice IGC (Beach 2005: 160).[86] However, it was influential in shaping the agenda of higher-order rule making post-Nice that subsequently led to the European Convention in 2002–3 (Schiffauer 2004). The Parliament's active promotion of a change of meta-rules reflects the claim

H: Shifting levels/arenas to accelerate institutional change
'Given a choice between different levels/arenas of decision-making an actor may, by opting out of one arena and shifting the decision to another, improve his prospects of obtaining an institutional change according to his preferences.'

What emerges across the IGCs is that the Parliament pursued a long-term strategy in promoting such higher-order institutional changes. Even if its mostly ambitious institutional goals were not realized at one IGC, this did

---

[86] France and the UK were still opposed to full EP involvement in the IGC. The delegates of the Parliament did not participate in the political level meetings (Beach 2005: 160, 170).

not keep it from reformulating them the next time round (Schiffauer 2004; Beach 2005: 175). In 1999 it had proposed a *new meta-institutional rule*, the Convention method, for the revision of the treaties which would give itself an important role in the shaping of higher-order institutional rules. The protocol to the Nice Treaty declared that a new IGC should be held by 2004 in order to tackle more extensive reforms. And in order to achieve these reforms, a different institutional form of treaty revision should be employed (European Policy Centre 1998; Christiansen and Jorgensen 1999).

4.2.5. From the Nice Treaty to the Constitutional Treaty

The Parliament was an important, but not the only actor who pressed for more extensive institutional changes in the face of enlargement and external challenges of the Union. Member states in the declaration of Laeken called for a Convention on the Future of Europe to prepare the agenda for the next IGC of 2004. A change of the method of treaty reform was considered to be a crucial condition for achieving more ambitious reforms. The Parliament immediately seized on this opportunity of changing the procedure of revising of higher-order rules.

The Convention comprised 204 delegates and 3 chairmen (one representative from each of 15 member governments and from 13 candidate countries; 16 MEPs; 2 representatives from each national parliament; 2 Commissioners; and an alternate for each member. The European Parliament with sixteen members plus sixteen alternate delegates held an important position. It also occupied two seats on the presidium.[87] This offered an opportunity to take influence on the negotiations and to shape the selection of proposals put to the plenary (Magnette and Nicolaïdis 2003; Norman 2003; Maurer 2003). The Commission was represented by two Commissioners in the plenary and held two seats in the presidium. However, the delegates from the European organizations, that is Parliament and Commission, did not outnumber national delegates (Ludlow 2002: 59). The mandate of the Convention was to produce 'options' for a treaty change (Beach 2005: 179). The decision-making rule to be applied was not clearly specified in the mandate, except that the final text should be decided on the basis of consensus (CONV 9/02).

---

[87] The Presidium played a very important role in the negotiations of the Convention. It set the agenda, and drafted texts. The Presidium members also chaired the working groups which gave them an important agenda setting function in these groups, too (Beach 2005: 200).

The Convention started out with a phase of hearings, a 'deliberation' phase in a number of working groups and finally decided. Given the large number of actors, negotiations could not take place in the plenary, but occurred in the working groups. The final text was drafted in the presidium Secretariat under the leadership of the presidium chairman, Giscard d'Estaing. The Convention members submitted thousands of amendments to the draft from which Giscard and the Secretariat selected those that were to be incorporated into the draft sent to the presidium for approval (Beach 2005: 201). In the end a clear majority of delegates supported the final draft in the plenary, with a disagreeing minority text (Maurer 2003; Norman 2003; Beach 2005: 180).

As mentioned, the initial formal mandate given to the 'conventionnels' was quite limited, that is to consider the key issues arising for the Union's future development and to try to identify the various possible responses. The members of the Convention chose to ignore this mandate and went much beyond it to propose a single, simplified Constitutional Treaty which should replace the existing treaties. Arguably (Norman 2003) the Parliament had played an important role in bringing the notion of developing a Constitution into play.

The institutional rule of interest here, co-decision, was not at centre stage in the Convention discussions, except in its link with the extension of QMV. By the beginning of 2003 there was broad support for an extension of co-decision and QMV,[88] albeit not to the extent that the Parliament had wished (i.e. to include justice and home affairs and agricultural policy). The final text, however, did not extend QMV to all policy areas, but established a 'passerelle' providing for the possibility that, on unanimity decision of the Council, a particular policy area could be subject to QMV (Beach 2005: 188).[89] Other difficult institutional questions, implying a redistribution of competences between the organizational actors were not tackled during the Convention, but in the IGC following the Convention.

The Convention text was approved as a starting point for the upcoming IGC negotiations at the European Council in Thessaloniki in 2003. As usual, the main actors submitted their positions. The Commission called for a generalization of QMV and co-decision. The Parliament, back in its observer status, defended the Convention draft and called on member states to avoid negotiations on the main decisions put forward by the Convention. It even envisaged a rejection of the final Constitutional Treaty if its new powers in the

[88] MEPs were successful when they were realistic in their claims and formed large coalitions often along political party lines (Jonsson and Hegeland 2003; Maurer 2003).

[89] The Convention draft also included codecision powers for the Parliament in compulsory budgetary expenditures.

budget were to be eliminated (Beach 2005: 209). The Italian Presidency tabled the controversial institutional issues for the final European Council.[90] The ensuing breakdown of the negotiations reflected member states' fundamental disagreement on institutional questions, such as QMV, if not co-decision. The incoming Irish Presidency, in numerous informal bilateral talks, step by step prepared the ground for a compromise between supranationalists defending the Convention text (e.g. Germany and Belgium) and intergovernmentalists[91] 'wanting to chip away integrative elements of the draft' (Norman 2003; Beach 2005: 203). While the Parliament's extension of budgetary powers to CAP remained untouched, the right to ask the Commission to table a new budget in case of disagreement with the Council was eliminated (Beach 2005: 209; CIG 60/03 Add 1). The process of institutional change incorporated in the Constitutional Treaty and accepted in the IGC was halted by the referenda held in France and the Netherlands.

Theoretical Conclusion: From the Nice Treaty to the Constitutional Treaty

The causes of the institutional change in the period between the Nice Treaty and the Convention and Constitutional Treaty was a response to the functional needs of enlargement, that is to make institutional rules fit for a decision-making process encompassing a larger number of members. Hence it can be interpreted in terms of a:

H: Functionalist transaction cost-based argument
'If, due to an external event, the benefits of rule A have decreased, the rule will be changed, if the gains of the proposed altered rule B including the transaction costs will be higher.'

There were *no endogenous developments of informal institutional change* at the lower-order rule level in order to extend the application of the co-decision procedure. The reform objective was directed immediately to a *change at the higher-order rules level* in the course of which the Parliament together with the Commission had pushed for a new mode of treaty revision, that is the Convention method. The Parliament had strong institutional interests in choosing the Convention method since it meant that the Parliament finally would gain access to the circle of the *actors (re)designing institutional rules.*

---

[90] And a poor management of the negotiations by the Italian Presidency.

[91] The UK maintained its concern about the extension of majority voting in sensitive areas such as taxation and foreign policy (Beach 2005: 189).

H: Shifting levels/arenas to accelerate institutional change
'Given a choice between different levels/arenas of decision-making an actor may, by opting out of one arena and shifting the decision to another, improve his prospects of obtaining an institutional change according to his preferences.'

But it was also the discontent with the cumbersomeness and lack of success of the intergovernmental decision-making process in the negotiation of the Nice Treaty that exerted a pressure to come up with new methods of adapting the decision-making rules in legislation to the exigencies of a Community that was to be drastically enlarged. Hence, a functionalist explanation of why redesigning the mode of changing the higher-order rules and to hold a Convention holds plausibility. However, in the work of the Convention which had been instituted by member governments at Laeken, there was a clear endogenous element of institutional development. The Convention by aiming for a Constitution drastically redefined the agenda and went clearly beyond the formal mandate defined by the European Council. This is not surprising in view of the actors composing the Convention, that is a large number of member of national parliaments and the European Parliament. The Parliament, arguably, was the driving force behind this redefinition of the agenda of the Convention. Due to its representation in the presidium and a skilful strategy of coalition building among political groups in the plenary in the second half of the Convention process, it was also successful in inserting its objectives into the Treaty text, that is the expansion of QMV and co-decision in all policy areas.

The Convention was supposed to push out the Pareto frontier and propose institutional solutions acceptable to all. This reflects the hypothesis on integrative vs. defensive bargaining:

H: Problem type and integrative vs. defensive bargaining
'If redistributive issues are at stake the process of institutional change will be characterized by defensive bargaining. The outcome will reflect the asymmetry of power of the involved actors.'
'If in a first, institutionally separate stage of negotiation, actors focus on problem-solving, they may identify institutional solutions beneficial to all; the developing of such solutions may have an impact on the second stage defensive bargaining because the space of feasible options has been extended.'

While problem solving oriented behaviour may have prevailed in some working groups, towards the end of the Convention bargaining in view of the positions of member states seems to have played an important role.

In the IGC which followed and decided on the draft Constitutional treaty submitted by the Convention defensive bargaining clearly prevailed. Here the Parliament did not have a role.[92] The process was subject to the goal-oriented behaviour of member state governments in negotiating over issues with redistributive implications. This reflects the claim

H: Problem type and integrative vs. defensive bargaining
'If redistributive issues are at stake the process of institutional change will be characterized by defensive bargaining. The outcome will reflect the asymmetry of power of the involved actors.'

4.2.6. Conclusion

What were the main forces driving the expansion of the Parliament's rights in legislation from consultation to codecison? From the process perspective it is striking how the Parliament on the basis of a given formal institutional rule negotiated informal rules extending its power. It frequently was able to obtain the formalization of these informal rules. A distributive power-based bargaining theory of endogenous institutional change may explain this pattern of change. If this practice would give rise to a conflict between Parliament and Council, it was submitted to third-party dispute resolution, that is the ECJ. The subsequent Court ruling would have an important influence on the subsequent rule application. This development is well grasped by the theory of rule development through adjudication.

Strong exogenous problem pressure also constituted an important factor of change prompting actors to engage in a redesigning of the formal institutional rules. Thus, the completion of the internal market and monetary union and various enlargement rounds triggered rounds of redesigning of existing formal rules. This corresponds to the functionalist argument that new tasks alter the cost–benefit calculations regarding existing institutional rules and, after calculating transaction costs, actors may be willing to redesign the existing institutions. Once this rules have been formally adopted in a treaty revision, the daily application of the rule engenders new informal rules which in a next round of formal rule revision may be confirmed in a bargaining process in the context of unanimity rule.

From a structural perspective (levels and arenas of change and types of actors) this case demonstrates that the multilevel aspect of change plays an important role for the dynamics of institutional change. The Parliament, tired of the only modest success obtained at the level of intra-treaty changes, shifted its ambitions of institutional reform to the higher-order level and, indeed, the

[92] The Parliament did threaten not to support the treaty revision in case that the codecision power in compulsory budgetary expenditure should not be accepted at the IGC, but to no avail.

meta-rules, that is the rules about higher-order rule-making. It was successful in setting the agenda for a treaty revision by constantly reiterating its requests for a treaty revision and was supported in these claims by the new functional requirements of the Single Market project. Moreover, the Parliament strongly advocated the Convention method under which it obtained the status of a designing actor and engaged in the changing of treaty provisions. However, the shift to another level or arena as such would simply open up another opportunity of change, by no means the guarantee of a change in the desired direction.

In order to exert some pressure on the direction of formal institutional change in an arena in which the Parliament was not a designing actor, for example the IGCs, the Parliament with some success took recourse to a linked-arena veto. It established a link between the arena of redesign and another arena in which it did have a formal vote. By withholding or rejecting the decision in the latter, it exerted pressure on the decision in the first. To give an example, the Parliament by delaying its decision in an arena of daily Community policymaking (refusing budgetary means, delaying the delivery of an opinion in consultation) or by forming an alliance with other formal veto-players (national parliaments or individual member state governments), attempted to influence the decision in a higher-order rule arena. This strategy of influencing institutional change is well captured by strategic bargaining theory in a given institutional context.

The distinction of actor types offers further insights. The designing actors of higher-order institutional change are the member states only. The Parliament is only an implementing actor. Because it does not have a voice in the designers' arena, it had an incentive to engage in a process of endogenous institutional change between treaty revisions to shift powers in its own favour. At the same time, it constantly sought to gain direct access to the table of the designing actors. But it was not until the Nice IGC that the Parliament was informally accepted 'at the table'. Under the Convention process it finally gained the status of a formal designing actor in drafting the Constitutional Treaty.

Alternatively to the rational institutionalist account of the expanding role of the Parliament in legislation, one could hypothesize that a normative social-ization process has occurred in the course of which the democratic legitima-tion argument convinced the Council and the Commission to yield power to the Parliament. Being the only directly elected political body, and therefore, able to refer to its direct democratic legitimation did help the Parliament to push its cause. This reflects the argument of sociological institutionalism that a change of institutional rule comes about through the force of normative ideas. Yet bearing in mind the multiple obstacles the Parliament had to overcome in order to achieve its institutional objectives and to how many bargaining and pressure strategies it resorted to in order to achieve its purpose, makes it seem questionable whether the normative power explanation by itself would be sufficient. The democratic legitimation argument was certainly used by the Parliament to push its goals. This explanation would be perfectly compatible with the argument of strategic bargaining. What becomes evident is that the functional causes of rule change, that is the new exigencies of the Single Market Programme and the democratic legitimation arguments were linked in a bargaining process. Some member states were only willing to shift the competencies necessary for the completion of the internal market to the supranational level if this shift would be connected to a strengthening of the power of the Parliament.

4.3. INSTITUTIONAL RULE TWO: THE PRESIDENCY OF THE COUNCIL

What are the institutional rules that govern the Presidency of the Council and how have these rules changed over time? The rules governing the Council Presidency have mostly developed in an informal way and have only partly been formalized. This constitutes a stark contrast to the rapid increase of the tasks performed by the Presidency, starting out from a mere administrative function, as the rotating chair of the meetings of member states to 'a vital part of the EU's institutional structure and a critical component of the institutional balance' (Hayes-Renshaw and Wallace 2006: 133) as a business manager, manager of foreign policy, promoter of initiatives, package-broker, liaison point, and collective representative (Edwards and Wallace 1976).

As in the case of the institutional rule governing the role of the Parliament in legislation, the empirical account and theoretical explanation of the development of the institutional rule governing the Presidency will be divided into a number of periods which are delimited by the events of formal (higher-order) rule revision, that is the treaty revisions

1. from 1957 to mid-1960s;
2. from the Empty Chair Crisis/Luxembourg compromise (1965–6) to the establishing of the European Council (1974);
3. from the establishing of the European Council (1974) to the SEA (1986);
4. from the SEA (1986) to the Maastricht Treaty (1992);
5. from the Maastricht Treaty (1992) to the Amsterdam Treaty (1997);
6. from the Amsterdam Treaty (1997) to the Nice Treaty (2001);
7. from the Nice Treaty (2001) to the Constitutional Treaty (2004).

4.3.1. From 1957 to 1965

When first formally established under the Treaty of Rome in 1957, the Presidency possessed only weak procedural responsibilities that were clarified in the Council's Rules of Procedure (Tallberg 2006: 45). A crucial operating rule of the Presidency is the system of rotation. Each government holds the Presidency for six months.[93] The rotation rule not only determines 'the order in which the member states exercise the Presidency, but also their place at the negotiating table at all levels of the Council hierarchy.... It may also determine the order in which they are called on to speak and, where applicable, to vote at meeting' (Hayes-Renshaw and Wallace 2006: 138). The Presidency chairs all working groups, committees, and ministerial meetings in the Council of Ministers. Subsequently, as we will see, the initially limited managerial responsibilities of the rotating Presidency changed, mostly as a consequence of a loss of power of the Commission and a functional widening of the Community tasks European Political Cooperation (EPC).

4.3.2. From the Empty Chair Crisis and Luxembourg Compromise to Establishing the European Council

In the second half of the 1960s two factors played an important role in changing the institutional rules governing the Presidency. The first factor concerns interorganizational relations between the Council and the Commission. The weakening of the Commission due to the 'Empty Chair Crisis' and the Luxembourg compromise strengthened the role of the Presidency in the Council; the second factor concerns the increasing tasks of the ECE that, after the completion of the customs union, had led to an increased fragmentation of decision-making in the Council, and as a consequence, to a strengthening of the leadership of the Council Presidency (Tallberg 2006: 46/47).

As regards interorganizational relations, the Empty Chair Crisis in 1965–6 weakened the Commission's capacity to control the agenda of policymaking. In its famous 'triple deal' which set off the Empty Chair Crisis, the Commission bundled very diverse issues when it proposed the financing of the CAP, but also unexpectedly introduced two new dimensions: to create its own financial resources and to give the European Parliament new authority to oversee the Community budget (White 2003: 124). France resisted the attempts

---

[93] The Treaty of Paris Art. 27 had provided that the Presidency would be held for three months following alphabetical order. The Treaties of Rome (EEC, Art. 146 and Euratom Art. 116) extended the term to six months, the Merger Treaty of 1965 adopted a six-month period for all three communities (Hayes-Renshaw and Wallace 2006: 138).

of the Commission to extend the application of QMV in Council decisions and boycotted the decision-making process in the Council. The conflict was solved with the Luxembourg Compromise in 1966 providing for the continued application of unanimity rule in the Council and a postponement of the introduction of majority voting, moreover, obliging the Commission to consult national governments before proposing new legislation. The Empty Chair Crisis and the Luxembourg compromise clearly impinged on the authority of the Commission as a formal initiator of new policies and 'as the principal motor of European integration' (Tallberg 2006: 46; Palayret, Wallace, and Winand 2006). This, in turn, led to a series of proposals to give more formal power to the Council Presidency which should act as a broker balancing diverse member state interests. In the wake of the Empty Chair Crisis the Commission, which in the 1950s and early 1960s had played this role, was now 'distrusted for its supranational intentions ... and increasingly excluded from central bargaining processes' (Tallberg 2006: 58). New institutional rules to define the Presidency's role were called for.

Another aspect of deepened interorganizational interaction contributed to the strengthening of the Presidency: the requirement to interact with the Parliament in the budgetary process. The agreements of 1970 and 1975 revising the budget procedure of the EEC had provided for a formal role of the Parliament in the budgetary process. In order to negotiate with the Parliament, member governments delegated authority to the Presidency which, initially, the Presidency did not have. Since the negotiation proved to be very difficult, a conciliation procedure was introduced in 1975 under which the Presidency could negotiate on behalf of the Council (Hayes-Renshaw and Wallace 2006).

Yet another factor leading to a change of institutional rules concerning the Presidency resulted from the rapid growth of Community tasks. After the successful completion of the customs union and the rapidly widening tasks of Community policy it became clear that the decision-making processes in the Council were increasingly fragmented and lacking in coordination (Tallberg 2006; Hayes-Renshaw and Wallace 2006). One important extension of Community tasks was the establishing of EPC in foreign policy at the end of the 1960s. European Political Cooperation was introduced outside the Community, which meant that the Commission did not have a right of agenda setting, coordination, and brokerage. Therefore these functions automatically fell to the Presidency. In the Luxembourg Report of 1970, member states defined the procedural arrangements, according to which all governments had the right to propose subjects, and the Presidency should set and structure the foreign policy agenda. These expanding functions increased the problems of fragmentation, pointing to the need for a better coordination of the Council work, and concomitantly, a reconsideration of the institutional rules guiding the work of the Council Presidency (Hayes-Renshaw and Wallace 2006: 135). 'The growth in the scope and effectiveness of political cooperation was made possible only by the constantly increasing authority vested in the Presidency' (de Schoutheete 1988: 82 quoted in Tallberg 2006: 53). Member states agreed to these modifications and wrote them down in reports (Hayes-Renshaw and Wallace 2006: 140). Interestingly, these changes first emerged as an informal practice which was only subsequently written down (Hayes-Renshaw and Wallace 2006: 140). Thus, coordination and execution was added to the presidential tasks in the Copenhagen Report of 1973. European Political Cooperation also strengthened the function of the Presidency in representations and negotiations with external actors. And the Luxembourg Report charged the Presidency to function as a liaison actor between member states and the new four applicant countries. This link function involves 'a process of brokering an internal agreement before external negotiations are initiated, renegotiating this position in the light of the other party's counter-demands, and eventually seeking member states' support for a final deal involving new compromises' (Tallberg 2006: 143).[94]

An alteration of institutional rules governing the work of the Council was also discussed in a more salient form, such as in a report on institutional reform commissioned by the Council (Tindemans Report) in 1974. The report confirmed the need for coordination and urged for a reinforcement of the Presidency. In 1974 the European Council was founded as a body for summit meetings chaired by the Presidency *outside* the existing formal Community organizations: since the beginning of the 1970s the member states had begun to meet more often in the European Council which began to assume crucial agenda-setting functions.[95] Its decision-making mode is intergovernmental and follows the unanimity rule. The preparation and implementation of the summits very quickly became a task of the Presidency (Tallberg 2006: 54). 'The presidency-in-office has a clear discretionary role in narrowing down the agenda from the rather large set of topics that emerges initially' (Bulmer and Wessels 1987: 52) from the meetings of foreign ministers. In order to define concerns and policy priorities, the Presidency would undertake a 'tour des capitales'.[96]

---

[94] The Copenhagen Report (1974) additionally asked the Presidency to present the Community in negotiations with friendly states. The Presidency also began to speak on behalf of member states in the UN Assembly.

[95] The Commission does not have a right to set the agenda.

[96] Previously the conclusions from the records of meetings were bargained among representatives of the member governments, the 'sherpas'. The issues that could not be agreed on were 'bracketed'. This would happen frequently since 'the sherpas lacked the authority to reveal

A reform of the rotation rule was considered in the mid-1970s and solutions such as the extension of the period of the Presidency and the introduction of some form of group presidency were discussed. However, none of the proposed solutions were able to produce a consensus (Tallberg 2006: 76).

Theoretical Conclusions: From the Empty Chair Crisis and Luxembourg Compromise to the Establishing of the European Council

Viewing the empirical development from the Empty Chair Crisis and Luxembourg Compromise in 1965–6 until the establishing of the European Council in 1974 through *theoretical lenses*, two important sources and processes of institutional change may be identified. Theoretically, they may be interpreted as the outcome of the loss of weight of another actor, the Commission, and the concomitant gain in importance of the Council; secondly, as a response to changed *functional demands* of the external environment calling for a redesigning of the institutional rules.

As regards the first cause and ensuing process of institutional change the argument is that one organization (the Commission) losing importance in a particular function, the other (the Presidency of the Council) compensates this vacuum by gaining in influence and that this is reflected in a change of the institutional rules governing the Presidency.

The second source of institutional change, that is the increased functional demands deriving from new policy tasks of the Community and the ensuing strengthened role of the Presidency in coordinating these tasks within the Council, may be interpreted in functionalist terms as a pressure to redesign institutional rules in response to new external exigencies. This corresponds to the claim

H: *Functionalist institutionalist transaction cost-based hypothesis*
'If due to an external event the benefits of rule A have decreased, the rule will be changed, if the gains of the altered rule B including the transaction costs will be higher.'

The new functional demands were met by introducing the European Council which, in turn, strengthened the Presidency. An *informal institutional rule* was developed to better coordinate agenda setting in the face of growing decision-making tasks and an increasing compartmentalization and fragmentation of decision-making in the EEC. This new informal institution was only later formalized. The rule formation followed 'an already established practice, rather than prescribing new practice' (Hayes-Renshaw and Wallace 2006: 140).

bottom lines, effectively producing unnegotiable draft texts' (Tallberg 2006: 64–65). In 1982, the drafting of conclusions was handed over to the Presidency (Tallberg 2006: 65).

The functionalist explanation of the growing importance of the Presidency within the Council may also be formulated as a *principal–agent relationship.* Member states delegated the negotiation to the Presidency. The agent/Presidency may gain some latitude in his actions because he has more information than the member states/principals due to the knowledge of his own objectives, the tours of capitals, bilateral talks and the support of the Council Secretariat (informational asymmetry) (Tallberg 2006: 144, 191). The agent, therefore, to some extent, may pursue its own interests when fulfilling its task, creating the risk of agency loss (Tallberg 2006: 141).[97] To prevent this, the principals may devise institutional rules to restrict the risk of moral hazard. This is reflected in hypothesis:

H: *Agency loss as a cause of institutional change*
'If the divergence between the principal's and the agent's preferences has become too large, the principal will redesign the contract, i.e. change the institutional rule in order to rein in the agent.'

Thus, Tallberg argues and shows empirically that most agents/Presidencies use their institutional resources in the *negotiation of changes* in order to achieve objectives that are favourable for them. 'If the zone of agreement (in negotiations, A.H.) permits a number of efficient outcomes with varying distributional consequences, presidencies promote the agreement closest to their own preferences...' (Tallberg 2006: 112). Similarly Hayes-Renshaw and Wallace argue that the Presidency tends to suffer from a 'structural bias in favour of its own government's position' (Hayes-Renshaw and Wallace 2006: 149). However, they also point out that there would be 'deep resistance to the explicit peddling of sharp national interests' (Hayes-Renshaw and Wallace 2006: 148) because of 'strong-minded national representatives and because of the segmentation of the Council' (Hayes-Renshaw and Wallace 2006: 148).

An institutional rule that reins in the Presidency/agent is the unanimity rule. Each member state having a veto position, the actor least willing to change the status quo, must somehow be accommodated. As Scharpf (1997) argues, it needs only one to prevent a change, while it takes all members to

---

[97] The agent/Presidency disposes also of several informal institutional rules that offer leverage in the negotiation process over the change of institutional rules (Mateo Gonzalez 2006). One important institutional rule the Presidency applies in order to forge a compromise in the negotiation among member states is the so-called 'confessionals'. They are employed in order to overcome a deadlock in negotiations. In these bilateral discussions the Presidency is given a privileged insight into the negotiation position of a member state and its possible room for manoeuvre. It also has an opportunity to put pressure on a member state. The Presidency has committed itself not to reveal this information publicly, but only to use it in order to gain an overview of the possible latitude for a compromise (Tallberg 2006: 115, 153; Haynes-Renshaw and Wallace 2006; Mateo Gonzalez 2004). The 'tour de capitales' serves the same purpose (Hayes-Renshaw and Wallace 2006).

bring a change about. Under unanimity rule, the Presidency can only push its own goals if its own position is close to that of the government least willing to change the status quo. However, even under unanimity, is it possible to change the status quo if opponents are offered compensations (Kaldor 1939; Tallberg 2006: 119). This presupposes a widening of the scope of issues on the agenda allowing to 'buy off' resistance in one area by offering compensation in another area (Davis 2004). Under QMV the Presidency's strategic possibilities increase. Extreme positions may be overruled more easily. 'Even if actual voting rarely occurs, negotiations take place in the "shadow of the vote" ' (Tallberg 2006: 119).[98]

Most importantly, the risk of agency loss through delegation to the Presidency is attenuated in the eyes of member states by the fact that it is a delegation limited in time. This is the key answer to the question why member states were willing to delegate authority to the Presidency in the first place, and even more so to strengthen this power of the agent/Presidency over time. Since the Presidency is rotating, the delegation is temporary and each member state has its turn to be the agent. The rotation principle is the reason why the granting of more power to the Presidency is not considered as a *redistributive* problem of a permanent power shift from member states to the Presidency, but as a *coordination* problem from the solution of which all member states benefit. This reflects the inverse claim from:

H: *Problem type and integrative vs. defensive bargaining*
'If redistributive issues are at stake, the process of institutional change will be characterized by defensive bargaining. The outcome will reflect the asymmetry of power of the involved actors.'
'If coordination issues are at stake, the process of institutional change will be characterized by consensus.'

As we have seen, the new exigencies with which the EEC was confronted, constituted an important reason why the Presidency's powers were increased and why the European Council was introduced. A crucial function of the European Council is to coordinate diverse policy preferences[99] and solve conflicts in case that member states cannot agree in sectorial Councils. This reflects two

[98] As Tallberg describes, the process based on information from Council officials: 'You note that there is a qualified majority in favour of the Presidency proposal, you invite the remaining states to join in and you propose minor modifications in order to increase acceptance, and then you make it clear that it is time to take a decision. Usually, the minority then accepts the proposal without a vote' (Interview with Council official, quoted in Tallberg 2006: 119).

[99] As a broker, the Presidency relies on the General Secretariat which keeps detailed records of the member state preferences and their negotiation positions. 'No actor is so familiar with the complex decision-making procedure of the EU and the formal instruments available to the Presidency as the Council Secretariat. Tactical advice on negotiation procedure is part and parcel

theoretical *institutionalist bargaining arguments*: What is not solved in one arena is transferred to another arena. What differs across the two arenas is the institutional rule defining the scope of the agenda. This change of *institutional rule governing the negotiation process*, as Davis (2004) has shown, makes a difference with respect to outcomes. The wider scope of the agenda makes it easier to thrash out a compromise because there are more issues that can be accommodated in package deals and issue-linkages and included in compensation payments (Tallberg 2006: 59). This corresponds to the claim:

H: *Distributive, power-based bargaining of institutional change mediated by institutions*
'The institutional rules governing the bargaining process make a difference with respect to the outcome, i.e. the changed institutional rule.'
'A wider scope of decision-making issues and simultaneous voting on all issues will lead to more redistributive outcomes of the negotiation process than voting on single issues sequentially.'

The Presidency in the Council can come up with a 'Presidency compromise', that is 'stitch together unorthodox deals that stretch across a number of issue areas' (Tallberg 2006: 117) and propose a compromise, reflecting the role of the Presidency as a broker of compromises. The creation of the European Council as an additional decision-making arena shows that a shift of decision-making across arenas can lend a new dynamic to a decision-making process allowing to form new alliances and to overcome sectorial veto-positions (Davis 2004).

H: *Shifting levels/arenas to accelerate institutional change*
'Given a choice between different levels/arenas of decision-making an actor may, by opting out of one arena and shifting the decision to another, improve his prospects of obtaining an institutional change according to his preferences.'

In its function as a broker in Council negotiations, the informal institutional rules provide that the Presidency can define the speed and format of negotiations (Sherrington 2000), for example whether it should be a full session or a restricted session (Tallberg 2005: 154; Hayes-Renshaw and Wallace 2006: 149).[100] It is untypical that the Presidency calls a vote; rather it assesses whether a maximum consensus has been obtained and no actor objects to the proposed compromise (Westlake 1999: 43; Tallberg 2006: 119).[101] In its

---

of the Secretariat's support function as is legal advice on possible courses of action' (Tallberg 2006: 114, 152).

[100] The Council Rules of Procedure allow the Presidency to determine the number of delegates in the meeting room, the duration of discussions and even individual interventions (Hayes-Renshaw and Wallace 2006: 149).

[101] It is important that a Presidency does not prematurely propose a compromise. All positions have to be carefully listened to in the course of tours de table. A prematurely proposed

function as a broker of compromises the power to decide whether there is consensus among member states or whether an issue should be voted on, wields considerable power on policy outcomes.

4.3.3. From Establishing the European Council to the Single European Act

The Three Wise Men Report (1979) once more underlined the need of certain fixed responsibilities of the Council Presidency (Westlake 1999: 40; Tallberg 2006: 60, 64). The ever expanding tasks of the Community and another round of enlargement (the accession of Spain and Portugal in 1985) continued to strengthen the Presidency. The informal rules which had been developed to reduce the fragmentation of Council work were formally adopted (Tallberg 2006: 64) and the functions of the European Council were strengthened. The London Declaration explicitly granted the Presidency a role in the advance preparation of the agenda, and the writing of a record of conclusions. The European Council was also designated as the bargaining arena for the final negotiations on treaty revisions. Under the London Report (1981) the agenda-management tasks of the Presidency remained the same, but an EPC secretariat was created to support the Presidency in its work. It also empowered the latter to issue collective declarations and conveyed on it the right to meet with third parties. Only under the SEA was the European Council incorporated into the treaties. It also formalized EPC as an area of European policymaking, thereby the role of the Presidency and the institutional rules governing the Presidency's role in EPC. To ensure continuity in the policy positions taken across Presidencies in all policy areas, member states created the institutional rule providing for the cooperation of three successive presidencies ('troika') (Nuttall 1992: 179; Westlake 1999: 41) which was included in the Stuttgart Solemn Declaration (1983) (Tallberg 2006: 68, 91–4).

Continuity in policymaking was enhanced by introducing a three-year strategic programme drawn up by the six presidencies following each other in consultation with the Commission.[102] Each incoming presidency is to draw up a work programme with specified targets (Hayes-Renshaw and Wallace 2006: 148) that is to be discussed with the Commission, presented to the Parliament

---

compromise could thwart the prospects of gaining concessions from the negotiating partners in a compromise viable for all (McDonagh 1998).

[102] And submitted to the General Affairs and External Affairs Council for adoption by the European Council.

and evaluated at the end of the Presidency (Hayes-Renshaw and Wallace 2006: 148).

These attempts at an improved coordination were all the more urgent since this period was dominated by budgetary conflicts among member states[103] which made it difficult for the Presidency to exert effective leadership (Middlemas 1995: 105).

Increasingly an interorganizational interaction of a new type created additional demands on the Presidency: the interactions with the Parliament. In the budget procedure of 1982 a so-called budget trialogue had been introduced to facilitate conciliation which often had proven to be difficult.[104] Moreover, as mentioned above, in 1983 the Presidency was obligated to formally render accountability of its work programme to the Parliament by presenting the programme before and after its term (Westlake 1999: 42; Tallberg 2006: 48, 65).

Theoretical Conclusions: From Establishing the European Council to the Single European Act

From a theoretical viewpoint, the changes in the institutional rules governing the role of the Presidency in this period point to the importance of increasing demands on the Council workload. External exigencies created a pressure to strengthen the role of the Presidency and to contain the fragmentation in the Council work, lending plausibility to a functionalist claim.

H: Functionalist institutionalist transaction cost–based hypothesis
'If due to an external event the benefits of rule A have decreased, the rule will be changed, if the gains of the altered rule B including the transaction costs will be higher.'

Moreover, we observe a formalization of informal institutional rules that had been developed for the same practical purposes of managing the increased workload of the Council and to reduce the ensuing fragmentation of the Council work by strengthening the position of the Presidency. These rules served to reduce transaction costs by shifting power to the Presidency, or in principal–agent theoretical language, delegating more tasks to the agent. Although competences were shifted from member states to the Presidency, this was not considered to be redistributive because of the rotation principle. Due to the latter, member states did not object to some formalization of this shift, either.

---

[103] i.e. the British budgetary question.

[104] In which the chairman of the Parliament's budget committee, the Presidency representing the Budget Council and the responsible Commissioner were represented (Hayes-Renshaw and Wallace 2006: 43).

Additionally, the deepening of interorganizational cooperation contributed to the further strengthening of the Presidency. The requests of another organizational actor, the Parliament, to be informed about the work programme of the Presidency, had an impact on the institutional rules applied by the Presidency. The reasons which induced the Council to oblige with these requests of the Parliament, may be due to the fact that, with the direct elections of 1979, the Parliament had gained additional legitimacy. It speedily issued an entire battery of institutional reform proposals meant to strengthen its power vis-à-vis the other bodies. This suggests that *the force of normative democratic legitimation and democratic responsibility argument* may have some plausibility in explaining why Council acquiesced to present the Presidency's work programme to Parliament. However, through its role in the budgetary process the Parliament also had a practical lever to exert some pressure.

4.3.4. From the Single European Act to the Maastricht Treaty

The implementation of the SEA under the Delors Commission was followed by numerous proposals for a new finance package, steps towards an Economic and Monetary Union, and the creation of a European Economic Area (Westlake 1999). The planned completion of the internal market programme brought a new heavy workload for the Council; moreover the SEA had extended European cooperation into new policy areas, such as environmental policy and regional policy. Additionally, the change from EPC to a Common Foreign and Security Policy (CFSP) added to the tasks of the Council (Hayes-Renshaw and Wallace 2006: 146). Exogenous events reinforced this development: the Council was confronted with major political changes, that is German reunification, the collapse of the Soviet Regime and the ensuing opening up to Eastern enlargement. These new tasks led to a further call for a strengthened leadership in the Council and a deepening of the cooperation between the Presidency and the Council Secretariat.[105] Throughout the 1980s and 1990s the Presidency maintained its central role in the management of EPC and then foreign policy cooperation. The Maastricht Treaty, finally, established formal procedures for the CFSP (Tallberg 2006: 52).

More specifically, governments reacted to the increasing pressure on the Council machinery by giving the Presidency additional authority, such as to prioritize among competing policy concerns, by conferring on the Presidency the right to introduce the Presidency programme which assigns priority to particular issues on the political agenda (Tallberg 2006: 10, 17). Additionally,

---

[105] The Commission, too, played a central role in reacting to these events.

the existing rules meant to secure a continuity of policymaking and agenda setting across presidencies were strengthened. They provide for a regular preparation of policies in pre-negotiations between the concerned member states and a defining of the central agenda issues. Each European Council formulates an agenda for the next European Council. This reduces the individual Presidency's capacity to set the agenda (Tallberg 2006: 56, 75–6).[106]

With the increasing tasks and enlargement, the Presidency's reliance on the Council Secretariat increased. Since—with more members—the intervals between presidencies grew longer, making 'it harder for individual governments to accumulate on-the-job experience' (Hayes-Renshaw and Wallace 2006: 141), the continuous experience of the Secretariat became more and more important. The rotation rule was modified in that new members were 'slotted in among pre-existing members' (Hayes-Renshaw and Wallace 2006: 139). The TEU (1992) formalized the troika under which the preceding, incumbent, and successor presidencies share the responsibilities of representing the Union and common actions.

Theoretical Conclusions: From the Single European Act to the Maastricht Treaty

From a *theoretical perspective* institutional change in the role of the Presidency in this period was mainly driven by the pressure of exogenous events, that is the consequences of the end of the cold war and enlargement, giving rise to new tasks in CFSP and the external representation of the Community (Westlake 1999: 43). These demands led to an initial *informal change* of the institutional rules, and subsequently to a formalization of some of the rules under the Amsterdam Treaty, reflecting a *gradual process of institutional adaptation to functional pressure* (Tallberg 2006: 43). The functionalist explanation does account for an important part of the institutional change occurring in this period.

H: Functionalist institutionalist transaction cost-based hypothesis
'If due to an external event the benefits of rule A have decreased, the rule will be changed, if the gains of the altered rule B including the transaction costs will be higher.'

The more pronounced delegation of tasks to the Presidency and simultaneous introduction of institutional rules reining in the Presidency (such as the

---

[106] The rotation principle also has the effect of creating competition among member states to outdo each other. The increased political saliency of Union policies and in particular the European Council '... confronted each incoming presidency with increased domestic expectations and also tempted it to make more of a public spectacle during its presidency' (Hayes-Renshaw and Wallace 2006: 137).

establishing of the troika-rule and the obligation to report to the Parliament) may also be interpreted in terms of *principal–agent theory*.

H: Agency-loss as a cause of institutional change
'If the divergence between the principal's and the agent's preferences has become too large, the principal will redesign the contract, i.e. change the institutional rule in order to rein in the agent.'

Again, we also encounter a factor of *interorganizational dynamics* that deepened the importance of the Presidency (Westlake 1999: 44). The negotiations with the Parliament grew increasingly important and strengthened the position of the Presidency. The only actor in sight to conduct these negotiations was the Presidency in office. The more intense interorganizational interaction, that is joint decision-making, therefore had an impact on the internal structure of the Council and contributed to the change of rules governing the processes within the organization (Farrell and Héritier 2004).

4.3.5. From the Maastricht Treaty to the Amsterdam Treaty

The Maastricht Treaty (1992) had confirmed the position of the Presidency in the CFSP and its mandate for external negotiations, subject to the unanimous support of the Council for the negotiated agreements (Tallberg 2006: 68). The Amsterdam Treaty empowered the Secretary General of the Council Secretariat to act as High Representative for CFSP. Accordingly, the troika was reshaped to include the Presidency in office, the new High Representative of CFSP, and the Commissioner in charge of external policy (Westlake 1999; Tallberg 2006: 53, 68). As in the previous periods, the continuously widening Community tasks and the danger of fragmentation spurred the need for the Presidency to function as an integrating element between the different bargaining arenas'.

Additionally, the importance of the Presidency was augmented by intensified interaction with the Parliament under the co-decision procedure which had been introduced in the Maastricht Treaty. As discussed in Section 4.2 on the role of the Parliament in the legislative process, the development of trialogues and early agreements under the co-decision procedure tended to reinforce the role of the Presidency (Farrell and Héritier 2003). The Presidency's power of initiative 'is now strengthened thanks to the increasing possibility of reaching agreement at first reading' (Council Report on Co-decision 2000: 15). It can select the issues on the agenda that should be subject to fast-track legislation instead of the two readings process, even enter into negotiations with the Parliament before the Council has come to common position. Early agreements at first reading open new possibilities for the Presidency to shape the legislative agenda during its six months in office. It can influence the progress of a dossier much more easily and seek to accelerate proposals that it would like to see enacted during its presidency (Farrell and Héritier 2003, 2004; Interv. Commission, Sep. 2001; Shackleton and Raunio 2003).

In negotiating with the Parliament, the Presidency has some latitude when reporting back to member states which it can use for its own purposes (Farrell and Héritier 2003: 9). 'During trialogues, the Presidency is the single voice of the Council...' (Council Report on Co-decision 2000: 15). In order to reach an agreement with the Parliament things are kept provisional much longer: '...if you negotiate with the Parliament you should not go too early with a position to the Council of Ministers. Because ministers say: "We cannot agree to this, we cannot agree to that". So everything is done early on between COREPER and the Parliament' (Interv. Perm. Repr. C, Jan. 2001 in Farrell and Héritier 2004: 1203). Even if the Presidency has a negotiating mandate from the Council, it has considerable leeway in bargaining. It usually uses this latitude in such a way as not to damage national interests (Tallberg 2006: 3). When trialogue negotiations are successful, the Parliament and Council do little more than sign off on a deal that has already been negotiated among a small group of actors, the Council presidency being a crucial one (Farrell and Héritier 2003: 24).

With another external demand in mind, that is the perspective of Northern enlargement, the system of rotation was redebated in the mid-1990s. One proposal was to introduce a Presidency shared among several member states which would serve together for a longer period of time and divide the different sectors of Council work between themselves. However, the Reflection Group, preparing the 1996–7 IGC, did not pursue the proposal. Rather, the act of accession of 1995 established with Austria, Finland, and Sweden revised the balanced rotation system providing that the troika would always include at least one larger member state and group a neutral member state with non-neutral member states (Hayes-Renshaw and Wallace 2006: 139). In view of the impending enlargement by ten or twelve new member states, after a renewed debate on institutional reform, the Solana Report (2002) proposed a rotation between five to six groups of states as an alternative to the present system (Tallberg 2006: 79), but again without any practical consequences.

Theoretical Conclusions: From the Maastricht Treaty to the Amsterdam Treaty

Interpreting this period in *theoretical terms*, it emerges that the further development of the institutional rule governing the Presidency continues to be driven by the functional needs of enlargement, and new policy tasks, that is an increased importance of CFSP. A *functionalist institutional redesign* explanation seems therefore plausible.

H: Functionalist institutionalist transaction cost–based hypothesis
'If due to an external event the benefits of rule A have decreased, the rule will be changed, if the gains of the altered rule B including the transaction costs will be higher.'

As in the previous periods, with widening Community tasks, the importance of the Presidency as a mediator between the different bargaining arenas (Tallberg 2006: 58) increased even further. The broader policy agenda offered opportunities for cross-cutting issue packages proposed by the Presidency in the European Council. As bargaining theory posits, with a wider defined scope of the agenda, obstacles within one policy sector or issue area may be overcome more easily (see Davis 2004).

As in the previous period, the more extensive delegation of tasks to the Presidency and simultaneous institutional controls on the Presidency may also be interpreted in terms of *principal–agent theory.*

H: Agency-loss as a cause of institutional change
'If the divergence between the principal's and the agent's preferences has become too large, the principal will redesign the contract, i.e. change the institutional rule in order to rein in the agent.'

Moreover, as previously, but more pronouncedly so, the increased *interorganizational interaction* in joint decision-making underlined the need of cooperation with the Parliament, and, as a consequence, led to a gain of importance of the Presidency within the Council. This development was reinforced by the use of early agreements (see Chapter 4.2) (Farrell and Héritier 2003). The Presidency's power of initiative 'is now strengthened thanks to the increasing possibility of reaching agreement at first reading' (Council Report on Co-decision 2000: 15) thereby offering new possibilities to adopt its legislative agenda during its six months in office. The organization theoretical argument would run as follows: the increased interaction with another organization created new demands within an organization to effectively deal with interorganizational cooperation. The likely actor to whom this task would fall was the Presidency. Therefore, the internal institutional rules of the Council needed to change to adjust to this strengthening of the Presidency giving it more leeway in the negotiations with the other organization.

Why would an intergovernmental organization, such as the Council, accept the institutional rules clearly privileging the Council Presidency? As pointed out, the answer is, that the latter is clearly limited in time. The Presidency is granted this privileged position because the system of rotation renders the distributional implications acceptable for member states. The alternation of the Presidency avoids the concentration of chairmanship power in one member state or supranational institution, by granting each government, in turn, a privileged opportunity to shape EU policymaking. Governments accept the 'exploitation' of the Presidency in the present, because they will get their opportunity in the future.[107] At the same time, there is the awareness that if a member state/Presidency would go too far, there could be a possible retribution next time round. This has a disciplining effect. In general terms, one may conclude that the Presidency does not develop institutional interests identified with one actor over a longer period of time because the rotation principle prevents that such institutional interests develop.

4.3.6. From the Amsterdam Treaty to the Nice Treaty

The most important feature of institutional change between the treaty revisions of 1996 and 2001 was the strengthening of institutional rules securing continuity. Member states developed new rules on the cooperation between consecutive presidencies and extended the functions of the Council Secretariat. The Nice IGC negotiations which were supposed to deal with the institutional leftovers from Amsterdam, that is 'the institutional triangle' questions of extending QMV, the reweighting of votes, and the number of Commissioners, did not directly address the institutional rules governing the Presidency in the Council.

Theoretical Conclusion: From the Amsterdam
to the Nice Treaty

Only minor institutional changes occurred in this period seeking to further develop the continuity between the Presidencies' work. These minor changes took on the form of informal institutional rules intensifying the coordination of the activities of different Presidencies over time. Theoretically this further rule development may be interpreted as a functional reaction to an expanding number of members of the European Union and an increasing workload for the Council.

---

[107] As a Commission official expressed it '... When you are not the Presidency, you are swallowing bitter pills every day, only because you know that you will have the Presidency one day and the others will have to swallow their bitter pills. You suffer for six years and in the seventh you get to bash the others. The Presidencies are always overstepping the limits of neutral behaviour' (Interview Commission official, Feb. 9, 2001, quoted in Tallberg 2006: 11).

H: Functionalist institutionalist transaction cost–based hypothesis
'If due to an external event the benefits of rule A have decreased, the rule will be changed, if the gains of the altered rule B including the transaction costs will be higher.'

4.3.7. From the Nice Treaty to the Constitutional Treaty

After the Nice Treaty further changes of the institutional rules governing the Presidency were, once more, developed at an informal level. In 2002 a multi-annual strategic programme was introduced which was based on the rules of a deepened cooperation of consecutive presidencies (Tallberg 2006: 50, 69; Hayes-Renshaw and Wallace 2006). The rules governing the Presidency were not an issue that was discussed and decided on at the Convention.

Under the Convention a Franco-German proposal calling for a long-term Union President chairing the European Council and the creation of a foreign minister sitting both in the Council and in the Commission, was rejected by the smaller states. Sixteen smaller states proposed to maintain the rotating Presidency (Beach 2005: 182). The final draft submitted by the presidium to the plenary did not contain the rotating presidency (Beach 2005: 186). At the end of the day, the Convention did not decide on a solution of the delicate institutional questions.

During the IGC negotiations, by contrast, the institutional issues were at centre stage, among them was the proposal to maintain the rotating Presidency (Agence Europe 9.9.03). The outcome of the process was that the six-months rotation of the Presidency should be preserved within the form of a team Presidency of three governments. The institutional change provided for in the Constitutional Treaty, however, did not enter into force because of the rejection of the latter in the French and Dutch referenda.

Conclusion

The most typical feature of institutional change emerging from the description of the rules governing the Presidency of the Council over time, is a step-by-step adjustment to external functional demands. Member states transformed the institutional rules such as to make decision-making in the Council more efficient by giving the Presidency more prerogatives. The changes can theoretically be explained as responding functionally to exogenous problem pressure, that is enlargement and salient political events. The triggers of institutional change were exogenous. At the same time, an increasing delegation of tasks to the Presidency may also be accounted for in terms of *principal–agent theory*, with the principals/governments, temporarily delegating a task to the agent/presidency while simultaneously exerting some control over the agent.

Another striking feature is that most of these institutional changes of the rules concerning the Presidency, in a first instance, did not occur as formal treaty revisions but as informal and incremental changes. Although some of them, such as the agenda-setting function of the Presidency, and the co-ordination function of the European Council, were subsequently formalized, this does not hold for all of them. Some stayed at the level of informal daily application, and have been carried to the *higher-order institutional level* of treaty change.

What is perhaps most striking in the development of the rules governing the Council Presidency is that member states consider these rules to be efficiency-oriented *despite* a redistribution of power in favour of the Presidency. The reason is that the rotation principle limits this shift of power in time and each member state will enjoy it in its turn. This fundamentally important institutional rule distributing the power of the Presidency equally among member states, large or small, takes the redistributive sting out of the decision-making processes, because each state knows that it would, in turn, be able to exercise this power. As a result, the adjustment of the institutional rules to new challenges could be easily achieved.

With respect to the types of actors involved in the changing of the insti-tutional rules, it is obvious that the *designing actors are also the implementing actors*, engaged in incrementally devising the changes and immediately imple-menting them as well. The formalization that occurred in some instance again occurred relatively smoothly. No threshold between designing and application had to be overcome The threshold between the level of daily application of institutional rules and their formalization at the level of macro-institutional rule change was easily achieved, the reason being again that all member states saw themselves as the winners of the new formalized rule.

One further important factor influencing institutional change that emerges from the empirical account which has not been discussed in Chapter 3 is the importance of an intensified *interorganizational interaction* and its repercus-sions on the rules within the Council. Pressure to change the institutional rules governing the Presidency not only derived from external problem pres-sure, but also from endogenous institutional causes. The increasing legislative *interaction* with other Community bodies, in this case with the Parliament in the cooperation and the co-decision procedures, had the consequence that the Presidency gained in power because it is at the centre of this interor-ganizational bargaining process. We argued that the increasing interaction with another organization in joint decision-making may strengthen the actor controlling the exchange of information with the other organization (Farrell and Héritier 2004). Again, however, individual member states allowed for this shift of power because of the rotation principle.

4.4. INSTITUTIONAL RULE THREE: THE PARLIAMENT AND THE INVESTITURE OF THE COMMISSION

Adrienne Héritier and Catherine Moury

The Parliament, virtually out of a nothing, 'created' for itself competences in the investiture of the Commission. How did it achieve this and what does this tell us about the change of institutional rules? Until the SEA the Parliament had no powers regarding the investiture of the Commission; it eventually acquired a right to be consulted on the appointment of the President of the Commission as well as the right of investing the Commission as a whole; in a further step, it gained the right of the formal approbation of the Commission President and finally it was granted the right to 'elect' the President of the Commission under the Constitutional Treaty. In analysing the emergence and change of these rules, we focus on four periods:

1. from the beginnings (1957) to the Single European Act (SEA) (1986);
2. from the Single European Act (1986) to the Maastricht Treaty (1992);
3. from the Maastricht Treaty (1992) to the Amsterdam Treaty (1997);
4. from the Amsterdam Treaty (1997) and Nice Treaty (2001) to the Constitutional Treaty (2004).

4.4.1. From 1957 to the Single European Act

The Treaty of Rome very clearly stated that the President of the Commission was to be appointed by the common agreement of the governments of the member states. The Parliament, then Assembly, initially did not have any right in the appointment of the Commission. However, the Treaty of Rome provided that the Commission be responsible to the Parliament and granted the latter the right to censure the Commission in its entirety (if not individual Commissioners) by a two-thirds majority of the votes cast, representing a majority of the members.

Calls from the Parliament to be given the right to formally invest the President of the Commission and the Commission as a whole emerged as early as 1960. Over the years, the Parliament requested this right in several reports. Thus, the Faure report of 1960 on the fusion treaty (1965) demanded the investiture of the Commission by the Parliament (Commentaire Mégret, vol. 9, Bruxelles 1979: 218). The two Furler reports (1963, 1972) were in favour of the nomination of the President and the members of the Commission by the Parliament on the basis of a list proposed by the governments (Commentaire Mégret, vol. 9, Bruxelles 1979: 218); the Vedel report of 1972 proposed that the President of the Commission should be invested by the Parliament (Bulletin CE, supplement 4/72); and the Kirk report of 1974 suggested that the governments should design the members of the Commission on the basis of a list compiled by the Parliament; the Tindemans report, finally, recommended that the President of the Commission should be nominated by the European Council and be confirmed by the Parliament and would then, in consultation with the European Council, appoint the Commissioners (Bulletin CE, supplement 1/76).

After the first direct election of the Parliament in 1979, it set up a subcommittee of its Political Affairs Committee that was given the task of dealing with institutional questions (see also Chapter 4.2). In 1980 the subcommittee, in its Rey report demanded that the Parliament be given the right to debate the Commission President's programme and vote on the candidate for Commission President proposed by the member state governments. It also claimed that the Political Affairs Committee should conduct a debate on the Commission's programme with the designed Commission President before the individual Commissioners were appointed. After the nomination of the Commission there should be a public debate terminated by a vote of confidence and investiture (JOCE, Nr. 117, 12.5.1980: 53). The report derived these claims from the Parliament's *right of censure* of the Commission's policy. An extensive interpretation of the right of censure led to the request of an institutional rule allowing the Parliament to scrutinize the Commission's programme and confirm the President of the Commission as well as the Commission. The demands of the Rey report were adopted as a resolution in the plenary of the Parliament in 1980.

The newly appointed President of the Commission, Gaston Thorn, concurred with the view that the Parliament had a right of scrutinizing the Commission's programme and confirming the Commission President. Thorn came to the plenary and participated in a debate that the Parliament described as 'confirmation hearings' (Westlake 1994). Ever since, the nominated President of the Commission has regularly presented his programme in a parliamentary debate. A *de facto rule* was created according to which the Commission is subject to a vote of consultation of the Parliament.

The 'Genscher–Colombo[108] initiative' in 1981 seeking to relaunch the development of the European Community, among other things, proposed to grant the Parliament a formal right of investiture of the Commission. Both Germany and Italy traditionally favoured a strong Parliament. More specifically, the initiative proposed that the *President of the Parliament* should be consulted regarding the nomination of the President of the Commission. The foreign

---

[108] The then foreign ministers of Italy and Germany.

ministers' in their meetings, however, could not agree on such a provision. Only two years later in the 'Solemn Declaration on European Union' (Bulletin of the European Communities, No. 6/1983) at Stuttgart, they agreed that, before nominating a President of the Commission, the Council Presidency should seek the opinion of the *enlarged bureau* of the Parliament. Moreover, after the nomination of the Commissioners by governments the Commission should present its programme to the Parliament to be debated and voted on. Hence, with the Stuttgart Declaration, the Parliament was granted the power of being consulted in the nomination of the President of the Commission. This procedure was applied for the first time to appoint Delors in 1984: the President of the Council met the enlarged bureau of the Parliament to discuss the proposal before Delors was nominated. And the Commissioners of the Delors I Commission delayed their oath-taking ceremony at the Court of Justice until they had obtained the Parliament's confirmation. Thus, thanks to the Commission, there was a move from the Stuttgart Declaration to something approaching a parliamentary vote of confidence as a condition for the Commission taking office.

In 1983 the Parliament had presented a draft Treaty on the European Union suggesting that the term of office of the Commission coincide with the mandate of the Parliament. It also proposed that the appointment of the President of the Commission by the European Council would follow each parliamentary election. The President would constitute a team of Commissioners, submit a programme and a parliamentary vote of confidence would allow it to take office (Corbett 1998). These ambitious objectives were supported by a declaration of Italy in the run-up to the IGC of 1984; it stated that Italy would only ratify a new treaty if it were accepted by the Parliament (Corbett 1998: 223). This declaration offered a useful lever for the Parliament to exert pressure on the content of the negotiations for one member state's veto could question the success of an agreement of treaty revisions.

The Dooge report[109] presented to the European Council in Milan in 1985, too, proposed that the Commission, on the basis of its programme, be subject to the investiture of the Parliament. The Dooge report's proposal was supported by an initiative of the Dutch government which went even further and called for a parliamentarian right of consultation on the designation of the Commission President. However, this proposal was not accepted as part of the negotiations of the SEA. The President of the Commission came out in favour of a procedure under which the Parliament holds an investiture debate and a vote (Corbett 1998: 241). Yet, the foreign ministers' meeting in Luxembourg

---

[109] Consisting of the representatives of the heads of governments under the chair of Dooge, Majority Leader in the Irish Senate (Corbett 1998: 180).

in 1985 settled more modestly on a package of reforms providing for a right of consultation of the enlarged secretariat of the Parliament, sticking merely to the Stuttgart Declaration of 1983. Italy restated that its approval of the IGC outcome would hinge on the support of the Parliament. The latter declared that the results were unsatisfactory (Corbett 1998: 252). However, the foreign ministers negotiating the details of the reform a few months later, ignored the warnings of the Parliament and finalized the texts. Despite its previous threats the Italian Parliament eventually ratified the SEA because the Parliament, although dissatisfied with the outcome of the SEA, did not encourage national parliaments not to ratify the SEA (Corbett 1998: 249).

Thus, the SEA did *not* turn the informal rule allowing the Parliament to hold a hearing that had been agreed on between the Parliament and the Commission into a formal right of confirmation in spite of the threat of non-ratification of one member state.

Theoretical Conclusions: From the Beginnings to the SEA

Viewing this first period from the beginnings until the SEA through *theoretical lenses*, it emerges that a first institutional change occurred when the Parliament introduced an *informal rule* which the Commission went along with, that is that the candidate for Commission President appears for a hearing in the Parliament. This new informal rule had only a rather loose foundation in the treaties which very clearly provide that the appointment of the Commission President rests uniquely with member states. But, by referring to its right of censure of the Commission, the Parliament legitimized the introduction of the informal rule providing that the Parliament may scrutinize the Commission's programme and confirm the President of the Commission as well as the entire Commission. Once the Commission obliged with the rule, it gained practical importance. Why did the Commission acquiesce to play along? The Parliament could exert some pressure by threatening to delay the process by withholding its opinion.[110] Thus, thanks to the Commission, there was a move from the Stuttgart Declaration to something approaching a parliamentary vote of confidence as a condition for it taking office. This development corresponds to the hypothesis that:

H: Institutional change through a formal/informal/formal dynamic
'Formal rules at t1 that are ambiguous give rise to informal rules that further develop the formal rules. These informal rules will reflect the bargaining power of actors, as

---

[110] Also the two Commission Presidency candidates in question (Thorn and Delors) both had previously been MEPs.

determined by formal institutions and the fallback position of the negotiating actors reflected in different time horizons and a different sensitivity to failure.'

However, this claim needs qualification in the light of this empirical story. The institutional rule in question is *not* ambiguous in the strict sense of the word, rather it just does not exclude the possibility that the Parliament may hold hearings on the candidature of the Commission Presidency. In that sense every institutional rule is 'ambiguous', because it may invite the development of informal institutional rules complementing, modifying, or indeed undermining the formal rule unless it explicitly excludes them. The latter, obviously, is impossible. As Caporaso argues, a complete contract or unambiguous institutional rule would have to be '... impossibly long, it would have to imagine every possible contingency, and in doing so it would have to duplicate all the real life events to which the rule is supposed to apply. Rules and complete contracts are contradictory notions, since the function of rules is to provide short cuts and summary guidance' (Caporaso forthcoming).

The informal rule, agreed between the Parliament and the Commission, however, was not transformed into a formal rule. The designing actors, that is the member states, entered the decisions-making process over the SEA and rejected the proposal. This development reflects the hypothesis concerning the:

H: Formalization of informal institutional rules
'The outcome of the formal negotiations at t2 will reflect informal institutions bargained if all designing actors agree to accept the informal change.'

4.4.2. From the Single European Act to the Maastricht Treaty

Disappointed with the outcome of the SEA, the Parliament had announced that it would exploit its provisions to the fullest (Haensch quoted in Corbett 1998: 249). It passed three consecutive resolutions (1986, 1987, and 1990) to underline its demands insisting that the Parliament should be consulted well in advance regarding the nomination of the Commission President and the Commissioners and that, furthermore, this consultation should be followed by a parliamentarian vote (JOCE, n. C 283, 10.11.1986: 36). Going beyond these requests one year later, it asked for a vote of investiture and a vote of confidence in the renewal of the mandate of the President of the Commission linked to the presentation of the annual Commission programme (JOCE, n. C 76, 23.3.1987: 137). Another resolution in 1990 called for the Parliament's right to '*elect*' by an absolute majority the candidate for Commission President proposed by the Council and to vote on the entire Commission (Resolution

Martin, doc. PE 144/2177 def. 31.10.1990). This should occur in a two-stage procedure: first, it would elect the President on a proposal of the European Council; and second, it would hold a debate and a vote of confidence on the Commission as a whole before the latter could take office.

By constantly repeating its institutional demands, the Parliament succeeded in putting the item on the agenda of the IGC of 1990–1 (Corbett 1998). In the run-up to the IGC, the Parliament organized a consultation between the parliamentarian political groups and their national counterparts, and held a conference with the national parliaments, 'the Assizes' (see Section 4.2). The Assizes, with an overwhelming majority of its members, endorsed the Parliament's demand of electing the presidential candidate proposed by the Council and supported a parliamentarian scrutiny of the Commission as a whole and its programme to be followed by a vote of confidence. Moreover, it requested that the Commission's term of office should be adjusted to the length of mandate of MEPs (i.e. five years) (Rome Declaration §18). To build further support, representatives of the Parliament visited all national governments and parliaments to explain the Parliament's position. Finally, as described in Section 4.2, at the Parliament's request four 'inter-institutional conferences' were organized in order to discuss issues to be dealt with during the IGC. It may well be that all these activities of the Parliament contributed to the willingness of several national parliaments (those of Germany, Italy, and Belgium) to link their ratification of the revised treaty to a positive vote of the Parliament.

During the negotiations of the treaty revisions the Parliament continued to press for a parliamentarian right of election of the Commission President. Support came forth from the German government which tabled a similar proposal. The Commission submitted a proposal to the same effect which was endorsed by Germany, Belgium, Italy, and Spain. However, other member states (the UK, Ireland, Portugal, Denmark, and the Netherlands) were strictly opposed (Corbett 1993: 58–9). Towards the end of 1990 three options were on the table: (*a*) the Parliament approves the candidate for Commission Presidency nominated by the member states; and it approves the Commissioners nominated by member states as a body; (*b*) the President of the European Council consults the President of the Parliament regarding the candidate for Commission Presidency and the candidates for Commissioners. The entire Commission is then presented to the Parliament which shall proceed to a vote. The entire Commission is then formally appointed by member states; (*c*) The President of the Commission is elected by the Parliament. The other members of the Commission are appointed by the member states and confirmed by the Parliament (Internal note, Commission 9.10.1990; Conference of permanent representatives 16.1.1991). While Germany, Italy, France, Belgium, and Spain supported the more far-reaching second and third options, the Netherlands and Ireland favoured the more limited first option and Denmark, Portugal, and the UK opted for the institutional status quo. One member state insisted on a 'simple consultation' by the Parliament (Internal note of the Commission, January 1991). In view of these diverging member state preferences, it is not surprising that the IGC settled for a relatively modest solution, that is a consultation right of the Parliament regarding the Commission President and a right of approvement for the members of the Commission (Internal note 25.1.1991). In a further round of discussion of the permanent representatives, Germany made another attempt to achieve a decision which was more favourable for the Parliament and presented a proposal providing for the Parliament electing the Commission President. It was supported by Belgium and Italy. The latter also asked for a five-year mandate of the Commission and the obligation to submit the Commission's programme to a parliamentarian vote. Strong opposition was voiced by Denmark and Portugal[111] and the UK which wanted to stick with the Stuttgart Declaration (Internal note Commission 31.1.1991).

In early 1991 the Presidency noted a majority that was in favour of giving the Parliament a consultation right on the nominated candidate for Commission President and a vote of approval for the Commission members. It also noted that there was no majority supporting the proposal that the Commission should submit a programme on the basis of which it would be invested by the Parliament; nor was there support for the extension of the length of the mandate of the Commission. A number of member states (Belgium, Italy, Germany, and France) supported a two-stage procedure or double investiture (first a nomination by member states, then an election right of the Parliament). Other member states, by contrast, only wished to incorporate the procedure of the Stuttgart Declaration in the Treaty (Internal note Commission 11.3.1991, 27.6.1991). The final text provided that member states will nominate the members of the Commission in consultation with the nominated President of the Commission for five years and that the Commission in its entirety will be submitted to a vote of approval by the Parliament; the Parliament will also be consulted in the nomination of the Commission President (DOC. SN 1919/91, 15.4.1991). In the eyes of the Parliament not much institutional ground had been gained under the revised Treaty. 'Even member states not enthusiastic about increasing Parliament's powers were prepared to accept this change, which could be presented as being little more than entrenching existing practice' (Corbett 1993: 58–9). The informal institutional rule according to which the Commission can only take

---

[111] Which however was in favour of the Parliament having to support the Commission programme.

office following a vote of confidence of Parliament was formalized. However, the Parliament's request that the Commission should present its programme was not integrated in the treaties.

As a consequence, the Parliament immediately set out to interpret the right of consultation as extensively as possible. In summer 1992 (before the entry into force of the Maastricht Treaty), it adopted a resolution regarding the nomination of the Commission President under the Maastricht Treaty (still called the Stuttgart procedure) in which it is stated that the consultation of the enlarged Bureau of the Parliament confers a power of nomination onto the Parliament. It also called for an extensive interpretation of Art. 29 of the Maastricht Treaty such that the plenary would give its view on the nomination after a public hearing.[112] This resolution was supported by most political groups (Internal note Commission 19.6.1992).

Theoretical Conclusions: From the SEA to the Maastricht Treaty

Which are the main factors driving institutional change between the SEA and the Maastricht Treaty and how can the process *theoretically* be accounted for? The Parliament in three resolutions, first, initiated a comprehensive campaign of institutional self-promotion to underline its demands for an extension of its rights. In so doing it did take influence on the definition of the agenda of the upcoming IGC. In a second step, it organized a lobbying campaign with potential allies in national parliaments which would have to confirm the treaty changes. As a result, some member states and their parliaments threatened not to accept treaty revisions if not supported by the Parliament. This attempt of taking indirect influence through mobilizing veto-actors in a linked arena reflects hypothesis:

H: *Bargaining leverage through arena-linking*
'Actor A, using a formal veto in one arena X, can create a leverage in another linked arena Y, in which actor A has no formal vote.'

To be true, in this case the veto in the linked arena could not be used by the Parliament itself since it does not play role in formal treaty ratification. However, it sought to induce 'allies', that is the national parliaments, to threaten to veto the revised treaty if the Parliament's institutional interests were not taken into account.

In the final negotiations of institutional change in the IGC, the diverse preferences of member states led to a compromise between member states favouring an extension of the Parliament's rights and those preferring the

---

[112] Spearheaded by M. Cot, President of the socialist political group.

status quo. Germany as a particularly eager defender of parliamentarian rights had acquiesced to the proposal of the Presidency allowing only for a consultation right, but, in return, obtained an adjustment of the length of the mandates of the Parliament and the Commission. This corresponds to a classic bargaining theoretical interpretation as proposed in distributional bargaining theory:

H: Institutional change through distributive bargaining
'Given a change of preference of a powerful actor(s) or a change of power balance between actors, an existing institutional rule may be subject to renegotiation in order to alter the rule in such a way as to reflect the (changed) preferences of actor(s) or the changed power balance.'

As soon as the Treaty amendments had been adopted, the Parliament set out to endogenously change the existing formal rules by interpreting them extensively in its own favour.

4.4.3. From the Maastricht Treaty to the Amsterdam Treaty

As described above, the Maastricht Treaty brought a new procedure for appointing the Commission, whereby the member states first agree on a candidate for President, on whom they must consult the Parliament. Then the Commission as a whole is subject to a vote of confidence by the Parliament. While on the nomination of the Commission President the Parliament only had a 'soft' right of consultation, Maastricht had granted it a 'hard' right of vote of confidence on the entire Commission.

Two elements were decisive for the further institutional development, the fact that the treaty did not specify how the Parliament should be consulted. And the fact that there was a 'soft' right of consultation for the Commission President and a 'hard' right of vote of confidence for the entirety of the Commission. These two elements were exploited by the Parliament in order to extend its competences. In a first step, the ambiguity of the consultation provision was used: The Parliament amended its internal rules and interpreted the Maastricht Treaty generously in its own favour by stating that the Parliament's opinion on the nomination of the presidential candidate shall be determined in a plenary session by a majority of its members. In case that the plenary should come to a negative opinion, it would notify the Council and the governments that it would not be possible to proceed with the approval of the Commission as a whole. As a second measure, before the contentious vote on Jacques Santer as candidate for Commission Presidency, the Parliament threatened not to invest the entire Commission if its negative vote regarding the Commission President were not considered. 'The European Parliament points out that, if it delivers a negative vote on the name of the person whom the governments of the member states plan to appoint as President of the Commission, it will refuse the investiture of the Commission if the governments of the member states present the same candidate again' (European Parliament, 'Résolution sur l'investiture de la Commission 21.4.1994).[113] In other words, by linking the 'hard' rule with the 'soft' rule, the Parliament transformed the 'soft' rule into a 'hard' rule. By failing to anticipate the obvious link between the two rules the Council had tied its own hands. There is no indication that during the permanent representatives' and foreign ministers' meetings, member states were aware of such a possible linkage. On the contrary, several member states and the Commission explicitly declared that 'granting a right of consultation to the EP would not grant it a veto power on the Council's choice' (CEC internal note, June 1992). In the concrete case, the candidate for Commission President, Jacques Santer, obliged with the unilaterally stated rules of the Parliament by confirming that a negative vote in the Parliament would require the European Council to find another candidate. In the event, the Parliament approved his appointment only by 260 votes to 238. De facto, the merely 'consultative' vote as specified in the treaty had been transformed into a de facto vote of confirmation.[114]

In another resolution of May 1995, the Parliament sought to formally institutionalize this de facto institutional development by calling for a formal provision that the President of the Commission be elected by the Parliament on the basis of a list proposed by the European Council. In the Reflection group, established to prepare the revisions of the Maastricht Treaty, some member states (e.g. Greece and Austria) supported this request while others (e.g. the UK and Ireland) were opposed (Internal note Commission, Dec. 1995). The Commission itself favoured the *approval* of the designated President by the Parliament and a common accordance of the governments and the President of the Commission in nominating the Commissioners (Internal note Commission, Febr. 1996).

The Nordwijk conference of ministers in 1996 supported the proposal of a Commission Presidency with a double legitimation by member states and the Parliament to be negotiated in the end negotiations, considering it as a mere formalization of an already existing practice. 'C'est la consécration d'une

---

[113] In Journal officiel des Communautés européennes (JOCE, 09.05.1994: n. C 128, p. 358).

[114] Moreover, at the moment of choosing the Commission President in 1994, the Parliament recalled to the Council that the Stuttgart Declaration had not been abrogated, and that the Council therefore ought to consult the EP on the name it was going to present to the EP before it was to hold a vote on the candidate presented by the Council (Internal note Commission, June 1992).

pratique' (Internal note Commission, 23.5.1996). By mid-1996 there was a common view among member states that the Parliament should indeed have a right to *approve* the Commission President nominated by member states. However, the idea of an *election* of the Commission President by the Parliament on the basis of a list put forward by member states enjoyed only limited support (Internal note Commission 12.6.1996). This was confirmed during the Italian Presidency towards the end of 1996. The Irish Presidency, finally, proposed the amended Art. 158, 2, TEU 'The governments of the member states design by common accord the personality they wish to nominate as President of the Commission. This designation is approved by the European Parliament.' It is noted that the case of a direct nomination by the Parliament is not an item of negotiation (Internal note Commission 31.1.1997). By contrast, the parliamentarian members in the conference of permanent representatives[115] argued that the Parliament already had a de facto right of 'election' of the Commission President, for if the Parliament in the process of consultation would reject the candidate, the latter would have little chances to maintain himself as a candidate. '... le vote est donc, en fait, une confirmation, et le traité devrait au moins reconnaître cette réalité.' (Internal note Commission 29.1.1997). Therefore the President of the Commission should be elected by the Parliament on the basis of the names proposed by the European Council. The Commission itself opted for a designation of the Commission President by the European Council, which then should be subject to the *approval* of the Parliament. The Parliament insisted in its demands to elect the President of the Commission on the basis of a list of names put together by the European Council. It was supported by a minority of member states (Ireland, Italy, NL, and Austria). The majority of them came out in favour a right of *approval* of the Parliament. The UK, Finland, and Ireland, however, were still opposed and wished to stick to the Stuttgart procedure.

Finally, without too many struggles, the Treaty of Amsterdam came to amend Art. 214 of the EC Treaty. The President, who was previously nominated by the governments of the member states after consulting the Parliament, is now nominated by common accord of the governments of the member states, with the nomination having to be approved by the Parliament. The point in time of intervention of the Parliament was changed. Before the Amsterdam Treaty, it was consulted *before* the appointment by the Council. Now its intervention is necessary *after* such an appointment. Technically, the President is subject to two votes of approval by the Parliament, initially the approval of his or her nomination and, subsequently, the approval of the Commission as a body (President and Commission). Thus, while under the Treaty

---

[115] Elisabeth Guigou and Elmar Brok.

of Maastricht (Art. 158–61) the Parliament had a consultation right for the nomination of the candidate and a vote of approbation for the Commission, under the Amsterdam Treaty (Art. 213–14) it had an approbation right for the Commission President and a formal investiture vote of the Commission in its entirety.

Theoretical Conclusions: From the Maastricht Treaty to the Amsterdam Treaty

How can we *theoretically* interpret the institutional changes that have occurred between the Maastricht and the Amsterdam treaties? What emerges imme-diately after the adoption of the Maastricht Treaty is that the Parliament seeks to *endogenously* change the existing formal rules by interpreting them as extensively as possible in such a way as to expand its own institutional role giving rise to an *informal rule*. The Parliament interpreted consultation as a confirmation or a vote of confidence. It engaged in an implicit bargaining process with the Commission and member states in the application of the formal rule stated in the Treaty. This corresponds to the claim:

H: Institutional change through a formal/informal/formal rules dynamic
'Formal rules at t1 that are ambiguous give rise to informal rules that further develop the formal rules. These informal rules will reflect the bargaining power of actors, as determined by formal institutions and the fallback position of the negotiating actors reflected in different time horizons and a different sensitivity to failure.'

And

'The outcome of the formal negotiations at t2 will reflect informal institutions bar-gained if all designing actors agree to accept the informal change or if the implement-ing/affected actors can exert pressure through a linked arena veto.'

The Parliament derived its bargaining power from the second hard element of the provision of the Maastricht Treaty purveying on the Parliament the formal right of a vote of confidence on the Commission as a whole. By withholding this vote of confidence on the Commission or voting against the Commission in its entirety, as the Parliament threatened to do in the case of the Santer Commission inducing the latter to resign,[116] it could lend 'a bite' to its consultative role regarding the Commission President and transform

---

[116] 'Somehow the balance of power (between the EP and the Commission) changed follow-ing the resignation of Santer. . . . Forcing the Commission to resign really changed the bound-aries' Interview with G. Amato, Feb. 2004, quoted in Boucher 2006) and 'Following Santer's resignation, the Parliamentary puppet-master can tweak the string if he thinks the Commission is not being obedient and respectful enough. The Commission will always have to jerk in

the latter into a de facto rule of approbation. In short, by making under the 'hard' rule the acquiescence to the Commission as a whole dependent on the willingness of the Council and Commission to come to an agreement with the Parliament regarding the Commission President under the 'soft' rule, the Parliament turned the 'soft' rule in a de facto 'hard' rule.

This is how the Parliament successfully obtained a de facto voice in the investiture of the Commission President and a shift of power in its favour. But could it also transform this informal rule into a legal right? As we have seen, member states views were split in that respect. The right of the Parliament to approve the Commission President introduced under the Amsterdam Treaty formalized the existing informal rule created by the Parliament. As our empirical account shows, this solution emerged in the course of the IGC negotiations as an acceptable compromise between the governments asking for the election of the Commission by the Parliament, and the governments insisting on the status quo. The compromise allowed the most Parliament-friendly governments to claim that they had reduced the democratic deficit and the less integrationist ones to claim that the new formal provision did not change the status quo, *the* status quo *being the informal rule created by the Parliament.* This corresponds to the classical bargaining argument:

H: Institutional change through distributive bargaining
'Given a change of preference of a powerful actor(s) or a change of power balance between actors, an existing institutional rule may be subject to renegotiation in order to alter the rule in such a way as to reflect the (changed) preferences of actor(s) or the changed power balance.'

What is important is that the informal rule which the Parliament had successfully obtained interstitially, changed the status quo of the options negotiated during the IGC.

At the same time the Parliament could still threaten to block the confirmation of the Commission in its entirety. Therefore it seems plausible that, although the Parliament was not a designing actor in treaty revisions, it could exert some pressure through a linked arena mechanism:

H: Bargaining leverage through arena-linking
'Actor A, using a formal veto in one arena X, can create a leverage in another linked arena Y, in which actor A has no formal vote.'

the direction Parliament wants' (Interview with C. Day, Dir. General, March 2004, quoted in Boucher 2006).

4.4.4. From the Amsterdam Treaty and Nice Treaty to the Constitutional Treaty

The Amsterdam Treaty provided that the Commission as a whole should be put to a vote of confidence by the Parliament. For the implementation of the provisions the Parliament adjusted its rules of procedure and stated that the nomination for the office of the President of the Commission should take into account the outcome of the European elections. It also unilaterally changed its procedural rules regarding the approbation of the Commission President, by replacing the term 'approbation' by 'election' (Agence Europe 10.3.1999).[117]

The Nice Treaty (Art. 213–14) did not change the provisions for appointing the Commission President and the Commission as a whole. Like the Amsterdam Treaty it states that the Parliament has to approve the nominee for Commission President and formally vote on the investiture for the Commission in its entirety.[118]

In the Declaration of Laeken, the European Council established the European Convention with the task 'to pave the way for the next IGC'. It was the Parliament which first proposed such a preparatory conference or a 'constituante' to prepare treaty revisions (see Schiffauer 2004). The Convention members were split regarding a possible election of the Commission President by the Parliament and so were the MEPs in the Convention. The members of the Parti Socialiste Européen (PSE) wanted an election directly by the Parliament on the basis of candidates proposed by the European Council; while the members of the Parti Populaire Européen (PPE) supported the 'election of a candidate named by the Council' in view of the outcome of the elections to the Parliament.[119] Finally, the Parliament as a whole issued a declaration advocating the 'election of the Commission President by the EP with a majority of its members'. The Commission was in favour of its President being elected by a majority of three-fifths of the Parliament's members. As regards member states' representatives in the Committee of permanent representatives, Greece, Germany, and Luxembourg were in favour of the President of the Commission being elected by the Parliament, the UK and Spain (under Aznar) were opposed (Internal note Commission 25.9.2002).

The Presidium, in control of the Convention agenda, first presented a draft set of articles, that was accepted in its principal features but to which

---

[117] PE/Traité d'Amsterdam: les principales modifications du règlement du PE approuvés afin de l'adapter au niveau du traité.

[118] For the Council the Nice Treaty introduced QMV for the appointment of the President of the Commission and the other members of the Commission.

[119] CEC, Thème de la future Communication institutionnelle de la Commission—principales prises de positions exprimées à la Convention, 25.9.2002, http://European-convention.eu.int.

numerous amendments were tabled (Crum 2004: 7). The draft proposed that, taking into account the elections to the Parliament, the European Council, deciding by QMV, shall put forward to the Parliament its proposed candidate for the Presidency of the Commission. The Parliament by a majority of its members shall elect this candidate. If this candidate does not receive the required majority support, the European Council shall within one month put forward a new candidate, following the same procedure as before. The Presidium's first draft is almost identical to the internal rules of the Parliament except for the requirement stating that the European Council should decide on the President by QMV rather than by unanimity. This formulation was a compromise between the countries wanting a direct election by the Parliament on the basis of one or several candidates presented by the Council (Benelux, Greece, and Portugal) and the five member states favouring the status quo (Aznar's Spain, Finland, Ireland, the UK, and Sweden) (Papers presented by governments and the European Commission, http://european-convention.eu.int).

During the IGC, in the meeting of the permanent representatives, eighteen representatives expressed their views in favour of such an election while five were asking for the election to be held by a mixed electoral college (composed of MEPs and national parliaments).[120] The final text adopted by the Council of Ministers incorporated the Presidium's text without amendments, that is the provision that the Commission President should be elected by a majority of MEPs. It states that, taking into account the elections of the Parliament, the European Council proposes with a qualified majority a candidate for the Commission Presidency to the Parliament. This candidate is elected by the Parliament with a majority of its members. If the candidate does not obtain a majority, the European Council proposes a new candidate to the Parliament. The text also provides that each member state, designed under the rotation system, establishes a list of three persons, that it deems qualified to exercise the function of European Commissioner. The President of the Commission retains one person from each of the proposed lists, and thereby designates the thirteen Commissioners. Subsequently, the President of the Commission and the members of the Commission collegiate, including the minister for foreign affairs, are jointly subject to a vote of approbation of the Parliament.

[120] The Parliament's Committee for Institutional Affairs held a preparatory discussion of the election of the Commission President with invited guests and, as a result, decided in favour. A minority of participants (Philippe de Schoutheete, Yves Mény, and Peter Sutherland) argued that this would disturb the institutional balance and would lead to a politicization of the Commission and bargaining within the Parliament. De Schoutheete and Mény proposed an electoral college including MEPs and members of the legislative Council. Corbett retorted that the advantage of a direct election by the Parliament would be that citizens would see what impact their choice of MEPs had on the Commission President (Internal note Commission 19.2.2003).

The duration of the mandate of the Commission is five years (Art. 26 Constitutional Treaty).

Having acted so successfully at the *higher-order level*, however, did not mean that the Parliament reduced its efforts to obtain institutional changes *within the existing institutional rules* of the Nice Treaty. On the contrary: it turned its efforts to the next strategic goal of institutional change, the appointing of *individual* Commissioners. Spurred by the recent large enlargement round and the need to appoint additional Commissioners, it decided to hold public hearings for the new Commissioners and to take a parliamentary vote on the basis of these hearings. As Pat Cox, the then President of the Parliament, put it: 'Immediately after the parliamentary *vote* (*emphasis added*), the designated Commissioners could take the oath-of-office at the Court of Justice' (Pat Cox, President EP 10.1.2003). By contrast, the Council in its internal discussion argued that legally there is no requirement for the Parliament to be involved in the appointment of the new members of the Commission since the draft Accession Treaty provided a simplified procedure. It stated that for such a purpose 'a national of each of new member states shall be appointed to the Commission as from the date of its accession. The new members of the Commission shall be appointed by the Council, acting by qualified majority and by common accord with the President of the Commission' (Art. 32(2) in MD 190/8/02, p. 2). Nonetheless, the Council accepted to involve the Parliament after having asked the acceding states whether they consented to the Parliament being informed of their nominees.[121] Moreover, it should be made clear that the 'parliamentary vote' would only apply to the appointment of the *new* Commissioners and not to the Commission as a whole including present members (Internal note Council 15.1.2003). The Maastricht Treaty states that the nominated college of Commissioners *as a whole* be subject to a vote of approval by the Parliament before being confirmed by the member state governments. It was exactly from this provision, however, that the Parliament derived its presumed right of qualitative control over the member states' individual nominees.

As early as 1996 the Parliament had adopted an internal rule of procedure according to which the individual nominees for Commissioners had to appear before its parliamentary committees which would be evaluating their proposed policy competences. The internal rule stated that the vote of approbation of the entire Commission would be held only after the individual confirmation hearings. Moreover, the Parliament set up several criteria for Commissioners to be chosen (some of the members must be MEPs; women

[121] Under the condition that the Parliament does not express its views before 1 May 2003, the entry into force of the Accession Treaty.

should be equally represented, etc.). The Commission contested this provision (Interview Commission, Nov. 2004; Interview Council, Nov. 2004). In response, the Parliament made it clear that it would simply not schedule a vote on the new Commission until the latter had complied with this requirement (Internal note Commission, June 1994). One more time, the Council had been caught in the Parliament's trap; it had not anticipated how powerful a lever the formal vote of confidence for the entire Commission would be to extend the Parliament's soft powers with regard to the Commission President and individual Commissioners. Santer and his colleagues therefore accepted to go through the procedure which, in turn, required a prior agreement on the distribution of portfolios. Some MEPs strongly criticized the performance of some candidates, but rather than rejecting the Commission as a whole, the Parliament pressed for a reallocation of responsibilities.[122] After the Commission had complied with the wishes of the Parliament, the latter expressed its confidence in the new Commission as whole.

Thus, in another successful move to extend its competences, this time in the appointing and discharging of individual Commissioners in 1999, the Parliament used its right of collectively rejecting the incoming Prodi Commission in order to obtain from the Commission President an additional concession. Prodi informally conceded that he would consider requesting any Commissioner to resign if the Parliament expressed a lack of confidence in him or her (Nugent 2000).

In yet another successfully deployed strategy in 2004, the Parliament decided to conduct public hearings of the Commissioners to be under the Barroso Commission. In some cases, the Parliament expressed concern and—as before—threatened it would not express its vote of confidence for the entire Commission if the incoming Commission President Barroso did not replace and reshuffle some of the Commissioner-nominees. The parliamentary committee in charge narrowly voted to oppose the Italian Rocco Buttiglione as Justice Commissioner. Barroso initially resisted the pressure to reshuffle his team, but the PSE, which with 200 seats makes up the second biggest group in the Parliament, along with the Communists and the Greens, insisted that Buttiglione be not appointed. Finally Barroso backed down and asked some government leaders to withdraw their nominees and proposed new candidates. Member states finally accepted this; two Commissioners were replaced and one reshuffled. As a result the Parliament expressed its confidence.

In all three instances the Parliament had successfully bargained a new informal rule expanding its own competences, that is the rule to hold hearings of individual Commissioners in order to judge their competencies, and to

---

[122] This took place in the case of Commissioner Flynn.

reserve the right to ask the Commission President to reshuffle or replace some members of his team. In short, the Parliament implicitly bargained an informal rule of quasi-investiture of the individual Commissioners. It drew its bargaining power from the formal right of approving the Commission in its entirety. Once this had been granted under the Maastricht Treaty, all other competences followed quasi-automatically because the Parliament had an overall lever to block the functioning of the EU by refusing to vote, or threatening to vote against, a new Commission.

Why did the Parliament never ask that this rule of parliamentarian investiture of individual Commissioners be incorporated into the treaty? The formalizing of the informal rule was no topic during the IGC. Member states were not interested in formalizing this informal rule, but neither did they seek to abolish it. The Parliament did not request it because there was no need to do so since the de facto rule could be directly derived from the right of vote confidence over the Commission as a whole. The new 'inter-institutional agreement' reached between the Commission and the Parliament in mid-2005 does not introduce this principle of individual investiture, either, but only recognizes that when a member of the Commission should be replaced, the President of the Commission shall present the nominee to the Parliament 'in full compliance with the prerogatives of the institutions'.

Theoretical Conclusions: From the Amsterdam Treaty and Nice Treaty to the Constitutional Treaty

How can we *theoretically* account for the change in the institutional rule on the investiture of the Commission in this period from the Amsterdam and Nice Treaties to the Constitutional Treaty? A first pattern emerges immediately in the aftermath of the Amsterdam Treaty negotiations. We can identify another successful attempt of the Parliament to *endogenously* change the institutional rules governing the appointing of the Commission President by developing a modified *informal institutional* reinforcing its own institutional interests. What is notable, is that—by changing its procedural rules—the Parliament unilaterally altered a rule which concerns the *interaction with other actors*. The latter, however, were *not* involved in the decision about the change. Rather, the Parliament sought to *impose it unilaterally* in an informal decision.

When with the decision to hold a Convention the prospect of large-scale institutional change offered itself,[123] the Parliament fully set its stakes on this change of *levels, that is the change of higher-order rules and the change of the*

---

[123] The Parliament had proposed a 'constituante' much earlier (Schiffauer 2004).

scope of designing actors, that is, a change of the meta-rules (rules about how to change the higher-order rules) in order to obtain further institutional changes to its own advantage. In the Convention for the first time, it became itself a *designing actor* was, therefore, able to play an important role within the Presidium and to formally shape the institutional outcomes in its favour. The Convention proposal regarding the election of the Commission President was identical with the provision in the procedural rules of the Parliament. This is reflected in the hypotheses:

H: Rules-mediated distributive bargaining hypothesis
'The institutional rules governing the bargaining process make a difference with respect to the outcome, i.e. the changed institutional rule.'

And

H: Shifting levels/arenas to accelerate institutional change
'Given a choice between different levels/arenas of decision-making an actor may, by opting out of one arena and shifting the decision to another, improve his prospects of obtaining an institutional change according to his preferences.'

Having acted successfully at the higher-order level, however, did not mean that the Parliament eased its efforts at obtaining institutional changes *within the existing rules* of the Nice Treaty. It engaged in another effort of endogenous institutional change in the appointing of *individual* Commissioners and successfully bargained a new informal rule expanding its own competences, that is an informal rule of quasi-investiture of the individual Commissioners. From where did it draw its bargaining power? Simply from the formal right of approving the Commission in its entirety. Once this had been granted under the Maastricht Treaty, all other competences followed because the Parliament had an overall lever to block the functioning of the EU by refusing to vote, or vote against, a new Commission. This reflects the hypothesis:

H: Bargaining leverage through arena-linking
'Actor A, using a formal veto in one arena X, can create a leverage in another linked arena Y, in which actor A has no formal vote.'

4.4.5. Conclusion

Which were the most important factors and *processes* that drove the change of rules governing the Parliament's role in investing the Commission? One typical pattern of change that emerges consists in the exploiting of an existing formal rule in such a way as to extend the Parliament's power. Typically, the informal rule would be unilaterally stated by the Parliament and—depending on the Commission's and Council's alternatives—would be obliged with or not. This informal rule would subsequently be formalized or not, depending on the negotiation process and the preferences of the *designing actors*, that is member states. The point of departure would be an existing formal rule giving the Parliament the right of censure over the Commission; this *existing formal rule* in practical application would be extensively interpreted and would give rise to an *informal rule* shifting the power in favour of the Parliament. The change of rule would be *unilaterally* decided by one actor, the Parliament, however, would have implications for the Council and the Commission. Referring to its right of censure of the Commission, the Parliament legitimized the introduction of the informal rule allowing the Parliament to scrutinize the Commission's programme and confirm the President of the Commission as well as the entire Commission. Once the Commission obliged with the rule, it gained practical importance. The Parliament could exert some pressure by threatening to delay the process by withholding its opinion. This pattern corresponds to the argument of *distributive bargaining theory of institutional change* giving rise to an *informal* rule. The formalization of the informal rule does not necessarily follow. The designing actors, the member states, might decline the formalization, such as in the negotiations of the SEA when member states granted the Parliament only a right of consultation concerning the candidate for the Commission Presidency.

The Parliament also used the occasions of planned treaty reforms *at the higher level* to press for an institutional change in its favour. Not being a *designing actor*, it had to rely on the support of other actors. Thus, in the run-up to the Maastricht Treaty negotiations, the Parliament engaged in major lobbying efforts and built an alliance with veto-players (national parliaments) to set the agenda for the IGC. This strategy can be accounted for by *bargaining theory*, too: One actor seeks to gain leverage through arena-linking, that is *mobilizing veto-actors in a linked arena*. In the negotiations of the IGC of 1992, the diverse preferences of member states led to a compromise between governments favouring an extension of the Parliament's rights and those preferring the status quo, an outcome that can be explained by *bargaining theory*, as well. Once the new formal rules had been adopted, the Parliament set out to *endogenously change* the existing formal rule by interpreting it extensively in its own favour, giving rise to an *informal rule*. The treaty being vague on what consultation means, the Parliament had latitude to extend the notion to a de facto vote of confidence. It did so by engaging in an implicit bargaining process with the Commission and member states, linking its 'hard' right of a vote of confidence on the Commission as a whole with the 'soft' consultation right on the presidential candidate, that is making the former dependent on the latter. Since the designing actors were split among themselves a compromise had to be struck between designing actors favouring the Parliament' empowerment and designing actors favouring the status quo. The willingness of the recalcitrant designing actors increased when the Parliament threatened to block the confirmation of the Commission in its entirety, that is the intergovernmental negotiations occurred under the shadow of *linked-arena veto* of the Parliament.

Once the higher-order rules were reformed under the Amsterdam and Nice treaties, the Parliament made a renewed effort to *endogenously* change the formal rules. Once more, it proceeded to do so unilaterally although the rule involves the interaction with the other players. It stated that the nomination for the office of the President of the Commission should take into account the outcome of the European elections and changed its internal procedural rules accordingly replacing the term 'approbation' by 'election'. The Parliament also successfully endogenously changed another rule of investiture, the appointing of *individual* Commissioners, and established a de facto right of investiture of individual Commissioners. Again it drew its bargaining power from the closely related hard formal right of approving the Commission in its entirety, that is from a *linked-arena veto*.

With the Convention an opportunity of a large-scale change of higher-order rules emerged which the Parliament seized on. The changed meta-rules allowed it, for the first time, to have access to the circle of *designing actors*. This opportunity to have an impact on revision of higher-order rules and to change them in its favour was fully used. The provision on the election of the Commission President in the Convention draft of the Constitutional Treaty was identical with the provision in the procedural rules of the Parliament.

4.5. INSTITUTIONAL RULE FOUR: THE COMPOSITION OF THE COMMISSION

In this section the change of the institutional rule governing the composition of the Commission will be analysed. This rule has been remarkably stable over time. What are the underlying reasons and how can they be interpreted theoretically? The periods that will be investigated are

1. from 1957 to the Single European Act (1986);
2. from the Single European Act (1986) to the Amsterdam Treaty (1997);
3. from the Amsterdam Treaty (1997) to the Nice Treaty (2001);
4. from the Nice Treaty (2001) to the Constitutional Treaty (2004).

4.5.1. From 1957 to the Single European Act

The original institutional rule concerning the appointment of Commission-ers provides that each member state appoints at least one, and—by tacit agreement—the large five member states two, Commissioner(s) (Spence 2000: 12). They can resign, but cannot be sacked by their governments. In the course of enlargement the number of Commissioners grew steadily until it became to be perceived as a problem compartmentalizing the Commission's work and rendering it very cumbersome and hard to coordinate. In a report (the Spierenburg Report of 1979), commissioned by Commission President Roy Jenkins, it was recommended that member states appoint only one Com-missioner each; however, this recommendation was not followed by prac-tical measures. With the Greek (1981) and Spanish and Portuguese acces-sions (1986) the situation of 'too many Commissioners chasing too few jobs' (Jenkins 1991: 376) was exacerbated. Similarly to the Spierenburg Report, the Dooge Report of 1985 recommended only one Commissioner per member state, and so did the House of Lords Select Committee Report on the European Communities of 1985. However, in the negotiations of the SEA no adjustment to the institutional rule was made (Spence 2000: 14).

Theoretical Conclusion: From 1957 to the Single European Act

From a *theoretical process perspective* two aspects emerge from this brief empir-ical account of the period from 1957 to the SEA. In spite of exogenous func-tional pressure due to enlargement, there was *no* change of the institutional rule governing the composition of the Commission. This disconfirms the functionalist expectation that:

H: Functionalist transaction cost-based hypothesis
'If due to an external event the benefits of rule A have decreased, the rule will be changed, if the gains of the altered rule B including the transaction costs will be higher.'

How can this resistance to change be explained? The most obvious answer is that the change of the rule would have implied a *redistribution* of power between member states with the result that one member state's gain would have been another member state's loss. The redistributive nature of the issue was deepened by its coincidence with the small states versus large states cleav-age (Galloway 2001: 46). Redistributive issues are notoriously difficult to be dealt with in *bargaining* processes under *unanimity rule*. This reflects the claim

H: Problem type and integrative vs. defensive bargaining
'If redistributive issues are at stake the process of institutional change will be charac-terized by defensive bargaining. The outcome will reflect the asymmetry of power of the involved actors.'

In this case, no preparatory value-increasing negotiations took place in which actors proposed solutions beneficial to all, that would have widened the options for the subsequent defensive bargaining. The status quo defending negotiations immediately came to bear and failed before they had really started *in spite of* the functional pressure of the imminent enlargement.

4.5.2. From the SEA to the Amsterdam Treaty

Neither did the Maastricht Treaty revise the institutional rule governing the composition of the Commission although the latter's inefficiency was regularly pointed out. In a renewed effort, the Turin European Council of 1996 called for an analysis of how the Commission could improve its functioning 'having regard to its composition' insisting on the long 'accepted wisdom ... that the number of Commissioners was already too great' (Spence 2000: 12). The imminent eastern enlargement which would extend the Commission from twenty to twenty-eight members once more underlined the urgency of an institutional reform.

In the run-up to the Amsterdam IGC individual figures from member states came forth with proposals seeking to influence the debate. Weidenfeld (1994: 38) argued that Commissioners should not be appointed on a national quota basis. Member of Parliament Bourlanges proposed that the link between member states and Commissioners should be entirely severed (Bourlanges 1996) and Lamers (spokesman of the Christian Democrats in the German Parliament) called for a reduction of the number of Commissioners, an elimination of member states' right to a Commissioner as well as a gentlemen's agreement on having alternating national rights to propose Commissioners (Ross 1995; Spence 2000: 15). Former Commissioner Brittan proposed a system of senior and junior Commissioners. Each large state should always have a senior Commissioner, the rest of senior and junior Commissioners should be drawn from a rotating basis (Spence 2000: 15).[124] The Commission itself supported a reduction of the number of Commissioners to one per country (Beach 2005: 124).

But one more time, member states could not agree on a change of the institutional rules in the negotiations leading to the Amsterdam Treaty. The debate in general made clear that each member state wanted to ensure its national representation in the Commission and that the status of Commissioners should be equal (Spence 2000: 13). The discussion among member

[124] Each senior Commissioner chosen by large states should have two votes, junior Commissioners just one vote that should not be used against his or her senior Commissioner (Spence 2000: 15).

states underlined that 'all member states must retain the right to appoint a Commissioner regardless of size, budget contributions and political clout in the Union, if legitimacy and public acceptance nationally are to be guaranteed. Indeed, the smaller member states have made it clear in the past that their idea of the EU did not include domination by the larger countries' (Spence 2000: 13).

Eventually, some of the large member states, that is Germany, France, and Britain, came forward and agreed to renounce to one Commissioner, (Davignon 1995: 16). At the Nordwijk Special Council in 1997, held to prepare the Amsterdam IGC, however, a cleavage between large states and small states re-emerged. Small states, such as Denmark and Sweden 'were adamant about not giving up "their" Commissioner' (Beach 2005: 119). They argued that '... the efficiency and effectiveness of the Commission required not an ideal "management" size ... but rather a composition which would continue to reflect the sensitive and central role of the Commission in the most important pooling of sovereignty ever undertaken by independent democratic countries' (McDonagh 1998: 159). The smaller states regarded the right of nominating a Commissioner 'as a sort of safeguard for national interest in the policy formulation stage' (Svensson 2000: 164). When pushed hard in negotiations, the larger states, with the exception of France and Italy, admitted, too, that a system without an automatic right to appoint a Commissioner would not be acceptable for them; additionally, the newer member states pointed out that the right to at least one Commissioner had been guaranteed to them during accession negotiations (Petite 1998: 30 cited in Svensson 2000: 164).

In the negotiation over the revision of the Maastricht Treaty, the question of the composition of the Commission was closely linked with the issues of QMV and the weighting of votes (McDonagh 1998: 156), all similarly thorny and contested issues. France had requested a rebalancing of the votes in the Council to remedy the relative overrepresentation of the smaller member states (Devuyst 1998: 627). The Dutch Presidency proposed that after the accession of two new member states, the large member states should give up their second Commissioner and, as a compensation, the votes in the Council would be reweighted in their favour.[125]

The entwinement of the three issues, two of them of redistributive nature, made that—unless solutions were found for the two redistributive ones—most countries saw no reason to give up the status quo on the third

---

[125] Twenty-five votes for Germany, France, the UK, and Italy; twenty votes for Spain; twelve votes for the Netherlands; ten votes for Belgium, Greece, and Portugal; eight votes for Sweden and Austria; six votes for Denmark, Finland, and Ireland; and three votes for Luxembourg.

(Svensson 2000: 164). In this situation of gridlock, it appears that Germany proposed to delay the decision. The federal government's initial support for the decision was challenged by the veto of the regional governments (Länder) which vetoed the proposed solution for the extension of QMV in areas of their competences (Beach 2005: 120). Other countries, though, such as Belgium, set great store by the extension of QMV as a prerequisite for any reweighting of votes, and were not willing to proceed without a change in QMV. Spain, for its part, insisted on its goal of reweighting of votes. After a tour de table on support the Presidency apparently sensed, that no compromise was possible and the German idea was accepted (Svensson 2000: 164; Ludlow 2004).

The result was that the negotiations '... on Council votes and the number of Commissioners slipped out of the hands of the heads of state and government' (McDonagh 1998: 193)[126] and, at the end of the day, no agreement was found. The Amsterdam Treaty only included a declaration[127] stating that the institutional reform of the Commission's composition would be a precondition of the next round of enlargement (Spence 2000: 12).[128] Given that the preferences of member states were far apart on these contested institutional issues, 'the failure to reach a more permanent solution should come as no great surprise' (Svensson 2000: 165).

Theoretical Conclusion: From the SEA to the Amsterdam Treaty

Through *theoretical lenses* the same two patterns emerge as in the previous period. From a *process perspective*, it was shown that the institutional rule was not altered *in spite of* exogenous functional pressure. This tends to disconfirm a simple functionalist argument:

---

[126] Different accounts have been given for the failure: according to one, Spain was unwilling to support an agreement since the compensation offered for giving up its second Commissioner (the latter having been guaranteed during accession negotiations) was not considered as sufficient. It insisted on being given the same number of Council votes as the large states (Devuyst 1998: 628). The Belgian government was afraid to lose an important bargaining chip if it agreed to the reweighting of votes in the absence of a change of QMV. Finally France refused a new dual majority system which would give Germany a greater weight than France (Devuyst 1998: 628).

[127] By France, Italy, and Belgium.

[128] The protocol to the Treaty reads: 'Article 1: "At the entry into force of the first enlargement of the Union ... the Commission shall comprise one national of each of the Member States, provided that, by that date, the weighting of the votes in the Council has been modified, whether by re-weighting of the votes or dual majority, in a manner acceptable to all Member States taking into account all relevant elements, notably compensating those Member States which give up the possibility of nominating a second member of the Commission".'

H: Functionalist transaction cost-based hypothesis
'If due to an external event the benefits of rule A have decreased, the rule will be changed, if the gains of the altered rule B including the transaction costs will be higher.'

Again, the underlying reasons are that the issues at stake were of a *redistributive nature coinciding with the cleavage of small vs. large member states.* Therefore, a bargaining solution under unanimity decision-making was unlikely to come forth.

H: Problem type and integrative vs. defensive bargaining
'If redistributive issues are at stake the process of institutional change will be characterized by defensive bargaining. The outcome will reflect the asymmetry of power of the involved actors.'

What compounded the negotiation problem was the fact that the composition of the Commission was entwined with two other, just as thorny issues, the weighting of votes in the Council and QMV. Both of them are of a redistributive nature as well. This meant that *widening the scope of negotiations* to other highly contested, redistributive issues did not ease the bargaining difficulties with respect to the number of Commissioners. This points to the necessity of further specifying the argument made in the theoretical part according to which a widening of the scope of the agenda as such increases the opportunities to come to an agreement. Rather, it seems to depend very much on the nature of the other issues on the agenda and, if redistributive in nature, who is winning and who is losing and how possible losses in one issue area can possibly be compensated by gains in another (Benz, Scharpf, and Zintl 1992).

Adding the *structural perspective,* it emerges that a *multilevel aspect* was important, too, when accounting for the failure of negotiations. If it is true that the agreement on QMV failed because of the veto of the German Länder tying the government's hands, the multilevel aspect of bargaining contributes to the explanation of the failure (Benz 1992; Benz, Scharpf, and Zintl 1992). As regards the *types of participant actors,* there is a coincidence of *designing and implementing* actors. The actors designing the rule, that is member states, are the ones which are also implementing the rules.

4.5.3. From the Amsterdam Treaty to the Nice Treaty

The Amsterdam Treaty left a number of unresolved issues, among them the size of the Commission and the reweighting of votes in the Council that were to be renegotiated at the foreseen next IGC. From the viewpoint of institutional politics both these issues are highly salient and delicate, therefore were carefully scrutinized by member states. Little preparatory leadership was left to other organizations, such as the Commission or Council Secretariat (Beach 2005: 165), or the Committee of permanent representatives preparing IGCs (Reh forthcoming).

The Parliament, in its Herman Report, called for a reform, too, suggesting that real portfolios and teams of Commissioners should be formed for each subject area, grouped into senior and junior Commissioners (Spence 2000: 14). The Commission argued in favour of the opposite solution, that is to increase the number of Commissioner posts to be distributed. Each portfolio should carry a significant area of work (Spence 2000: 16). One reason given was the increased workload deriving from the increased interactions with the Parliament.[129] In the IGC the Commission proposed two options: a Commission of twenty members with equal rotation or one Commissioner per member state (Beach 2005: 154).

The IGC negotiations were clearly dominated by the French Presidency. Its objective was to link the reweighting of votes in Council with the loss of Commissioners. Large member states, for renouncing to one Commissioner, should be compensated by getting more votes in the Council (Tallberg 2006: 131ff). However, the solution proposed by the Presidency to limit the number of Commissioners, was considered to be unfair vis-à-vis the small countries (Tallberg 2006: 131ff). Their suspicion was raised because France, in preparing the Biarritz summit in October 2000, had held secretive consultations with the four large member states in the course of which it was agreed that they would accept an alternation of the posts between *all* member states in a restricted Commission with fewer Commissioners than the number of member states. The large member states by agreeing among themselves on this position put pressure on the smaller member states to accept a reduced number of Commissioners, invalidating the small-state argument that in a capped Commission they would not be treated equally (Schout and Vanhoonacker 2001: 18). The proposal raised irritation among the smaller member states since it questioned the implicit bargain of the Treaty of Amsterdam according to which the smaller member states had signalled acceptance of a reweighting of votes in favour of the larger member states in return for guarantees that the smaller member states could keep their Commissioners (Beach 2005: 149).[130] By renouncing to one Commissioner, 'the large states placed the ball in the

---

[129] The College meets during the parliamentary session in Strasbourg and some Commissioners are always available for the other days. Commissioners frequently attend parliamentary committee meetings to defend the Commission's policies (Spence 2000: 17).

[130] The debate about the reweighting of votes quickly led to a conflict between small and large states. And between France and Germany, as well as between Belgium and the Netherlands regarding the parity of voting weights (Beach 2005: 150).

court of the small states. This proved to be a major breakthrough in the negotiations, which then shifted to the format of such a capping in the number of Commissioners' (Tallberg 2006: 133).

The final bargaining took place in the concluding session in Nice 'since any solution to this highly sensitive issue would require concessions that only heads of government could make' (Gray and Stubb 2001; Schout and Van-hoonacker 2001: 20; Tallberg 2006: 131f, 177). Immediately before the summit at Nice, the formal negotiations were more and more frequently accompanied by informal bargaining. The Presidency was engaged in bilateral talks meeting with all heads of state. When Germany agreed to a voting parity with France in spite of its larger population, the prospects for an overall agreement improved (Beach 2005). The concluding negotiations in Nice began with bilateral con-fessionals which served as a basis for the first draft submitted for negotiation. It provided that Spain be compensated with additional Council votes for giving up one Commissioner, maintained the parity of France and Germany in votes and introduced a demographic safety net. The latter provided that a proposal under QMV (if a member state asked for it) must be adopted by governments representing 62 per cent of the EU's population (Schout and Vanhoonacker 2001: 20). This proposal was supported by the large member states, but rejected by Portugal and Belgium, Austria, Finland, Greece, and Sweden (Beach 2005: 150) because it was considered to be biased in favour of the large states.[131]

A second and a third draft were presented and negotiations were frequently interrupted for bilateral consultations (Gray and Stubb 2001; Tallberg 2006). The bargaining on the last draft took place in a restricted session of heads of state and government. It was basically the same proposal as described above providing for a triple majority, and giving the medium-sized states an additional vote (Beach 2005: 150–1). After Belgium had been offered a side-payment,[132] the negotiations were concluded (Tallberg 2006: 136). With regard to the composition of the Commission, each member state would keep one Commissioner until a membership of twenty-seven is reached. At this point the size will be capped at a lower level than the number of members. However, member states did not agree on the actual number of Commis-sioners but only that an equal rotation system will then be put in place (Beach 2005: 152). The influence of the French Presidency was crucial for obtaining the necessary support for capping the number of Commissioners, and the principle of equal rotation. The Presidency did not thrash out a

---

[131] At this point the negotiations threatened to stall. Beach referring to Schout and Van-hoonacker (2001) emphasizes that the French Presidency appeared to be most interested in maintaining Franco–German parity instead of 'brokering a fair compromise' (Beach 2005: 150).

[132] European Council meetings would take place in Brussels in the future.

compromise from the divergent positions, an enterprise close to impossible given the opposing preferences of small and large states. Rather, it used its position to direct the debate in the direction of its own preferences (Schout and Vanhoonacker 2001: 19).

Theoretical Conclusion: From the Amsterdam Treaty to the Nice Treaty

Again, from a *theoretical process and a structural perspective*, bargaining theory in a zero-sum interest constellation explains the outcome, that is that *no change* of the institutional rule under scrutiny ensued, but a commitment was made to change it in the near future (after enlargement to twenty-seven members). The composition of the Commission, linked with the re-weighting of votes in the Council, has clear-cut redistributive implications that were tackled in negotiations at the *highest level* among *designing actors* exclusively. The difficulties of negotiating a compromise under unanimity rule could be overcome in the case of the reweighting of votes through the strong institutional leadership of the French Presidency that used its prerogatives to the utmost, proposing drafts and building coalitions on the basis of compensation promises in order to build support for its proposal. This supports the claim:

H: Problem type and integrative vs. defensive bargaining
'If redistributive issues are at stake the process of institutional change will be characterized by defensive bargaining. The outcome will reflect the asymmetry of power of the involved actors.'

And

H: Distributive, power-based bargaining of institutional change mediated by institutions
'The institutional rules governing the bargaining process make a difference with respect to the outcome, i.e. the changed institutional rule.'
'A wider scope of decision-making issues and simultaneous voting on all issues will lead to more redistributive outcomes of the negotiation process than voting on single issues sequentially.'

The sheer functional pressure of the imminent enlargement did not suffice to produce a more efficient institutional solution. Member states' vested institutional interests in nominating their Commissioner(s) linked with their interest in the maintenance or increase of the number of votes in the Council clearly prevailed in determining the negotiation outcome. Hence the functionalist redesign argument is not borne out empirically, whereas a power-based redistributive bargaining argument can account for the outcome.

4.5.4. From the Nice Treaty to the Constitutional Treaty

The very moderate success achieved during the Nice negotiations as regards the reform of the composition of the Commission, gave rise to the call for a more fundamental institutional reform of the Union. As described in Section 4.2 on the rule governing the Parliament's role in legislation, the solution was sought at a meta-level; an attempt was made to change the method of treaty reform. The Convention method was used to prepare the agenda for the subsequent IGC and widen the space of possible institutional solutions by transcending the limits of the IGC method based on unanimity rule.

To what extent did this new format affect the attempt to change the size of the Commission? The Convention under the leadership of the Convention presidium submitted a Franco-German proposal calling for a long-term Union President chairing the European Council and the creation of a foreign minister sitting both in the Council and the Commission. This provoked a conflict between smaller member states and larger member states. Sixteen smaller states proposed an alternative that insisted on the preservation of the rotating Presidency and the keeping of one Commissioner per member state (Beach 2005: 182). 'Institutional balance' became the keyword in the Convention discussion, meaning a balance between the organizations *and* between member states. The final draft submitted by the presidium to the plenary did not contain the rotating presidency and changed the voting weights introduced under Nice (Beach 2005: 186). This text gave rise to many amendments from the plenary, some of them arguing for the maintenance of the rotating presidency and the omission of a capping of the number of Commissioners. But most members of the plenary agreed that the text was negotiable (Beach 2005: 186). At the end of the day, the Convention did not decide on a solution of the delicate institutional questions of the number of Commissioners and the reweighting of Council votes, but left them to the IGC.

During the IGC negotiations, by contrast, the issues of the size of the Commission and the reweighting of Council votes played an important role. The smaller countries could lend more emphasis to their views and argued strongly in favour of keeping 'their' Commissioner and the rotating Presidency (Agence Europe, 9.9.03). Given the link with the re-weighting of votes in the Council, Poland and Spain insisted to return to the Nice compromise on the Council votes. Due to this divergence in views among member states and the lack of leadership of the Italian Presidency, the negotiations failed. The incoming Irish Presidency engaged in careful bilateral preparation of the renewed negotiations. The outcome of the process was that the Commission should be reduced to two-thirds of the number of member states in 2014 and that the six-month rotation of the Presidency should be preserved within the form of a team Presidency of three governments. The institutional change provided for in the Constitutional Treaty, however, did not enter into force because of the rejection of the latter in the French and Dutch referenda.

Theoretical Conclusion: From the Nice Treaty to the Constitutional Treaty

How can the change of the institutional rule governing the composition of the Commission that occurred between the Nice Treaty and the Constitutional Treaty be *theoretically* interpreted? A *two-level initiative*, altering the mode of Treaty change, was meant to overcome the decision-making impasse into which the change over this rule had run. Drastically changing the mode of revising the higher-order rules through the Convention method, however, did not produce a clear answer to the delicate institutional questions. They were bracketed and saved for the IGC. A change of levels from the higher-order level to the meta-level of rules about higher-order rule-making could not instil a new dynamic into a gridlocked process of institutional reform because the decisions subsequently would have to be accepted under the IGC method.[133] And, as we have seen, the entire process later failed on account of a veto in two national referenda, that is at a *lower level*. The dynamics involved in the changing of arenas reflects the claim:

H: Shifting levels/arenas to accelerate institutional change
'Given a choice between different levels/arenas of decision-making an actor may, by opting out of one arena and shifting the decision to another, improve his prospects of obtaining an institutional change according to his preferences.'

As was shown, in the case of the composition of the Commission and the reweighting of votes, the Convention did not fulfil a function of integrative bargaining, that is propose new solutions beneficial to all actors involved. Rather, these redistributive hot issues were bracketed.

H: Problem type and defensive vs. integrative bargaining
'If in a first, institutionally separate stage of negotiation, actors focus on problem-solving, they may identify institutional solutions beneficial to all; the developing of such solutions may have an impact on the second stage defensive bargaining because the space of feasible options has been extended.'

The IGC—although failing in the first round—under the *functional pressure* of imminent enlargement—ultimately produced a compromise of an *institutional redesign* representing a compromise between large states and small

---

133 And the likely veto of some actors was anticipated.

states which is to be applied at a future point in time. The thrashing out of a compromise between the conflicting actors can plausibly be accounted for in *bargaining theoretical terms*, based on issue linkages and compensation payments. Therefore, both claims, the functionalist and the bargaining theoretical explanation play a role.

H: Functionalist transaction cost-based hypothesis
'If due to an external event the benefits of rule A have decreased, the rule will be changed, if the gains of the altered rule B including the transaction costs will be higher.'

And

H: Problem type and integrative vs. defensive bargaining
'If redistributive issues are at stake the process of institutional change will be characterized by defensive bargaining. The outcome will reflect the asymmetry of power of the involved actors.'

4.5.5. Conclusion

What emerges very clearly is that the exogenously triggered change of this institutional rule which is clearly redistributive in its content and whose stakes are clear-cut, under unanimity rule is likely to be subject to a lengthy power-based process of distributive bargaining with an outcome not very different from the status quo. Moreover, in the case of composition of the Commission, the designing actors coincide with the implementing actors, that is the modification of the composition of the Commission is decided by the very actors who will implement this institutional change. This means that every loss incurred through negotiations has to be borne by the designing actors themselves; costs cannot be externalized to implementing actors. This adds to the difficulties of coming to an agreement. As we have seen, the functionalist efficiency argument as such did not suffice to bring the change of the institutional rule about. The old rule was maintained over a long period although its inefficiency was frequently bemoaned. The widening of the negotiation agenda to include several institutional rules, that is the reweighting of Council votes and the extension of QMV, did not facilitate the negotiations over the composition of the Commission either. This is not surprising since these two issues are just as contested and prone to polarize the political arena. Nor did the application of a two-level strategy or arena shift prove helpful to overcome the decision-making impasse. Switching from the IGC to the Convention method did not produce swifter changes as regards the composition of the Commission. Only under an overwhelming impression of a lack of practicability on the occasion of the extensive last enlargement round, could member states bring themselves to agree on a modification of the rule at a future point in time.

What this empirical case shows, too, is that—if an institutional rule is so clearly defined as the provision on the composition of the Commission—it is unlikely to be subject to creative interpretation and slight incremental modification. 'One commissioner per country' and 'two per large country' just does not lend itself to subtle alterations. Since the stakes are high and clear-cut, changes would not occur informally between higher-order rule revisions.

4.6. INSTITUTIONAL RULE FIVE: CONTROLLING THE IMPLEMENTATION POWERS OF THE COMMISSION (COMITOLOGY)

Carl-Fredrik Bergström and Adrienne Héritier

The Council has passed on a considerable part of its responsibility for implementing legislation to the Commission and has also reserved some implementation powers to itself. When delegating, it may impose particular requirements on the Commission when exercising these powers. These requirements provide for the use of committees in which the Commission cooperates with national representatives in the application of its implementation powers (comitology). In this section the empirical development of the institutional rules governing comitology and their transformation over almost fifty years will be described and theoretically explained. What were the most important processes driving change and what were their outcomes? And how can they best be grasped analytically?[134]

The institutional rule that the Commission must work together with committees consisting of national representatives was formally introduced in 1961 when a common commercial policy was initiated. In 1962 it was extended to the managing of CAP and in 1968 to measures regarding the free movement of goods. In the SEA it was formally institutionalized at the treaty level to be generally applied in all fields of cooperation. Today there are about 260 comitology committees which assist the Commission in the exercise of implementing powers. Thus, we testify a remarkable spread of comitology procedures across policy areas in this period.

In the following analysis we will distinguish a number of stages of development:

1. from 1957 to the establishing of the management committee system (1961);

[134] This chapter builds in large part on the empirical material presented and analysed in Bergström 2005.

2. from the establishing of the management committee system (1961) to
   The Hague Summit (1969);
3. from The Hague Summit (1969) to the SEA (1986);
4. from the SEA (1986) to the First Comitology Decision (1987);
5. from the First Comitology Decision (1987) to the modus vivendi
   (1994);
6. from the modus vivendi (1994) to the Amsterdam Treaty (1997);
7. from the Amsterdam Treaty (1997) to the Second Comitology Decision
   (1999);
8. from the Second Comitology Decision (1999) to the Nice Treaty and the
   Lamfalussy Reform (2001);
9. from the Nice Treaty and Lamfalussy Reform (2001) to the Convention
   (2003), IGC (2004) to the revised Second Comitology Decision (2006).

4.6.1. From 1957 to the Establishing of the Management Committee System

The EEC Treaty of 1957 pursued the objective of progressively introducing
a common market that was to be realized in stages, the transitional period
ending in 1970. A large number of provisions establishing a common market
and facilitating its operation were to be introduced during the transitional
period. The substantive areas to be covered included the 'four freedoms' and
the customs union with relatively precise provisions, and the common commercial policy, CAP, and transport policy with less specific provisions. It was
up to the Commission, the Council, and the Parliament to develop the actual
substance of the legislation in these areas.

The comitology procedure was developed while adopting the provisions
establishing a common market for agricultural products, that is a CAP. This
first transitional stage ended in 1962. The substance of these provisions were
to be discussed at an IGC immediately after the entry into force of the
EEC Treaty at a conference in Stresa 1958. The Commission submitted proposals for legislation by the Council in the form of regulations, directives,
and decisions that the governments at the IGC, however, were not willing
to accept. A major reason for this was that the Commission gave itself a
very strong role in the process (Bulletin EEC 5-1959). As a consequence,
the Commission submitted a revised proposal which clearly reduced its own
role in the future management of agricultural policy (Europe, bulletin quotidien 29.6.1959). The Council was still not willing to accept the rule and
the decision-making process stalled. Some governments wanted to leave the
Commission a lot of discretion, others wished to exert more control over

the Commission's implementing powers. In order to overcome the dead-lock, an ad hoc intergovernmental body, the Special Committee on Agriculture, was entrusted with further negotiations (Europe, bulletin quotidien 29.6.1959).[135] At the end of 1960 a conclusion was reached providing that CAP should be based on a system of levies and that the Commission should draft the regulations specifying the products to which the system would apply (Europe—documents 31.12.1960). The Commission completed its work and the Council took its decision at the beginning of 1962 (Europe, bulletin quotidien 14/15.1.1962). According to the decision (Council Regulations 19-24/62/EEC), common organizations were to be established for the markets in cereals, pork, eggs, poultry, fruit and vegetables, and wine. The regulation on the financing of CAP provided that, by the end of the transitional period, all incomes would go directly to the Community which would then bear all the costs.

In the second stage of transition it emerged that, beyond the difficulties to agree on the substantive questions of CAP, it was difficult to agree on the distribution of institutional power vested in the new system of managing CAP. The institutional rule allocating power to the Commission and the Council (and the Parliament) needed to be shaped. Some governments were unwilling to concede powers in an area which had not been more closely defined in the EEC Treaty. Their scepticism, however, also expressed the expectation that a question of general importance was at stake, the solution of which would be model for many other fields of activity (Europe, bulletin quotidien 28.11.1961).

In a first move, the Commission sought to assert its institutional position. It referred to the Treaty Article[136] providing that the Commission shall ensure the proper functioning and development of the common market, and that—for this purpose—the Council should delegate powers of implementation to the Commission. In order to fulfil this management task the Commission proposed that it should be permitted to run a number of so-called 'European Offices' (Bulletin EEC 5-1959: pp. 17–28). These offices, under the Commission's orders, would calculate intervention prices, make support purchases, and issue import certificates. A number of 'consultative committees' should allow to pursue a continuous dialogue with representatives of both governmental and non-governmental interests affected by the CAP (Bulletin EEC 5-1959: 17–28).

This proposal, not surprisingly, met with resistance on the part of the Council. It replaced the Commission's proposal for 'European Offices' by

---

[135] Still allowing the Commission to present the proposals.
[136] Art. 155 EEC 1958.

'Intervention Agencies' run by member states themselves. But, most importantly, the idea emerged that representatives of governmental interests should
be given greater opportunity to influence decision-making through participation in the consultative committees. In response, the Commission in 1960
suggested that the consultative committees should not include governmental
representatives. The latter should meet, instead, in 'directors' committees' that
the Commission would have to consult before taking any decisions (Bulletin
EEC 5-1959: 17–28). While governments accepted this institutional solution
in the area of competition policy,[137] they refused to accept it in CAP. The
French government argued that it would not provide sufficient opportunity to
'assure the effective direction' of member states and the German government
insisted that the final decision must always be taken by the Council. Finally, it
was concluded that some 'more supple institutional form should be found for
co-operation between the Commission and the national authorities responsible for the execution of agricultural policy measures' (Bulletin EEC 10-1960:
47).

Various new possibilities were discussed which finally led to the basic institutional structure of the present comitology system: the French government
proposed that the power to take certain management-related decisions should
be entrusted to management committees (comités de gestion) composed of
representatives of both the national administrations and the Commission
(Europe, bulletin quotidien 28–30.11.1961). The management committees
were not subordinate to the Commission, rather was the power to take
important decisions to remain with the Council. However, member states
could not agree. Some governments hesitated to take responsibilities from
the Commission to hand them over to intergovernmental bodies (Europe,
bulletin quotidien 30.11.1961). A first step towards a solution was made with
the proposal that measures of 'a practical nature' should be entrusted to the
Commission and management committees *jointly* (Europe, bulletin quotidien
30.11.1961). Management committees should exercise a control function and
an opportunity to prevent the adoption of measures which they did not
support.[138] If a measure proposed by the Commission would not be accepted
by a committee, the Commission could either adjust to the opinion of the
committee or submit a proposal for legislation to the Council.

The compromise negotiated in the Special Committee on Agriculture was accepted by most governments. Some governments, such as the
Dutch government, still held doubts and refused to place the Commission

---

[137] The Advisory Committee on Restrictive Practices and Dominant Positions (Council Reg.
17/62 EEC 6.2.1962) was agreed on.

[138] This had not been foreseen in the case of the directors' committees, or indeed, in the case
of the Advisory Committee on Restrictive Practices and Dominant Positions.

'under a tutelage of intergovernmental organs' (Europe, bulletin quotidien 30.11.1961). Notwithstanding, further steps in the same direction were taken although the Commission sought to claw back some power by proposing that only the Commission should take the actual decision on the adoption of a measure. However, it did not seek to change the essential element that management committees should be closely involved in the deliberations and also be permitted to exercise a control function. The control function, though, according to the Commission's proposal should only come to bear *after* it had taken its decision: if a committee with a qualified majority of the votes objected to a measure (negative opinion), the Council would have the competence to replace it by another.

The Council accepted the modifications proposed by the Commission at the end of 1961. There are reasons to believe that the rapid acquiescence of the Council was due to the fact that the Parliament had just become aware of the Commission's and Council's plan to create 'new organs' and had immediately issued a resolution in which it demanded that no decision should be taken before it had given its opinion. The Parliament is indirectly affected because under the Treaty it exercises a political supervisory power over the Commission. From the perspective of member states, if the Parliament were to be included in the decision-making process, an agreement on the management committees—already within reach—would be put into question. These concerns may explain why the first Council Regulations in the field of CAP in 1962 provided that the Commission should adopt 'measures for their application' in close cooperation with a management committee. Comitology was born. In the application of the rule the Commission developed a relationship with national administrations. After one year of experience it emerged that a well-functioning collaboration had developed '... which has permitted the resolution of divergent opinions on technical matters, without the need of involving an inter-change between the Council and the Commission, and to accomplish speedily a considerable volume of work' (Olmi 1963: 118).

The committee system typically operates as follows. The initiation of the process—at the difference from what the legal rules say—lies not only with the Commission. Before it is formally required to do so, the Commission will discuss with the representatives of the national administrations whether to proceed in a specific question. The Commission in spite of its formal right of initiative is not likely to push a matter which is not given sufficient support in a committee (Joerges and Neyer 1997: 279). The process for adoption of implementing measures is often triggered by the representatives of the national administrations.

Within the committee, national representatives are organized in delegations, containing normally two people, the 'representative' and the 'accompanying expert'. All formal contacts with and within the committee pass through the Chairman, appointed by the Commission. The Chairman has no voting rights and fulfils administrative tasks: to prepare and host meetings, to send invitations and distribute documentation, to write protocols, and to communicate with the Parliament.

If the Commission and the committee agree to initiate the process for adoption of implementing measures, a working group[139] consisting of national experts prepares the draft. Discussions on the draft continue until an agreement has been reached on a text which is supported by everyone. Test votes may be taken to get a 'clear picture' of the situation. Solutions are sought that satisfy all members in a cooperation characterized by professionalism and mutual respect. Once adopted in a working group, the draft text is passed on to the Chairman of the committee who will distribute it to the national delegations. It is unlikely that the debate is reopened in substance when the committee meets to give its opinion and the text is normally given consensual support. This explains the statistical fact that the situations in which the committee votes a negative opinion are virtually non-existent. If this is exceptionally the case, the matter will most likely be referred back to the working group for further discussion.

In sum: comitology as an institutional rule to control the implementing power of the Commission, should not primarily be considered as a mechanism of political control, but as a device for placing the responsibility for substantive discussion in the hands of the national administrations, in particular in the working groups. The role of the Commission, within a working group but also within a committee, is the role of coordinator or mediator rather than a decision maker. This holds in particular for regulatory committees, and less for market management committees where the Commission dominates the decision-making progress. (Interviews Commission Dec. 2005)

After 1962, the third actor, the Parliament, became increasingly preoccupied with the management committees. The mere fact that the Parliament had *not* been given the opportunity to state its opinion raised the suspicion of MEPs. It was not only the lack of control over the institutional rules governing the comitology procedure,[140] but a more basic question which has remained a contested issue until the present day, the question about the appropriate scope of delegation to the Commission and, concomitantly, of comitology procedures. Which matters ought to be dealt with under normal legislative procedures and which matters should be delegated to a 'mixed' administration in which the Commission and the Council were both involved, but the

---

[139] In matters of routine character a more simplified structure is used. No working group is set to work, rather everything is done within the committee. This is more frequently so in the case of management committees.

[140] The Parliament did welcome the new cooperation between the Commission and the national administrations in the management committees to the extent that national administrations would be induced to apply these decisions in a more uniform manner.

Parliament excluded? Thus, in its Deringer Report of 1962[141] the Parliament cautioned that the new management committees should not have the consequence that an increasing number of matters of political significance were dealt with under comitology procedures that did not permit the Parliament to discuss and promote its position publicly (Deringer Report 1962: 33–5).

The Parliament not only played no role in shaping the comitology rules, but found itself sidelined in another important respect: the exercise of its supervisory powers over the Commission established under the Treaty. From this concern it derived the demand that the Commission should assume the political responsibility for the new organs of cooperation (Deringer Report 1962: 33, 36), because the Commission, in turn, would be subject to the political supervisory powers of the Parliament. However, the Commission in its reaction to the Parliament's report, refused to assume a political responsibility for the new organs for cooperation, and insisted that the matters to be dealt with in comitology should neither be limited in scope, nor be subject to parliamentarian consultation.

Theoretical Conclusion: From 1957 to the Establishing of the Management Committee System

To draw a first *theoretical* conclusion: In view of the task to establish a common market, member states established an act of *delegation and* charged the Commission with implementing powers. In other words, the *principals*, that is member states, delegated authority to the *agent*, that is the Commission, to exercise the implementing powers. The Treaty also allows the Council to define procedures to control the Commission in exercising these implementing powers. In principal–agent theoretical terms: the principal will exert control over the agent in order to prevent agency loss. Put differently, the principals/member states only allowed for considerable delegation of implementing powers to the Commission, because they simultaneously maintained control and influence over, and indeed participate in, the exercise of this delegation. There is no zero-sum conflict in the allocation of institutional competences, but rather a sharing of competences.

This development is reflected in the hypotheses:

H: Functionalist transaction cost-based hypothesis
'If due to an external event the benefits of rule A have decreased, the rule will be changed, if the gains of the altered rule B including the transaction costs will be higher.'

---

[141] Summarizing the experience of twelve parliamentary committees in cooperating with the Commission.

And

H: Agency loss as a cause of institutional change
'If the divergence between the principal's and the agent's preferences has become too large, the principal will redesign the contract, i.e. change the institutional rule in order to rein in the agent.'

The institutional rules to supervise the agent do not simply derive from cost–benefit calculations (including transaction costs) of the principal and the agent, but are *bargained between principal and agent*. The particular shape of the institutional rule governing the implementing powers of the Commission is quite well accounted for by *distributive power-based bargaining theory*. In the first years, the Council and the Commission shaped the institutional rule which was to govern the member states control over the implementation powers of the Commission in a bilateral implicit bargaining process. In this process the Council prevailed because member states, formally responsible for the decision, are the sole designing actors. If national governments wish, they can specify the provisions in the Treaty and impose particular rules on the Commission in exercising its implementing powers. However, if member states disagree, which was the case, the outcome is more favourable for the Commission. The power-based distributive bargaining logic accounting for this outcome is reflected in:

H: Institutional change through distributive bargaining:
'Given a change of preference of a powerful actor or a change of power balance between actors, an existing institutional rule may be subject to renegotiation in order to alter the rule in such a way as to reflect the (changed) preferences of the powerful actor(s) or the changed power balance.'

What changed the dynamic of the implicit negotiation between two actors, the Council and the Commission, was the request of a third actor, the Parliament, claiming to play—at least a modest role—in these negotiations. This changed the actor constellation from a *bilateral to trilateral implicit negotiations*. The partner with the stronger hand in the bargaining process, the Council, made more concessions to the Commission in shaping the comitology rule to speed up the bilateral negotiation and avoid a trilateral negotiation including the Parliament. At this point, the Parliament was not successful in gaining a role in the implicit bargaining process between Council and Commission shaping the first institutional rule governing comitology. Again this may be accounted for in distributional bargaining theoretical terms: the Parliament, being neither a designing nor an implementing actor in shaping the comitology rules, but only an indirectly affected actor, had no bargaining clout in the adoption of the institutional rule. Neither did it have a veto power in a directly linked arena, therefore did not make any impact on the outcome.

The empirical story of institutional change directs the attention to the *link between institutional rules* and the unexpected effects that the change of one institutional rule had for another rule. In this particular instance, the new rule on the management committees (rule X) defining the interaction between Commission (A) and Council (B) affects a different institutional rule (Y) of the Treaty, that is the responsibility of the Parliament (C) to exercise the responsibility of political supervision over the Commission, touching on the interaction of the Commission (A) with the Parliament (C). Not surprisingly, the introduction of X, indirectly affecting the position of the third actor (C) under rule Y, calls forth the opposition of C.

Moreover, and very importantly, the conflict over competences centres around at the *scope* of application of the institutional rule (the dimension of Attribute according to Crawford and Ostrom 1995). Choosing comitology/delegation as an avenue of decision-making over another, legislation, deprives one actor, the Parliament, of its participation in decision-making. Therefore, the conflict also focuses on the question which avenue to choose in the first place. Accordingly, institutional change with respect to the scope of comitology rules has important implications on the *distribution of competences*, as Bergström, Farrell, and Héritier (forthcoming) have argued. The outcome of whether one avenue or the other is selected may be accounted for by an implicit bargaining process in which the powerful actors with the best fallback position prevail in determining the choice.

4.6.2. From the Establishing of Management Committees to The Hague Summit

After the adoption of the first CAP Regulations the comitology procedure was extended to additional areas of cooperation, in particular trade (GATT) policy. After the crisis caused by France's blocking the accession negotiations with the UK (which in turn led to the blocking of CAP) had been overcome, a period of advance in CAP and trade regulation[142] followed. In 1965, the final financial regulation of CAP shifted to centre stage[143] and became a hotly contested issue. The Dutch, Italian, and German governments were not willing to let the Community expend large sums of money without getting in exchange some kind of supranational 'préalable' in the form of an independent source

---

[142] Particularly in the context of the Kennedy Round.

[143] The other central issue was the merger of the executives of ECSC, EEC, and EAEC into a single Council and single Commission. The Merger Treaty was agreed in 1965.

of revenue for the Commission *and* a commitment to increase the supervisory authority of the Parliament. The French Presidency was strongly opposed to both proposals. In this situation the Commission did not present a compromise proposal trying to reconcile the different positions, but a very ambitious one: it suggested not only a mode of financing of CAP through agricultural levies, but also that customs duties should be designated as the Community's own reources *and* that the Parliament should be given an enhanced power of budgetary control. An attempt was made to 'buy off' the vehement French opposition by an extremely favourable financial arrangement, but to no avail. France took a principled stance trying to prevent that the Community should develop beyond the control of member states and declared that the 'Council had not been convened to examine suggestions about the future development of the Communities, but to resolve a very practical and pedestrian question, the financing of the agricultural policy for the next five years' (Edit. Comments, 1965–6, CMLR, p. 3). To underline its protest it stopped attending Council and COREPER meetings (Lindberg 1963: 248; Palayret, Wallace, and Winand 2006).[144] The other governments criticized France and supported the Commission. An extraordinary Council meeting (without a representative of the Commission) was scheduled to overcome the crisis and prevent new difficulties. It reached an agreement on the Council's mode of voting on the Commission's proposals and on the Council's relationship with the Commission.

With respect to the use of QMV all governments (except France) accepted that whenever 'very important interests of one or more partners at stake, the Members of the Council endeavour, within a reasonable time, to reach solutions which ((could)) be adopted by all the Members of the Council while respecting their mutual interests and those of the Community'.[145] In case of a lack of agreement an understanding was established that there would be an 'agreement to disagree'. As regards the cooperation between the Commission and the Council, the Commission was required to present its proposals to governments before unveiling them to the public in order to avoid that the Commission put pressure on governments by previously having addressed parties, interests groups, and the media and not to present its position to Parliament before it had been presented to Council.[146] Concerning the management committees, a method was to be defined on the basis of which the Council and the Commission would specify what type of implementing

---

[144] But not management committee meetings (Kaiser 1966).

[145] France demanded that, in such a situation, the discussion should continue until unanimous agreement is reached, but was not supported by member states.

[146] Moreover, the Commission was not to present proposals not dealing with the substance of the problems, but merely asking for general power to act later.

powers were to be entrusted to the Commission and what role was to be assigned to management committees.

After the solution of the empty chair crisis, the trade negotiations in the GATT Kennedy Round were resumed, albeit initially at a slow pace. The reason was that, as long the financial regulation of CAP had not been solved, the French government objected to the Commission being instructed for further negotiations in the Kennedy Round. By invoking the 'rule of synchronization', however, Germany helped achieving progress in both areas simultaneously.[147] Making progress in one area dependent on the progress achieved in the other gave bargaining actors an incentive to come to a compromise. Subsequently, step by step the use of management committees spread beyond CAP. It became the normal procedure of decision-making in all areas where the Council delegated powers to the Commission. But each time governments insisted on effective channels of influence and the retention of a right of control (Bertram 1967: 249).

With the customs union to be completed in 1968, a common commercial policy based on uniform principles regarding the changes in tariff rates, the conclusion of tariff and trade agreements, measures of liberalization, export policy, and measures to protect trade in case of dumping and subsidies was to be gradually introduced. In the first half of the 1960s member states had been hesitant to concede commercial policy powers to the Commission. Difficulties of the United States in the implementation of the Kennedy Round led to a conflict with the Community in 1968 which in turn forced member states to cooperate more intensively and to replace national trade rules by common rules. The Commission had already made preparations to use the same type of management committee procedures that were employed in CAP. But governments insisted instead on a more restrictive formula. The Regulations which were finally adopted, produced a new type of committee procedure, the regulatory committees.

The first regulation of common commercial policy was the Council Regulation on protection against dumping of 1968. It allowed the charging of a duty on imported products subject to dumping or subsidies in their countries of origin. For this purpose a procedure for a close cooperation between the Commission and governmental representatives was developed within the 'Committee on Protection against Dumping'. The Council made the Commission clearly understand that its role would essentially to be to mediate effectively between the interests of all governments and to examine the facts submitted by a member state. On the basis of this examination the Commission could then make a proposal to the Council that an anti-dumping duty should be

---

[147] The Kennedy Round completed its negotiations in Summer 1967.

introduced. The Commission could only choose not to propose a measure if none of the governmental representatives in the committee objected. In the case of objections, the Commission was compelled to submit the matter to the Council which could have the Commission reopen the examination. However, the Commission was empowered, on request of a national representative in the Committee, to introduce a provisional anti-dumping duty before the facts of a specific case had been established. Two further trade regulations followed in 1968, one on the concept of country of origin, and one for the valuation of goods for customs purposes.

The Regulatory Committee procedure constituted a more cautious version of the management committee procedure that was already in use in CAP. In both cases, the national representatives' influence in the committee was based on its ability to express its discontent with the measure proposed by the Commission. What was new, was that under the Regulatory Committee Procedure the Commission was only permitted to adopt a rule if it had previously been approved in a positive opinion. Should the Committee fail to approve the proposal (by qualified majority), the Commission would have to submit a proposal for legislation to the Council. Should the Council in turn fail to act within a certain period, the Commission could proceed as intended. This 'filet' or 'safety net' was to ensure that some sort of action would always be taken. In short, the rules governing committees in commercial policy were shaped more cautiously by member states. This fact reflects the wariness of governments vis-à-vis the Commission in the aftermath of the 'empty chair crisis'.

In spite of the abolishing of all customs duties in the summer of 1968 there were still many obstacles to a common market. Critically, the conditions that had to be met before a product could be sold needed to be harmonized. Notably the French and the Dutch government called for the harmonization of legislation relating to foodstuffs so that public health and consumer protection could not be used for protectionist reasons (Debré at Council meeting 4/5.11.1968). As a consequence, the Council adopted a programme for the veterinary sector. A procedural framework was established to enable the Commission to confirm or reject the protective measures in close and practical collaboration with the member states in the Standing Veterinary Committee.

The Commission proposed a procedure along the lines of the management committee. Some member states, however, insisted on exerting stronger control, in particular regarding the question of what should happen, if a matter had not been approved by the committee, would be referred to the Council, but the Council could not come to a decision within the specified period of time. Finally an agreement was reached that gave the committee an autonomous legal basis, that is Council Decision 68/361/EEC. The new Standing Veterinary Committee was to operate in accordance with a regulatory committee procedure similar to that established in common commercial policy. But its institutional rules secured member states even more control. A new 'double safety-net' or 'contre-filet' was introduced allowing the Council (by a simple majority) to prevent the Commission from acting even if the Council had not decided within a certain period.

What about the Parliament, the third—indirectly affected—player in the game? It had carefully observed all developments and issued a resolution (October 1967) and several reports expressing its concerns of being bypassed. It restated that new institutional rules were developed that undercut the power of the Commission and thereby indirectly the Parliament's power of political supervision of the Commission. It emphasized that there was a surge in legislative matters that were dealt with in the form of implementing measures and not legislative matters. The most important report, the Jozeau-Marigné Report set out an inventory of implementing measures and developed systematic criteria of their allocation to advisory, management, and regulatory committees. The report considered management and regulatory committees to be compatible with the EEC Treaty because Art. 155 (EEC) does not oblige, but only permits the Council to confer implementing powers on the Commission. Therefore, the Council is entitled to link the attribution of these implementing competences with certain conditions specifying their modalities. The report also acknowledged that the Council reserving to itself the right to decide at last resort is compatible with the Treaty (Jozeau-Marigné Report 1968: 27).

However, the Parliament's Report saw the Commission's executive authority endangered. It argued that the comitology system with its rapidly increasing management and regulatory committees contradicts the idea of the EEC Treaty that the Commission should be the Community's executive authority. The Report also concluded that the Parliament should be granted a 'droit de regard' in order to be informed about matters dealt with in management and regulatory committees and to offer it an opportunity to render an opinion whenever a problem arose that was beyond simple, technical implementation. Yet, the Parliament's wishes were not granted.

When, therefore, a legal challenge of a Commission decision was brought before the ECJ (Case 41/69 *Chemiefarma* v. *Commission*) by a private actor contending that the Commission's decision was of legislative nature, this was very much welcomed by the Parliament. It opened up a possibility of challenging the definition of the scope of the new rules. The Court argued that 'the Council *shall* confer powers on the Commission'. In a second ruling (Case 25/70 *Einfuhr—und Vorratsstelle für Getreide—und Futtermittel* v. *Köster, Berodt & Co*) the ECJ once more confirmed a wide interpretation of what constitutes an implementing measure.

Thus a fourth actor, charged with third-party dispute resolution, entered the scene, throwing its weight into the bargaining process and influencing the outcome. Given that management committees had in the meantime proved to be a well-functioning cooperation between Commission and member states, and given that not only the Council, but also the Commission and indeed the Parliament (in the Jozeau-Marigné report) had come out in favour of them, it would have been surprising if the Court would have condemned them. Instead it confirmed that Art. 155 provides that '... the Commission shall exercise the powers conferred on it by the Council for the implementation of the rules laid down by the latter. This provision, the use of which is optional, enables the Council to determine any detailed rules to which the Commission is subject in exercising the power conferred on it.... The function of the management committee is to ensure permanent consultation in order to guide the Commission in the exercise of the powers conferred on it by the Council and to enable the latter to substitute its own action for that of the Commission' (Judgment 25/70 see above).

Towards the end of the transitional period several economic and social developments in member states pointed to the need of a higher level of integration of monetary and economic policy in 1969 (Commentaries ch. 2, p. 433 CMLRev). Social turbulences in France triggered special safeguard measures, including quantitative restrictions on imports and subsidies for exports and the devaluation of the Franc. Germany imposed a levy on agricultural products and the Bundesbank revaluated the Deutsche Mark (Europe, bulletin quotidien 26.11.1968). A relaunching of integration was strongly promoted by French Commissioner Raymond Barre, however, the Council did not agree on necessary steps (Europe, bulletin quotidien 13.3.1968, 1/2.4.1968) After de Gaulle's resignation in 1969 his successor Georges Pompidou launched an initiative for a Summit Meeting of Heads of State or Government in The Hague. Here member states reached an agreement to close the transitional period by establishing a definitive arrangement for the funding of CAP and a system which would give the Community its own resources, and, more than that, to develop a plan for the creation of economic and monetary union. It was also decided to reopen the negotiations for enlargement (General Report 1969: 17). The crisis was overcome. Pompidou gained broad support for his notion of cooperation emphasizing the concurrent political wills of governments instead of supranational initiatives (French government spokesperson quoted in Bulletin EC 1970: 124). This new spirit was concretized and institutionalized in the regular meetings of heads of states and governments, which became to be known as the European Council. One more time the rule of *synchronization* was invoked in order to accommodate differing interests along parallel lines.

Theoretical Conclusions: From the Establishing of the Management Committee System to The Hague Summit

Which factors drove the changes of the comitology rules in this period? The empty chair crisis strikes as the consequence of an attempt of the Commission, who is not a *designing actor* in treaty revisions nor the revision of the comitology rules, to prompt such an alteration of these rules by boldly moving ahead and proposing changes (regarding rules of revenues and the powers of the Parliament in supervising the budget). This reflects the claim:

H: Shifting levels/arenas to accelerate institutional change
'Given a choice between different levels/arenas of decision-making an actor may, by opting out of one arena and shifting the decision to another, improve his prospects of obtaining an institutional change according to his preferences.'

The result was the empty chair crisis and member states' decision to apply the Luxembourg compromise, to take the Commission at a shorter leash and to chill its political ambitions. The Council competencies in the cooperation between the Commission and the Council in the management committees were strengthened. This outcome—an agreement among member states—may be interpreted in distributive power-based bargaining terms:

H: Institutional change through distributive bargaining
'Given a change of preference of a powerful actor or a change of power balance between actors, an existing institutional rule may be subject to renegotiation in order to alter the rule in such a way as to reflect the (changed) preferences of the powerful actor(s) or the changed power balance.'

The Parliament for its part considered the new procedures as a threat to its own status and its right to exercise political control over the Commission. In the implicit negotiation among the three actors, the Commission did not side with the Parliament against the Council because it had itself a lot to win through the introduction of the committee system. Although it had to share the new competences with national governments, it did gain considerable institutional power. With no formal say in the adoption of the comitology decision, no ally, and no indirect veto power through a linked arena (such as legislation) from which to gain bargaining clout, the Parliament had little impact on the shaping of the comitology rules. It did seek to obtain an institutional gain through supporting of a third-party dispute resolution to settle the institutional conflict over the rules governing comitology and the scope of delegation. The outcome, however, boosted the institutional position of member states. It reflects the general argument made about:

H: Third-party dispute resolution as a source of institutional change
'In a conflict over the application of ambiguous rules, actors may turn to a third party to settle the dispute. The decision of the third party subsequently becomes the authoritative reference point for interaction.'

Another factor playing an important role in prompting institutional change in this period was, once more, *exogenous functional pressure*. Domestic social problems and economic turbulences increased the need for a stronger cooperation among governments inducing them to proceed with integration through comitology procedures (in common commercial policy). This development lends plausibility to a functionalist explanation of why a change of institutional rules was accelerated by external pressure.

H: Exogenous functional pressure and institutional change
'If due to an external event the benefits of rule A have decreased, the rule will be changed, if the gains of the altered rule B including the transaction costs will be higher.'

4.6.3. From The Hague Summit to the Single European Act

The Hague Summit brought two important decisions of the Council: to establish a definitive arrangement for the financing of the CAP and a system that would give the Community its own budgetary resources. It also made a bold effort at renewal by announcing two important projects: to create an economic and monetary union and enlargement. But before long, the spirit of reform had evaporated and Community decision-making process was caught up in stalemate once more. Interestingly, though, during these years of 'political paralysis', the comitology decision-making machinery in CAP continued to churn out implementing decisions.

The Summit meeting at The Hague had established a group of experts, headed by Luxembourg's Prime Minister, Pierre Werner, to specify measures for initiating an economic and monetary union starting in 1970 and to be completed in 1980. Several governments were only willing to issue a nonbinding Resolution to coordinate economic and monetary policies and to accelerate the liberalization of the mobility of persons, goods, services, and capital, to harmonize taxation, and to secure monetary stability by agreeing that central banks should apply more narrow margins for the fluctuation of their currencies than required by the International Monetary Fund (IMF). Since the IMF had difficulties dealing with the sustained turbulences in the international currencies' systems, member states decided to make a renewed effort at an economic and monetary union by introducing a joint mechanism of floating currencies (the 'snake arrangement' (Council Directive 72/156 EEC 21.3.1972)).

In another important step, the accession negotiations for the first enlargement were successfully concluded after overcoming conflicts between France and the UK regarding CAP. The IGC in Luxembourg (1970) had required the applicant states to formally accept CAP, *before* the negotiations could be started. And The Hague Summit Meeting had asked that '... the solution of any problems of adjustment which arise must be sought in the establishment of transitional measures and *not* in changes of existing rules' (General Report 1971: 14; *emphasis added*). In other words, the scope of negotiations was drastically reduced by the requirement that the applicant states must not seek any changes of existing institutional rules.

However, once inside the Community in 1973, Britain sought to alter CAP by opening up the possibilities for trade with non-Community countries. The proposed changes of the sugar market[148] were not realized, but the old conflicts of the time before the Luxembourg compromise re-emerged. Although the Council could have forged ahead with a QMV vote against the opposition of the French, governments refrained from doing so. This attitude was reinforced by enlargement since the right of a Council veto had been a crucial condition for the UK's acceptance of the terms of accession. The 'streamlined veto' had become a fact of life (The Report of the Three Wise Men quote from Bulletin EC 11 1979). What was different, was that, with enlargement, the political balance had shifted away from France. However, in spite of the pressure of the oil shock and ensuing economic recession, governments again failed to reach an agreement needed for the transition to the second stage of an economic and monetary union.

The newly elected British Labour government made another attempt to renegotiate the terms of entry, in particular with respect to CAP.[149] It also refused to participate in financing the Community's own resources, as agreed, until a reform of CAP (Bulletin EC 1974, point 1104) and distrusted an economic and monetary union project that was not based on an agreed final objective. At the Summit Meeting in Dublin (March 1975) Britain obtained significant changes in the regulation of the sugar market as well as a corrective mechanism for the Community's own resources for member states faced with 'unfair financial burdens'.

---

[148] To cut the subsidies for surplus in sugar production.

[149] Which it considered to be a threat to world trade in food products preventing the access of low-cost producers outside Europe to the British food market (Bulletin C 3, point 1104).

The fundamental conflicts of interest, particularly between France and the UK, led to a relative inactivity at the legislative level (Nicoll 1998). At best, recourse was taken to the formula of synchronization and the attempt to solve several disparate problems at one stroke. To overcome the stalemate, the Commission and the Luxembourg Presidency presented an emergency plan to guarantee the most important common interests by proposing informal institutional means changes to avoid the application of a veto. One of them was to confer more implementing powers on the Commission,[150] another one to leave more decisions to COREPER, yet another one that the Council should make decisions without formal voting once it was clear that a majority had emerged. As a result, the Council widened the mandate of COREPER and reached a *gentlemen's agreement* to abstain from formal voting and conferred implementing powers on the Commission (Bulletin EC 6-1974, point 2506). The agreement was officially confirmed at the Summit Meeting in Paris in December 1974.

At the Paris Summit, Leo Tindemans, the Belgian Prime Minister, was asked to prepare a report on the possibility of converting the various fields of common interest into some form of European Union. In his report, Tindemans mainly presented a proposal of how to overcome the present crisis by proposing that the Council QMV should be the normal decision-making mode of the Council and that additional implementing power should be conferred on the Commission. The economic and monetary union should be given a new impetus by introducing a formula of *differentiation* allowing some members to forge ahead and others to wait. This formula would prove to be decisive for the success of economic and monetary union: in 1978 the EMS was introduced based on fixed but adjustable exchange rates allowing the UK to stay outside.

In the meantime there had been a further surge in comitology procedures spreading to other areas of policymaking, and the ECJ had confirmed comitology as a tool for improving the decision-making process. The basic function of all committees is the same: to ensure participation of the national administrations. The way, however, they define the relationship with the Commission when a committee wanted to prevent a measure from being adopted by the Commission differs. In advisory and management committees, the Commission can take its decision even if it does not comply with the opinion of the committee. Only after a measure has been adopted, does the control function of management committees enter into force providing the Council with an opportunity to react. In the case of regulatory committees, the control takes

---

[150] In accordance with Art. 155 EEC 1958.

place before a decision was adopted and the Commission can only take its decision if the opinion was positive.[151]

It was in particular the regulatory committees that rapidly grew in numbers (from six in 1970 to forty-six in 1980). This growth reflected member states' concern that the delegation of power to the Commission could alter the impact of a policy measure in an unforeseen way. In 1977 the ECJ issued a ruling concerning regulatory committees (Case 5/77 Pretura di Lodi) that confirmed the governments' rights of control. As mentioned, the General Programme for the elimination of technical barriers to trade, allowing the Commission to update the content of existing directives, used the regulatory committee procedure. The safety net under this procedure entailed the possibility of the committee to prevent a measure from being adopted. A number of commercial policy directives were agreed on in the Council making use of new regulatory committees such as the Committee on the Adjustment to Technical Progress of the Directives on the Removal of Technical Barriers to Trade in the Motor Vehicle Sector and the Standing Committee on Foodstuffs and the Standing Committee on Feedingstuffs.

In the first of the directives on feedingstuffs, the Commission exploited these rather far-reaching updating powers to the full. The directive provided that member states should ensure that national controls of feedingstuffs were carried out according to common methods of sampling and analysis, leaving their specification to the Commission with the Standing Committee on Feedingstuffs. It soon emerged that governments found it difficult to proceed in the same way with later directives concerning feedingstuffs, such as the directive concerning additives in feedingstuffs. Here, the Council reserved all powers to make decisions to itself and for the Commission to develop proposals together with the Standing Committee.

In the case of *Carlo Tedeschi* v. *Denkavit Commerciale* (Case 5/77), the Italian government had asked the Commission and the Standing Committee on Feedingstuffs to deal with the question of adjusting Council Directive 74/63/EEC by extending the existing list of undesirable substances to include potassium nitrates.[152] The proposal submitted by the Commission was not well received by most members of the Standing Committee on Feedingstuffs. The Commission reacted by withdrawing the proposal and sought independent expertise. Before this was provided, the Italian government formally invoked the application of a safety measure and stopped a truckload of feedingstuffs by Denkavit Commerciale Srl at the border. In response, one of its

---

[151] Some governments demanded that regulatory committee procedure should always be followed if matters at stake had political implications.

[152] That was added in the Netherlands to powdered milk.

buyers Carlo Tedeschi initiated legal proceedings against Denkavit before the Pretura di Lodi. The ECJ ruled that Council could prevent the Commission from implementing the proposal rejected by the Council even if the latter did not put forward an alternative solution. The message was clear: the Commission should focus its efforts on reconciling the differing interests of the member states.

The Parliament's position was ambivalent vis-à-vis this development. On the one hand, as shown above, it saw its own institutional position undermined; on the other, it was convinced that without regulatory committees there would be no integration progress at all. Therefore, rather than blocking the further increase of regulatory committees, it sought to carve a role for itself in the decision-making process.[153]

A new round of enlargement (Greece in 1981, Spain and Portugal in 1986) brought new challenges for the Council decision-making process. Anticipating the new exigencies posed by enlargement, the Commission in its Fresco Report of 1978 urged for an extension of QMV and the provision of a general competence for exercising implementing powers to the Commission. The Council, for its part, formed the Committee of the Three Wise Men[154] to propose an adjustment of institutional rules without any treaty amendments. The Three Wise Men Report of 1979 proposed a more frequent use of QMV voting and argued that the mere prospect of a resort to vote should encourage the Council to join in a compromise. And, of crucial future significance, the power to judge whether and when to vote should become an instrument of the Council Presidency. The report also recommended to delegate more implementing responsibilities to the Commission[155] and to establish a stock formula to cover each of the separate types of committees which could then be selected for insertion without dispute in each individual case. In general they identified a shift of power away from the Commission to the Council and cautioned against reducing the Commission to a secretariat (Report of the Three Wise Men 1979: 51–2).

Gradually, there were signs that the 'veto culture' was beginning to weaken. When the UK threatened to block a decision on increased agricultural spending, the Dutch Presidency called a vote since it did not see the British national

---

[153] See Jozeau-Marigné report above p. 83.

[154] Consisting of the former Dutch Prime Minister Barend Biseheuvel, the former Minister of State of Britain Edmund Dell, and the former Vice President of the Commission Robert Marjolin.

[155] In its view the Council was doing far too much itself, and should better distinguish between major and minor issues. They noted that difficulties were encountered to establish management-type committees in newer policy fields, because member states were afraid that there could be unforeseen political implications in delegating implementing powers in new policy areas.

interest directly affected.[156] When the proposal was adopted, with the UK, Denmark, and Greece not taking part in the vote, a precedent of overruling a vital interest of one government by the vital interest of other governments had been set. For first time, the right to invoke the veto had been questioned and even rejected (see also Palayret, Wallace, and Winand 2006). In the Solemn Declaration (Stuttgart 1983) all governments stated their interpretation of the veto stemming from the Luxembourg Compromise. Belgium, Germany, Luxembourg, Italy, and The Netherlands said that a vote must be called where the treaties allow for it. France and Ireland concurred with the qualification that the vote would be postponed if one or several member states requested it to defend a vital national interest of direct relevance to the subject at stake. Greece, the UK, and Denmark insisted that the discussion must continue until a unanimous decision has been reached where a vital national interest is at stake.

In the continuing debate on institutional reform (Fresco Report 1978, Three Wise Men Report 1979) the Parliament went much further and proposed an IGC to adopt a Treaty of the European Union to reconsider the existing institutional rules. Given the rapid increase of comitology committees from eighty-five (1980) to 154 (1985), it was increasingly concerned that the balance of powers would be upset. While the multiplication of comitology committees on the one hand was a sign that the Council had increasingly made a distinction between major and minor issues, the disputes regularly surrounding the establishment of committees, made the process slow, contested, and unwieldy (Three Wise Men Report 1979). The Parliament therefore reiterated its long-held view that the committees should only be given an advisory capacity and very directly used its consultation right in legislation to insist that provisions requiring cooperation with committees should be deleted or at least made less restrictive. Neither did it hesitate to use its powers of budgetary control, freezing the funding for committees, until specific demands had been satisfied.[157]

The budgetary power also helped the Parliament secure information about the work of committees and their organization. To drive the point home, the Parliament in 1983 froze a part of the Commission's funds until the latter explained the substantial increase in its expenditure for committees

---

[156] Britain had asked for a prior solution of the budget rebate question.

[157] The Parliament's powers of budgetary control had been increased by the Treaty of 1975. The Three Wise Men's Report argued that the main change in the relationship between Council and Parliament is to be traced back to the development of the Parliament's budgetary powers. The non-obligatory expenditure now constituted over 20% of the budget and covered most Community projects and policies apart from CAP (Three Wise Men Report: 74–6). To avoid conflicts in the budgetary process a conciliation procedure (later called concertation procedure) had been introduced by a joint declaration of the three organizations in 1975.

(EP Resolution 16.9.1983). After the Commission had presented a report, the funds were released. As we will see, the Parliament's powers of budgetary control also became a useful weapon in the inter-organizational battle which led to the adoption of the second so-called Comitology Decision in April 1999 and again in 2006.

The most ambitious demands of the Parliament, however, extended to the drafting of a Treaty of European Union. In this draft it proposed that new 'laws' should be introduced as the principal form of legislation to be adopted jointly by Council and Parliament. Thereby the Parliament could get rid of the comitology committees, or at least, give them a purely advisory capacity. Under the impression of the recent surge in the number of committees, it particularly attacked the use of Regulatory Committees when implementing powers were transferred to the Commission to adapt directives to technical and scientific progress allowing for strong member states' control. But it also emphasized that the Commission, with its entrusted powers should not be left without political supervision by the Parliament, and that the latter should be given a droit de regard. Accordingly, the Commission should be obliged to transmit to the Parliament every draft measure which it sent to regulatory committees, thus giving it the opportunity to express an opinion within a specified period of time. This opinion should be sent together with its draft measure to the Council. And in the case of a negative opinion of the committee and a subsequent revision of the decision, the Parliament should be re-consulted. The Commission rejected the Parliament's proposal arguing that it would lead to considerable delays (Bradley 1997: 232).

Independently from the Parliament's demands, the internal disputes concerning CAP and comitology procedures among governments were overcome and a modest reform was adopted under the French Presidency. Mitterrand also committed France to the Draft TEU of the Parliament and became the primary spokesman of a 'relaunch of Europe'. To spur the progress, the European Council at Fontainebleau (1984) made concessions to the UK granting it a budget rebate. The Dooge Committee[158] for institutional reform proposed a simplification of decision-making in the Council, modes of strengthening the legislative participation of the Parliament and increasing delegation of implementing powers to the Commission, however, could not agree on whether to call an IGC to reform the EEC Treaty. National representatives also failed to agree on the question of QMV: the UK, Denmark, and Greece insisted on making better use of existing provisions of QMV and, in case of important national interests, the possibility to invoke the veto. Most representatives, however, wanted to introduce QMV as a general principle. Given this disagreement on

---

[158] Composed of personal representatives of the heads of state and government.

an important institutional question, members decided to focus on economic and monetary union instead.

The new President of the Commission, Delors, known for his strong beliefs in a liberalized and deregulated market, led Margaret Thatcher plausibly to expect that the new Commission would share her ideas.[159] This was confirmed by the White Paper on the completion of the internal market to be achieved until 1992. The ensuing ambitious work programme including 297 proposals for the removal of non-tariff barriers to trade received strong support of governments, but also directed the attention to the need of institutional reform to be equipped for this ambitious project.[160] At first it seemed that member states would settle for a gentlemen's agreement on the extended use of the existing institutional rules. But the Italian Presidency of the EC under Bettino Craxi emphasized the urgency of more far-reaching reforms under an IGC. Pointing out that this required only a simple majority, he pressed for a formal vote, which brought a decision in favour of an IGC.[161]

At the IGC, the Commission under Delors sought to place the institutional question at the centre of the agenda, hoping to shake the conservative consensus and unblock the decision-process on measures required to implement Council decisions. However, Delors was aware of the risk that the Conference could end in deadlock if solely institutional issues were at centre stage. Therefore, the institutional issues were intimately linked with concrete substantive policy proposals designed to bring about progress regarding the internal market, that is the free movement of goods, persons, services, and capital; environment, economic and social cohesion, and research and technological development. The proposal, as all internal market measures, was to be subject to QMV (EEC Treaty 100a). Parallel to this, a limited effort was made to strengthen the role of the Parliament (see Section 4.2).

Before the SEA, the legal basis for the exercise of implementing powers by the Commission had been Article 155 EEC that refers to the Commission's duty to exercise the implementing powers conferred on it by the Council. According to the ECJ's interpretation this did not necessarily entail a *right* for the Commission to exercise implementing powers. Hence, the Council is free to keep implementing powers to itself but also, if conferred to the Commission, to determine the institutional rules governing the implementation by the Commission, such as the obligation to collaborate with advisory,

---

[159] Together with the nomination of Lord Cockfield as Commissioner.

[160] '... The rather sudden return to the question at a moment when Margaret Thatcher—the person who was most hostile to the institutional reform others felt was indispensable—had almost got what she wanted, was not a coincidence but a carefully planned tactic to ... oblige her to commit herself to more than she had intended' (Noel: 4–5, ch. 3, nr. 3).

[161] See also Section 4.2.

management, or regulatory committees. The Commission, not surprisingly, was discontent with this provision because, in its view, the Council all too often tried to deal with implementation matters itself (Commission Proposal to the IGC 1985, n. 221). In the words of Claus-Dieter Ehlermann 'What is so objectionable from the point of view of efficient decision-making is that people systematically re-open the question of what procedure to use and fiddle around with existing techniques in order to limit a little bit more here or there the powers of the Commission, or exercise the right of appeal to the Council. These constant attempts to re-discuss committee procedures are a waste of energy and a waste of resources.'[162]

The Commission therefore proposed an amendment to Art. 155 EEC providing that the Commission would be permitted to exercise implementing or management powers *without* prior authorization from the Council and that the Council should reserve the right to exercise such powers for itself in 'specific cases' only. Committee procedures should be limited and the Commission should get special powers to adopt implementing measures relating to the internal market under the advisory committee, without the prior authorization by the Council. But member states in the past had argued that implementing powers delegated to the Commission would then be outside the purview of the Council and that they were not willing to accept this. Instead, the Council stated in a non-binding declaration that the advisory committee should be given priority to speed up the establishing of the internal market. To underline their views, member states removed the special implementing powers from Art. 155 (Commission section of EEC 1987) to Art. 145 (Council section of EEC) and stated that the Council can reserve implementation powers to itself. However, they also accepted that the exercise of implementing powers must be consonant with the conditions and requirements imposed on the Commission and that the latter should follow rules laid down beforehand in normal legislation adopted unanimously by the Council after the Parliament has stated its opinion. And different from previous provisions, the Council under the SEA is *obliged* (not only enabled) to confer powers of implementation to the Commission.

Theoretical Conclusions: from The Hague Conference to the Single European Act

Which were the most important factors driving the change of the institutional rules governing comitology from the conference at The Hague 1969

---

[162] Oral evidence given by C.D. Ehlermann to the House of Lords Select Committee on the European Communities, 16.12.1986, pp. 18–19.

to the SEA 1986? What emerges as a regular factor driving the emergence and spreading of comitology procedures is the strong functional pressure of new policy tasks, expanding from CAP, to common trade policy, then the project of monetary and economic integration. In other words, a *functionalist (re)design argument* plays an important part in explaining the widening of the application of the comitology procedures: the decision to initiate a project of economic and monetary union pointed to the need to be equipped with a set of institutional rules that could tackle the new tasks. So there was an exogenous factor calling for new institutional rules suggesting that

H: Exogenous functional pressure and institutional change
'If due to an external event the benefits of rule A have decreased, the rule will be changed, if the gains of the altered rule B including the transaction costs will be higher.'

However, redesigning institutional rules was difficult during the Luxembourg compromise. Although multiple reports called for such a reform, change was slow to come about.

The difficulty of adjusting the institutional rules in the light of *new functional demands* is typical for the entire period. However, precisely because the decision-making process had slowed down during the Luxembourg compromise and higher-order rules did not change, the comitology procedures, at some distance from the central political arena, thrived, with decision-makers quietly shuffling along and producing decision after decision. The procedures rapidly expanded into more policymaking areas. The scope of application of the institutional rule on comitology procedures (the Attribute dimension in the terminology of Crawford and Ostrom 1995) was widened. Comitology filled an institutional vacuum resulting from the Luxembourg compromise and responded to the functional need of widened tasks. From an *across level perspective* this points to a *compensating role* of the lower level of comitology, reflecting the hypothesis:

H: Shifting levels/arenas to accelerate institutional change
'Given a choice between different levels/arenas of decision-making an actor may, by opting out of one arena and shifting the decision to another, improve his prospects of obtaining an institutional change according to his preferences.'

The two enlargement rounds constituted additional important sources of external demands which were likely to have an impact on the institutional rules governing comitology. What is notable, though, is that in the first round of enlargement, institutional stability was made a precondition of accession. By committing the new acceding countries, especially the UK, on the institutional rules of CAP *before* even starting the negotiations, and thereby taking the comitology rules off the agenda of the *accession negotiations*, the stability of rules was secured. By asking the applicant states *not* to question the existing institutional rules, the reverse of a flexibility clause (Koremenos 2005), a '*stability clause*' was employed to protect the interests of powerful old members in the accession negotiations. The stability of the institutional rules was maintained *in spite of* the exogenous change of enlargement.

Once the new members were inside, however, the divergence of interests resurfaced and Council legislative decision-making concerning economic and monetary union stalled. At a lower level, by contrast, the decision-making machinery of the comitology system functioned smoothly, regularly producing decisions. For this reason, the informal gentlemen's agreement seeking to overcome the paralysis at the Council level, suggested to move more decisions into the realm of the Commission's implementing powers and to extend the range of application of comitology procedures.

The fact that comitology became so important in driving the decision-making motor of the Community does not mean that its rules stopped being contested, quite on the contrary. The Council and the Commission continued to disagree on the nature of comitology rules. Both of them continued to disagree with the Parliament (until this very day) on what constitutes a matter of delegation or legislation, that is the scope of rule application. In both conflicts the involved actors sought to apply the institutional rule which would maximize their institutional powers (Bergström, Farrell, and Héritier forthcoming). A comitology rule allowing for a more stringent control of member states over the Commission, the regulatory committee procedure, came to be a continuing bone of contest between the Council and the Commission (and the Parliament). The Council favours regulatory committee procedures giving it a maximum of control over the Commission; the Commission and the Parliament, on the opposite, prefer the advisory committee procedure with limited member states' controls. The Parliament favours legislation over delegation because its role in delegation was and still is modest. In this conflict-ridden bargaining process, the Council with its formal powers under Art. 155, clearly had the upper hand. When challenged before the ECJ (*Tedeschi* v. *Prefetura di Lodi*), the Court ruled in favour of the Council, a rule interpretation which, henceforth, was binding for the two actors. Here we see the mechanism of *rule development through third-party dispute resolution* described by Stone Sweet (1999).

H: Third-party dispute resolution as a source of institutional change
'In a conflict over the application of ambiguous rules, actors may turn to a third party to settle the dispute. The decision of the third party subsequently becomes the authoritative reference point for interaction.'

Member states' successful attempt to exert stricter control over the Commission in the latter's application of the implementing powers can be interpreted in terms of *principal–agent theory* as well. Member states/principals seek to prevent the shirking of the agent/Commission by defining institutional rules allowing for a more stringent control of the agent's decision.

H: Agency-loss as a cause of institutional change
'If the divergence between the principal's and the agent's preferences has become too large, the principal will redesign the contract, i.e. change the institutional rule in order to rein in the agent.'

Another attempt at reforming comitology rules was taken in the Three Wise Men Report commissioned by the Council. Addressing the dispute about which comitology procedure to choose, it proposed an adjustment of institutional rules *without any treaty amendments*, such as a stock formulae to cover each of the separate types of committees which could then be selected for insertion without dispute in each individual case (Report of the Three Wise Men 1979: 51–2). This conflict between Commission and Parliament, on the one hand, and the Council, on the other hand, over the selection of a comitology procedure is well captured by Jupille's theory of procedural politics. Each actor favours the institutional rule under which she is provided the strongest institutional competences. The Court rulings, as we have seen, had settled the dispute in favour of the Council.

H: Procedural politics
'Faced with a possibility to choose among different rules, an actor will choose the rule under which she has most formal competences.'

Subsequently attempts were made and are being made—until the present day—to come to a priori classification of problems to be linked to a particular comitology procedure and thereby to prevent 'procedural politics.'

The Parliament, for its part, had observed the rapid increase of regulatory committees with growing concern and sought to curb the development, but unsuccessfully so. In order to, at least, gain some role in the procedure, it used its budget control powers to extricate more information about the comitology procedures. A bargaining theoretical explanation over institutional gains can account for this outcome.

H: Bargaining leverage through arena-linking
'Actor A, using a formal veto in one arena X, can create a leverage in another linked arena Y in which actor A has no formal vote.'

In the meantime at the *level* above comitology, that is the legislative level of the Council, the economic and monetary union project had been resumed.

By providing for a *flexibility clause* (Koremenos 2005), allowing the UK to remain outside the project the diverging views of member states could be accommodated. This reflects the hypothesis:

H: *Flexible contracts allow accommodating divergent preferences*
'With an opt-out rule, a stalled decision-making process may be set into motion again.'

Another round of *exogenous events*, that is the Southern enlargement, challenged again the extant institutional rules of the 'streamlined consensus' and the 'veto culture', and set off a renewed effort at *redesigning the existing rules*, confirming a *functionalist explanation*.

H: *Exogenous functional pressure and institutional change*
'If due to an external event the benefits of rule A have decreased, the rule will be changed, if the gains of the altered rule B including the transaction costs will be higher.'

In these reform endeavours, the Commission (Fresco Report) proposed a significant extension of implementing powers which was much more far-reaching than the proposals put forward by the Council (Three Wise Men Report). The latter suggested a general classification of issues linking them to corresponding comitology procedures. The Parliament, for its part, went much further than both the Commission and the Council, and called for a Treaty reform, that is a change of the higher-order rules, proposing that 'new laws' should be introduced and, as a consequence, comitology committees should be entirely abolished or have only advisory capacity. Having been unsuccessful at the *lower-order level* in influencing the rules governing comitology, the Parliament sought to achieve its ends at the higher level by proposing a draft for a reform treaty (DTEU). This reflects the claim:

H: *Changing arena changes outcomes*
'Changing the arena/level of decision-making with different formal institutional rules may improve the prospects of having an impact on the outcome.'

What emerges from the empirical account, too, is that institutional change involving a shift of power between actors at all levels is most likely to occur when closely intertwined with substantive policy issues, and in particular issues of market integration (see Héritier 1996, 2001). Thus, a change from unanimity to QMV or from the regulatory to the management committee procedure, implicates a shift of power and therefore is highly contested. When linked to substantive policy issues, bargaining space was created that was used for issue linkages and trade-offs, leading to an agreement in spite of the redistributive nature of the institutional issue. Thus when pressing for an institutional reform, Delors linked it to the internal market programme. For its realization, QMV was to be used; and in comitology questions it was informally agreed to use advisory committees only. This reflects the power-based distributive bargaining hypotheses under changing institutional conditions:

H: Distributive, power-based bargaining of institutional change mediated by institutions
'The institutional rules governing the bargaining process make a difference with respect to the outcome, i.e. the changed institutional rule.'
'A wider scope of decision-making issues and simultaneous voting on all issues will lead to more redistributive outcomes of the negotiation process than voting on single issues sequentially.'

4.6.4. From the Single European Act to the First Comitology Decision

The SEA provided that the Council should only be permitted to choose between a limited number of fixed comitology procedures. These procedures were formally established in a Council Decision, the first comitology decision of 1987. It requires the Commisson to discuss the definition of implementation measures with representatives of the national delegations within a committee, which then formulates an opinion.

Even though during the negotiations of the SEA the question of the Luxembourg Compromise had not been explicitly raised, the move to QMV was a clear indication that unanimity voting was to be abandoned. The informal practice that had emerged in the Council over the previous few years, allowing the Presidency to propose a vote, was codified by an amendment to its rules of procedure.[163] As a result, the decision-making process in the Council had become considerably smoother thanks to a regular recourse to voting and thanks to an effective extension of majority voting under the SEA. However, some governments, that is the UK and France, still insisted that the principle of protecting central national interests may be invoked. And the Commission, not having received special implementing powers for the internal market programme, was discontent with the outcome of the SEA. So was the Parliament. It therefore instructed its Political Affairs Committee to make sure that the provisions introduced by the SEA were exploited 'to the very limit'.

In 1986, with the surge in comitology procedures, the problem of delays involved in the choice of committee procedures had become more pressing than ever. There were more than thirty different variants of the basic procedures in operation and the Commission complained that it had to 'wage

[163] The Presidency can also open a voting procedure at the request of a member of the Council or of the Commission, provided that a majority of members of the Councils so decide.

a constant defensive battle against the Council's obsession with committees' (Debates of the EP, 9.7.1986, OJ 1986 Annex 2-341/130). It, therefore, presented a proposal for a Regulation laying down the procedures for the exercise of implementing powers conferred on the Commission. A codification of the three basic types of advisory, management, and regulatory committee procedures should be linked to particular matters. The Commission, anticipating the resistance of the Council, refrained from proposing criteria that would regulate the choice between the fixed procedures, knowing that governments would not accept it. Yet, refraining from the inclusion of criteria of selection of committee procedures meant that the Commission also refrained from proposing principles affecting the Parliament's droit de regard.

As a consequence, the Parliament refused to play along. The Political Affairs Committee presented a report (the Haensch Report) arguing that the management and the regulatory committee procedures jeopardized the 'institutional balance' because they enabled the Council to take back the power from the Commission, thereby depriving the Parliament of its rights to supervisory control over the Commission; and, crucially, contributing to a circumvention of the Parliament's right to participate in the legislative process. In its amendments to the draft of the comitology decision it therefore demanded that the Commission forward all draft measures to the parliamentary committees and, if the Council decided to take back the power, that the Parliament should be involved through consultation (Debates of EP, 9.7.1986: 118–19). It also called for the elimination of the regulatory committee procedure and the introduction of criteria requiring that precedence be given to the advisory committee procedure within the field of the internal market.[164] And, it decided not to deliver a formal opinion, but to refer the matter back to its Political Affairs Committee. Even if the opinion of the Parliament was merely of consultative nature, the proposal could not be adopted before it had been delivered. In the resulting delay it put pressure on the Commission which was anxious to get the new arrangement off the ground as quickly as possible. After some months the Commission 'reconsidered its position on the amendments adopted on 9 July 1986 and stated its willingness to bring it more into line with the position of Parliament' (EP Resolution 23.10.1986 OJ 1986 C 297/94 final). Now the Commission proposed that advisory committee should be given a predominant place in internal market measures and that the procedures of existing committees should be adapted to the new arrangement within a reasonable time. It also made a unilateral commitment to ensure comprehensive information for and consultation by the Parliament about

---

[164] Delors scolded the Parliament for unrealistic thinking. 'You always want the maximum' (Delors in Bergstrom 194).

planned draft implementing measures. Pleased with this development, the Parliament declared its willingness to resume the interrupted consideration of the proposal and delivered its opinion.

The proposal placed before the Council led to a heated discussion and was adopted by unanimity as a Council Decision (87/373/EEC) in mid-1987. The outcome was that close to nothing of the Commission's and Parliament's proposals was accepted by the Council. First of all, the Council chose the form of a Decision, not of a regulation, as proposed by the Commission. This reflected some governments' wish to limit the decision to its immediate addressees, that is the Council and the Commission. The Council also declined to apply the Decision to already existing committees as the Parliament had asked. It was keen to preserve the flexible nature of implementing powers, to establish boundaries only on a case-by-case basis and to avoid general definitions or principles. And more than that, the basic committee procedures proposed by the Commission were enriched by the inclusion of additional and more restrictive variants to the management and regulatory committee procedures. Additionally a special procedure, not explicitly involving the use of committees, had been introduced for the exercise of implementing powers with the so-called 'safeguard measures'.[165]

[165] Under the fixed *advisory committee procedure* the committee's opinion was not formally binding for the Commission. But it should take the utmost account of the opinion. Although expected to deliver the opinion by unanimity, the committee could proceed, if necessary to a vote by simple majority. This procedure is applied in areas where governments wish to leave the Commission with most discretion (competition policy). In an attached declaration the Council promised that this procedure should be given a predominant place within the field of the internal market.

Under the fixed *management committee procedure* the Commission adopts an implementing measure which would apply immediately. Only then would the committee give its opinion. If this were negative, the Commission would communicate the measure to the Council, which could modify or annul it. This procedure has been applied in CAP since 1962. The Commission can choose whether or not to suspend the application of a measure on appeal to the Council. Politically, it would be difficult for the Council to suspend the application of a measure that was already applied. The more restrictive variant of this procedure was used for the first time in 1975 in regional development policy when the Commission was obliged to suspend the application of a measure on appeal.

Under the fixed *regulatory committee procedure* the committee has the power to prevent an implementing measure from being adopted. Only if the committee has given a positive opinion the measure is adopted. In the case of no opinion or a negative opinion, the Commission has to submit a 'proposal' to the Council (without an opinion of the Parliament). The safety net or filet procedure (used for the first time in customs legislation in 1968) provides that, if the Council had not adopted the proposal within a limited period, then the power returns to the Commission which should adopt the proposed measure itself. Under the contre-filet or double safety net (used for the first time in veterinary legislation in 1968), the Council has the possibility to decide by simple majority against the proposed measure, thus preventing the power from returning to the Commission.

The fixed *safeguard procedure* is applied when the Council gives the Commission powers to introduce safeguard measures. The Commission would notify both the Council and the member

The Commission accepted the Council Decision with reservations and deplored the adoption of the restrictive contre-filet procedure which may result in the Commission's being prevented from adopting its proposed implementing measures where the Council failed to reach a decision. It also expressed its reservations with respect to the second variant of the safeguard procedure. Finally, it criticized the Council's failure to fix a deadline, however remote, for bringing the numerous existing committees into line with the principles of the framework decisions (Bulletin EC 6-1987, point 2.4.14). In return, it refused to include the contested procedures in its draft, thereby forcing the Council, to make formal amendments requiring unanimity, but did not withdraw its proposal.

The Parliament, for its part, was alarmed. The new Comitology Decision completely ignored its demands. It therefore marked the starting point for a long battle for parliamentarian competences in comitology, *and*, to set a curb on the increase of delegation. From then on the Parliament systematically used all opportunities when consulted on an (amended) proposal for legislation to ask for the elimination of committee procedures or the use of less restrictive ones. Specific guidelines were adopted to that effect: 'In first reading, Parliament should systematically delete any provisions for procedure III (a) or (b) (filet et contre-filet) and for proposals concerning the internal market put forward under Art. 100a of the EEC Treaty.... In second reading Parliament should continue to oppose any provisions in a common position for procedure III(b), but III(a) could be accepted exceptionally' (Guidelines of the EP cited in Corbett 1998: 258).

The Parliament's right to participate in legislation under the consultation and cooperation procedures did not entail, though, any obligation for the Council to comply with its opinion. Therefore, parallel to these attempts, other strategies were deployed: in 1987 it brought action before the ECJ in which it claimed that Council Decision 87/373/EEC was unlawful since the Council, when adopting it, had infringed the amended Art. 145 EEC 1987 (*Case 302/87 EP* v. *Council*). Before the SEA, committee procedures had been based on Art. 155 EEC providing that the Council is free to confer implementing powers on the Commission, and concomitantly to set conditions. According the amended Article 145 EEC the Council is *obliged* to confer

states of its decision to introduce such measures. Any member state can refer the Commission's decision to the Council. Then the decision adopted by the Commission should continue to apply if the Council by QMV has not taken a different decision within a limited time period. Or alternatively, the Council by QMV could confirm, or revoke the decision adopted by the Commission. If it had not acted within a limited period, the measure is revoked. The safeguard procedure does not require the use of any committee. But, in practice, its use e.g. (in the field of anti-dumping) is linked with the use of an ad-hoc committee.

implementing powers on the Commission. According to the Parliament this meant that the Commission now disposed of originating and autonomous powers in implementation. Therefore, committee procedures reserving the last word to the Council, in the Parliament's view, constitute an illegal attempt to impose conditions on the Commission and impinge on the political supervisory powers of the Parliament. The Court did not take up the issue, but dismissed it on procedural grounds. In its view, the applicable provisions of the EEC Treaty do not enable the Court to recognize the capacity of the Parliament to bring an action for annulment.

At the same time the ECJ was called on to adjudicate in another case, a dispute between the Commission and the Council over the use of the management committee procedure when adopting implementing decisions involving budgetary spending. Even if the matter involved was rather particular, the subsequent ruling had general significance. It confirmed the legality of the Council Decision 87/373/EEC and it made clear that the arrangement for the exercise of implementing powers had become a central element of the institutional legal order (*Commission* v. *Council* 1989 ECR 3457).

The Parliament was more successful in its bilateral dealings with the Commission. As mentioned above, the Commission had conceded to the Parliament an information and consultation right on matters before committee decisions preceding the Council Decision 87/373/EC. The Parliament subsequently sought to ensure that the Commission was keeping its promise. The President of the Parliament, Lord Plumb, sent a letter to Commission President, stating that all draft decisions relating to legislative documents' should be forwarded by the Commission to the Parliament at the same time as they were forwarded to the committees. Delors accepted these terms in a letter sent back to Lord Plumb (Plumb–Delors Agreement of 1988). For the first time a formal concession had been made to the Parliament's lifelong demand for a droit de regard.

Theoretical Conclusion: From the Single European Act to the First Comitology Decision

Looking at this period from the SEA 1986 to the first Comitology Decision 1987 through *theoretical lenses*, a number of factors emerge that may plausibly explain the change of the institutional rules governing comitology. Discontent with the outcome of the SEA, the Parliament announced that it would exploit all possibilities given in the formal rules in order to strengthen its position, that is its determination to *endogenously change the rules by implicitly bargaining for better results* that the SEA had produced. This is reflected in the claim:

H: Institutional change through a formal/informal/formal dynamic
'Formal rules at t1 that are ambiguous give rise to informal rules that further develop the formal rules. These informal rules will reflect the bargaining power of actors, as determined by formal institutions and the fall-back position of the negotiating actors reflected in different time horizons and a different sensitivity to failure.'

The Parliament started to realize this intention when reacting to the Commission draft proposal for a Comitology decision. This proposal anticipating a likely opposition of member states contained a proposal acceptable to the Council, that is not including general criteria for the selection of committee procedures meant to prevent *procedural politics*. This step of the Commission can be interpreted in *institutionalist bargaining terms*, reflecting the hypothesis:

H: Power-induced institutional change with distributive implications
'Given a change of preference of a powerful actor or a change of power balance between actors, an existing institutional rule may be subject to renegotiation in order to alter the rule in such a way as to reflect the (changed) preferences of the powerful actor(s) or the changed power balance.'

At this point the threat of the Parliament to exploit the existing rules to the limits was put into practice. By withholding its opinion on the Commission draft, the Parliament pressed the Commission to alter its proposal and incorporate some proposals of the Parliament. The change of the Commission draft can be interpreted theoretically in terms of *redistributive bargaining theory*, too, where one actor, by refraining from stating her opinion, can delay a process of decision-making and take influence on the substance of a proposal.

While this worked in the bilateral negotiations between *two actors*, that is with the Commission, it totally failed in the case of the Council which all but swept away the Commission's proposal. The *bargaining power* of the Council as the sole formal decision-maker accounts for this outcome. In order to claw back some power, the Commission in its drafts regularly introduced its preferred (least restrictive) comitology variants so that the Council would have to use unanimity if it wanted to replace it.

The Parliament felt totally bypassed and as an ultima ratio turned *to the Court to decide the conflict*. However, the Court was not willing to enter this institutional mining field and dismissed the case on procedural grounds, arguing that the Parliament had no legal standing to bring such a case to third-party dispute resolution. In yet another case, in which the Commission brought a case to the ECJ, the Court ruled in favour of the existing Comitology decision, that is did not bring about institutional change. This development is reflected in the claim:

H: Third-party dispute resolution as a source of institutional change
'In a conflict over the application of ambiguous rules, actors may turn to a third
party to settle the dispute. The decision of the third party subsequently becomes the
authoritative reference point for interaction.'

The Parliament, however, achieved some success in its bilateral negotiations
with the Commission. By withholding the budget funds for comitology, that
is *by using its formal veto power in a related arena*, the Parliament forced
the Commission to grant it the droit de regard under the Plumbs–Delors
agreement.

H: Bargaining leverage through arena-linking
'Actor A, using a formal veto in one arena X, can create a leverage in another linked
arena Y in which actor A has no formal vote.'

4.6.5. From the First Comitology Decision to the Modus Vivendi

Returning to the empirical account of the period from the first Comitology
Decision 1987, the Maastricht Treaty 1991, and to the Modus Vivendi 1994,
it soon became clear that the Commission was discontent with the implementation of the Comitology Decision. The Council did not predominantly
use the advisory committee procedure when realizing the internal market
programme, frequently replaced the advisory committee by a regulatory committee procedure,[166] and extended the use of the most restrictive variant of the
regulatory committee procedure including the contre-filet mechanism into
areas of cooperation. Hence, in the Commission's view, the Council tended to
make decision-making more difficult although the record shows that '... the
Commission has always been able to secure the backing of experts representing
the Member States and the instances referring a measure to the Council in
the absence of support from national experts are virtually non-existent and
the Council has never had to use the blocking mechanism designed to prevent
the Commission intervening in the event of the Council failing to take a
decision' (Commission Report Sept. 1989: 8–9).[167]

---

[166] According to the Commission, the Council opted for the advisory committee for twelve
out of thirty-seven proposals adopted in the field of internal market (Commission Report of
Sept. 1989: 8).

[167] In 98% of the cases in which the regulatory committee procedure had been involved
the Commission had secured the favourable opinion from the committee. In the 2% of cases,
where the matter had been referred to the Council, a decision had virtually always been taken
by the Council and recourse to the disputed contre-filet mechanism had not proved necessary.
With respect to the management committee procedure, in only eight out of 16.248 cases between
1962 and 1978 had the opinion been negative. And of 1,792 cases dealt with in 1988, there had

The Commission's implementation of the droit de regard, in turn, was unsatisfactory in the eyes of the Parliament. Since the status of the bilateral commitment was unclear under the EEC Treaty (Bradley 1997: 273), the 'right' granted to the Parliament only rested on the Commission's will and ability. As a result, the number of matters actually transmitted to the Parliament was relatively small[168] and the Parliament in 1990 adopted a resolution requesting the Commission to improve its performance.

Addressing the Council, the Parliament criticized the extensive use of the regulatory committees, and, as two years earlier, called for another Treaty reform to extend QMV, to increase the efficiency of implementing powers, to grant the Commission more responsibility, and to prevent the erosion of its supervisory powers over the Commission.

In its position for the upcoming IGC the Commission presented a fundamental overhaul of the existing arrangements by introducing a hierarchy of legal acts (Bulletin ECD Supplement 2-1991). Accordingly, 'laws' would be used in all fields of cooperation to determine the fundamental principles, general guidelines and the basic elements of the measures to be taken for their implementation. All other matters should be considered as implementation and would be covered by regulations or decisions. The adoption of Laws would be reserved for the Council and the Parliament under the new co-decision procedure, the adoption of regulations and decisions would be left to the Commission. Regulatory committee procedure would be abolished and replaced by a substitution mechanism under which the Council and the Parliament would be permitted to act in place of the Commission if they considered that the Commission was exceeding its powers or straying from the guidelines allowing them to block its entry into force. If either of the Council or the Parliament would object, the Commission would adopt a new regulation itself or present a proposal for regulation which would be adopted like a law. While both the European Council in Dublin and Rome had supported the claim to give the Commission a greater executive part in the implementation of Community policies, in the eyes of most member states this Commission proposal was overly ambitious. Yet, the Council was aware of the overcomplexity of the comitology system and the need of an institutional reform and, therefore, included a provision in the TEU declaring that a new IGC in 1996 would, among other questions, review a possible classification of Community Acts.

---

been 1.665 favourable opinions and 127 failures to give an opinion (Commission Report Sept. 1989: 9).

[168] Only 171 of 400 relevant draft measures during the first three years were transmitted and the Parliament received no indication of the time constraints involved in each case making it difficult to react (EP Resolution 19 April 1991).

Even though the TEU did not change the rules on the exercise of implementing powers, it was to have far-reaching implications for the future development because of the introduction of co-decision: the Parliament had received the right to block legislation. Prior to the entry into force of the TEU (Nov. 1993), the Parliament in a bilateral agreement with the Commission (the Klepsch–Millan agreement of 1993) had obtained the promise that the Commission would forward to the Parliament all draft measures relating to the implementation of structural funds.

After the adoption of the TEU, the Parliament did not lose time to emphasize its views on the implications of the co-decision procedure on comitology. It argued that now, being an equal partner in legislation, it was no longer acceptable that the Council reserve exclusive competence in the exercising of control over implementing powers. The latter, therefore, should no longer fall under Art. 145 EC 1993 referring to acts the Council adopts, rather both Art. 145 and Art. 155 should have been amended. Until this revision, only consultative committees consisting of national experts advising the Commission should be allowed. Moreover, the Parliament insisted that its droit de regard should be formalized and that, under a hierarchy of legal acts, a substitution mechanism should be introduced which would allow the Council and the Parliament to cancel implementing legislation. While the Commission welcomed the proposal, the Council's reaction remained cool.

In order to lend pressure to its claims, the Parliament launched an offensive: it had always sought to replace the regulatory committee procedure by a less restrictive procedure. But since it had lacked the formal power of asserting its view, it rarely was successful. With the introduction of co-decision this had changed. During the first year of operation of co-decision, the 'issue was fought out on each individual item of legislation' (Corbett 1998: 258, 347, 348). The precedent was set in the very first case dealt with under co-decision, the Open network provision to voice telephony. The Council replaced the advisory committee procedure by a regulatory committee procedure. The Parliament asked for a shift back to the original advisory committee procedure, as well as provisions to secure its droit de regard and a substitution mechanism. The Council did not accept these amendments and the conciliation committee was convened.[169] The conciliation negotiations ended in a deadlock; and the Council reintroduced the Common Position which was rejected by the Parliament in July 1994. Commissioner Bangemann called on MEPs not to fight their battle against comitology on individual substantive items. The Commission sought to settle the conflict by proposing an 'inter-institutional

---

[169] Apparently the Commission also rejected the amendments aiming at giving the Parliament a supervisory role with respect to the exercise of implementation powers.

agreement' on the exercise of the power of implementation to be adopted jointly by the Parliament and the Council. The agreement distinguished between legislative and non-legislative measures. For the latter advisory and management committee procedures should be employed, excluding the restrictive variant of the management procedure (IIb) and the regulatory committee. A substitution mechanism would be introduced allowing the Council and Parliament to agree to repeal an implementing act. Quite obviously, the agreement would have left the Commission in a stronger position. Not surprisingly, the draft agreement was rejected by governments.[170]

Under the impression of the intensifying conflict the Council Presidency proposed a compromise. The governments would commit themselves to examine the question of implementing powers in the upcoming IGC 1996. For the time being a modus vivendi should meet the demand for a droit de regard of the Parliament, while preserving the existing arrangements for implementing powers. As a reaction, the Parliament decided to place a substantial share of the proposed budget for committees in the reserve, in order to underline its role in the negotiation of the modus vivendi. It was signed by the Council, Parliament and Commission in December 1994 and provided that the Commission inform the appropriate parliamentary committee when adopting a measure and, in case of amendment, a second time; that the Council shall adopt a draft general implementing act only after informing the Parliament and take the latter's opinion in due account. What was new is that the Council confirmed not to adopt a draft general implementing act without first informing the Parliament and hearing its opinion. For the very first time the Council had placed itself under a direct obligation to the Parliament.

Theoretical Conclusion: From the First Comitology Decision to the Modus Vivendi

Which *theoretical insights* regarding the process of institutional change can be drawn from this period? The fact that the Council—to the discontent of the Commission—insisted on the regulatory committee procedure although committee decisions are almost always accepted, allows for two conclusions: the Council insists because it pursues institutional interests and does not want to forego the strong institutional position in regulatory committees. The high degree of acceptance of the committee decisions very likely derives from the fact that member state representatives strongly influence the work of the

---

[170] 'Under the cover of contributing to resolving a dispute, the Commission was first and foremost seeking to free itself of the constraints of Council Decision 87/373/EEC and secure largely uncontrolled implementing powers to itself' (Interv. Council Secretariat, March 2006).

committees. Committee decisions being an outcome of a collaborative effort, there is no need to object.

The Parliament deeply discontent with the outcome of the First Comitology Decision immediately urged for a *change of rules of a different order, that is a treaty change*, hoping to have more of an impact at the higher-order rule level.

H: Changing arena changes outcomes
'Changing the arena/level of decision-making with different formal institutional rules may improve the prospects of having an impact on the outcome.'

While all three actors agreed that the present process, in view of the tasks to be tackled, was not efficient enough and needed to be revised, that is that there was a *functional pressure to redesign the existing institutional rules*.

H: Exogenous functional pressure and institutional change
'If due to an external event the benefits of rule A have decreased, the rule will be changed, if the gains of the altered rule B including the transaction costs will be higher.'

They, however, disagreed on the specific aspects of the desired change. In preparing the Maastricht negotiations the Commission submitted a very ambitious plan of establishing a hierarchy of legal acts, clearly serving its own institutional interests. It was all but ignored by member states, the sole designing actors, in the negotiations, reflecting the claim of

H: Power-induced institutional change with distributive implications
'Given a change of preference of a powerful actor or a change of power balance between actors, an existing institutional rule may be subject to renegotiation in order to alter the rule in such a way as to reflect the (changed) preferences of an actor or the changed power balance.'

Yet, one higher-order rule change introduced in the Maastricht Treaty, co-decision, was to have a strong impact on the altering of comitology rules. Under the new co-decision procedure, the Parliament has a veto power in the legislative process. This provides the Parliament with an important lever to influence the institutional rules in the comitology arena, as well. It immediately set out to use this power in the open telephony case, blocking a substantive issue in order to obtain a change of institutional rule in comitology. This development is well explained by *redistributive power–based bargaining theory*. And in a further step of hostage taking, the Parliament froze the budget funds for comitology to take influence on the content of the modus vivendi. The strategy was successful. The Parliament obtained a formalization of the droit de regard agreed on in the modus vivendi. The Council, for the first time, committed itself directly to the Parliament in comitology matters. This development is captured by the hypothesis on:

H: Bargaining leverage through arena-linking
'Actor A, using a formal veto in one arena X, can create a leverage in another linked arena Y in which actor A has no formal vote.'

4.6.6. From the Modus Vivendi to the Amsterdam Treaty

Returning to the *empirical development* of the comitology rules, it can be shown that after the agreement on the modus vivendi in 1994, the Parliament was willing to accept the Directive on the Open Network, although the substance had remained the same and the Council had insisted on changing the advisory committee procedure into a regulatory committee procedure.

The Parliament considered the modus vivendi to be a step into the right direction, but wanted to see it applied to consultation and cooperation procedures, as well. As before, to underline its wishes, it used its powers of delay: it postponed votes and insisted on re-consultation whenever amendments were introduced by the Council, to emphasize its wishes. In the instance of legislation on ambient air quality (Council Directive 96/62/EC), the Parliament took almost two years to deliver its final opinion.

One consequence, paradoxically, was that both the Council and the Commission increasingly sought to circumvent the Parliament in legislation and to shift matters of potential controversy into the area of implementing legislation. This was explicitly acknowledged by Advocate General Philippe Léger in February 1995 (Léger Case C-417/93) who simultaneously emphasized that this should only be tolerated in areas of subordinate character and that the legislative participation of the Parliament was to be protected.[171] But the Court also made it clear that it was not prepared to support the Parliament's fight against the Council and the Commission. In the notorious power to delay question, the ECJ ruled that the Parliament was not entitled to complain when legislation was adopted before it had stated an opinion if it had failed to discharge its obligation 'to cooperate sincerely' with the Council. The Court

---

[171] In 1980 the Court had stated that the participation of the Parliament in legislation was an essential factor in the institutional balance. Since the Parliament had no standing before the Court, it had to rely on others. In 1987 the Court had declared that an annulment action at the suit of the Parliament was admissible if the latter seeks to safeguard its prerogatives. After that, the Parliament flooded the ECJ with applications, many of them relating to legal basis for legislation. But many of them also concerning procedural matters where the Parliament sought to secure interpretations which would make it difficult for the Council and the Commission to circumvent it. In several rulings during the 1990s the Court reconfirmed that the participation of the Parliament in the legislation was an essential factor in institutional balance and specified the duty to re-consult the Parliament if the text finally adopted departs substantially from the text on which Parliament had already been consulted.

also reduced the right to reconsultation with respect to the choice of committee procedure when amendments had been made. And most importantly, the Court in a number of rulings delimited implementation acts from basic acts in such a way as to encourage the Council and the Commission to circumvent the Parliament (C 156/93 *EP* v. *Commission* and C-417/93 *EP* v. *Council*). In the first case on organic production of agricultural products the Court showed passivity concerning the Parliament's concerns that important issues were included in implementation issues. In the second case implementation was interpreted very widely. The implications of these two rulings were far-reaching. Even if a provision was placed in legislation adopted under a normal procedure, it could be considered to be implementing in nature and therefore, made it possible for the Council, or the Commission to modify it under a simplified procedure which excluded the participation of the Parliament. In principle this did not only apply to consultation procedures, but also cooperation and co-decision procedures. Thus, the Court had curtailed the Parliament and had provided the Council and the Commission with a weapon for the future.

The application of the Parliament's droit de regard under the modus vivendi suffered from the same practical application problems as the Plumb–Delors and Klepsch–Millan agreements. Only a smaller part of the draft measures were transmitted to the Parliament. The Parliament reacted to this by placing 90 per cent of the proposed funding for committees in the reserve while demanding from the Commission a list of the matters these committees had been involved in during the previous year. The Commission swiftly produced an almost 2,000 page report listing 355 committees involved in the exercise of implementing powers. As a result, the Parliament released 50 per cent of the funds, and the other 50 per cent after the report had been studied. However, it pointed out that the information did not allow to assess whether the committees had acted within their mandate. In a resolution on the report the Parliament requested the Commission to set out guidelines for all executive committees to indicate the date of meetings, the terms of the advice given as well as the voting results. It also demanded that committees in general should meet in public. When the Commission did not meet these expectations, the Parliament continued to place the expenditure for committees in the budgetary reserve. Finally, the controversy ended when in 1996 an agreement (Samland–Williamson Agreement) was concluded meeting these demands plus allowing for a possible committee attendance of MEPs.

In preparing the revision of the Maastricht Treaty the Reflection Group focused on the classic issues of the extension of QMV and co-decision, but also on a possible hierarchy of legal acts and the rules for the exercise of implementing powers. Most member states favoured a minimal reform. The Commission and the Parliament, by contrast, were united in demanding an establishment of a hierarchy of legal acts. The Westendorp Report presented by the Reflection Group contained two conflicting positions: a number of representatives favoured the introduction of a hierarchy of legal acts and the granting of executive powers to the Commission, whereas the large majority of members rejected these proposals. All agreed, however, that a simplification of committee procedures was necessary. The European Council welcomed the report. Before the IGC could start, the Parliament had to be consulted. The Parliament stated that the Westendorp Report could not be considered as a sufficient basis, restating the need for a hierarchy of legal acts and of a simplification of the maze of comitology procedures. In the negotiations member states were not willing to consider an amendment to Art. 145 EC (now renumbered Art. 202 EC) and limited themselves to a declaration attached to the Treaty that requested to submit a proposal for amendments of the first Comitology Decision of 1987 by the end of 1998.

Theoretical Conclusions: From the Modus Vivendi to the Amsterdam Treaty

From a *theoretical viewpoint*, the change of the comitology rules between the modus vivendi and the Amsterdam Treaty was driven by the renewed delaying strategies applied by the Parliament. Co-legislation of basic acts was used as a lever to change the institutional rules governing comitology, a strategy well captured by *redistributive power-based bargaining theory*.

H: Bargaining leverage through arena-linking
'Actor A, using a formal veto in one arena X, can create a leverage in another linked arena Y in which actor A has no formal vote.'

One response of the Commission and the Council was to *change arenas* and to shift more issues from the legislative into the implementing/comitology arena, or to put it differently, to widen the scope of the comitology rules. Here the Parliament held no direct *blocking power*. This Commission/Council strategy is reflected in the hypothesis on:

H: Changing arena changes outcomes
'Changing the arena of decision-making with different formal institutional rules may improve the prospects of having an impact on the outcome.'

In the resulting conflict the Parliament turned to *third-party dispute resolution*, that is the ECJ. The Court in several rulings came down on the side of the

Council inviting the Parliament, when being consulted, to 'sincere coopera-tion'; moreover, delimiting normal acts and implementing acts in such a way as to encourage the circumvention of the Parliament. The authoritative inter-pretation of the institutional rule by a third party in this case confirmed the *institutional* status quo and did not drive institutional change favouring the Parliament. This interpretation would subsequently serve as point of reference in the interaction of the three actors in their negotiations.

H: Third-party dispute resolution as a source of institutional change
'In a conflict over the application of ambiguous rules, actors may turn to a third party to settle the dispute. The decision of the third party subsequently becomes the authoritative reference point for interaction.'

Another point of criticism from the Parliament's viewpoint concerned the implementation of the droit de regard included in the modus vivendi. To press for an improved practice it, once more, used the leverage of freezing comitology funds until a new agreement (Samland-Williamson 1996) was found. This—albeit—small institutional change extending to the droit de regard can be accounted for in terms of *distributive, power-based bargaining theory:* By using its blocking power in a linked arena, the Parliament obtained a change of the institutional rule that was to its advantage as claimed in hypothesis:

H: Bargaining leverage through arena-linking
'Actor A, using a formal veto in one arena X, can create a leverage in another linked arena X in which actor A has no formal vote.'

Finally, the ambitious demands of the Commission and the Parliament to establish a hierarchy of legal norms at the highest level of rule-making, the IGC, was not taken up in member states' negotiations. They shifted the question of comitology rules to the *lower level* of a mere amended Second Comitology Decision to be decided within a year. *Bargaining theory* accounts for this outcome. Since it is the member states which solely decide on the outcome of Treaty revisions, the ambitious proposals of the Commission and the Parliament which would have reduced the controlling power of mem-ber states over comitology, remained unsuccessful. This corresponds to the hypothesis:

H: Institutional change through distributive bargaining
'Given a change of preference of a powerful actor or a change of power balance between actors, an existing institutional rule may be subject to renegotiation in order to alter the rule in such a way as to reflect the (changed) preferences of the powerful actor(s) or the changed power balance.'

4.6.7. From the Amsterdam Treaty to the Second
Comitology Decision

As required by the Amsterdam Treaty, the Commission submitted a proposal for a revision of the First Comitology Decision. However, instead of proposing amendments, it aimed at an entirely new decision seeking to make the system less complex and to develop rules for existing and future committees. With respect to the regulatory committee procedure, a thorn in the Commission's flesh, it proposed that, if a draft-implementing measure was not approved by the committee, the Commission would present a proposal in the normal legislative process (instead of placing a proposal before the Council). For the Commission this would have offered the advantage of getting rid of the controversial contre-filet mechanism, would have strengthened its own right of initiative and made the system more open to parliamentary control. The Commission also drew up general criteria for choosing different procedures, similar to the logic of a hierarchy of legal acts according to which the scope of a measure would determine between legislative or executive authority. It also suggested a formalization of the Parliament's droit de regard. The latter would receive the agendas for committee meetings, the draft implementing measures within the area of co-decision, and the results of committee voting and matters transferred to the Council.

The Commission formally submitted its proposal to the Council in July 1998. The Parliament was consulted and submitted its view in the Aglietta Report. The report stated that the Commission's proposal was too complex and failed to render the system transparent, and that it would undermine the co-decision procedure. Also, according to the Parliament, too many matters were dealt with under implementing matters. It therefore asked for a voice in implementing decisions under co-decision and the insertion of substitution mechanism in order to able to repeal an implementing measure. The Commission, bearing its own institutional interests in mind and anticipating resistance from member states which in their majority favoured only a modest reform, did not oblige and incorporate the demands of the Parliament.

Therefore, the Parliament, which had been highly supportive of the Aglietta Report, launched an offensive to obtain a modification of the proposal. Members of Parliament from all camps urged their colleagues 'to be very careful with regard to any olive branches held out by the Commission' (Brian Crowley in Debates of EP of 15.9.1998) warning that the demand for reform of the committee system was a vexed issue with a legacy which had been passed on from one generation of MEPs to another and that it was time for a 'rupture' with the status quo. Instead of issuing an Opinion which would have closed the procedure of consultation for the amendment of the Comitology

Decision, a resolution was adopted in which the guidelines were laid down for further negotiations with the Commission and the Council. Yet, the strategy of delay was not as effective as in the consultation over the First Comitology Decision since the Commission was not as hard pressed as in 1987 when the Decision was a pre-condition for implementing the internal market. The power of delay was also diminished by the fact that the ECJ had decided that the right of consultation did not apply when the Parliament failed to discharge 'its obligation to cooperate sincerely with the Council' (see above p. 210). Therefore, the Parliament to lend more emphasis to its demands, used an additional lever through its power of budgetary control, and in November 1999, put just over half of the appropriations for committees in the reserve '... in order to maintain pressure on all sides to come to an equitable and effective solution on the new comitology structure' (EP Resolution, 17.12.1998 on the Draft General Budget of the EU for the Financial Year 1999).

In March 1999 the Parliament's Committee on Institutional Affairs had presented a revised version of the Aglietta Report. It requested that the Parliament be given an equal share of the powers of political supervision in the field of co-decision, called for the abolition of the regulatory committee, the delimitation of the substantive scope of implementing measures, as well as a protection mechanism for the legislative sphere consisting of a right to revoke a decision in the area of co-decision and, within the other areas, a right 'to blow the whistle'. As it happened, the second Aglietta Report and the draft Resolution were debated in Parliament on the same day it approved the nomination of Prodi for President of a new Commission, very likely an intentional coincidence. In the new Commission, the Commissioner responsible for relations with the Parliament, Neil Kinnock, supported the claims of the Parliament. While the Council still refused to make concessions, the Commission unilaterally offered the Parliament a right 'to blow the whistle'. But the Parliament aimed for a legally binding mechanism to protect the legislative sphere. Richard Corbett, one of the MEPs who was most actively involved in the negotiations, said 'I warn the Council that ... if the working group continues to be so restrictive on Parliament's rights to intervene, then there will be no agreement and we will continue in legislative procedure after legislative procedure to block the comitology measures and resist the adoption of such restrictive measures and we will be very restrictive on voting the budgets and the credits to allow comitology-type committees to continue to meet. We are not seeking to take powers to ourselves to intervene in the detail but we are seeking to have the safeguard. That safeguard is very important. It is the principle on which we will insist and unless agreement is reached in this matter I can tell Council that co-decision procedure after co-decision procedure will have to go all the way to conciliation and time after time there will be difficulty on this problem' (Corbett in the Debates of the EP of 5.5.1999).

Before delivering their opinion, the MEPs were advised by Neil Kinnock that they should prioritize their requests. The Council would be more likely to accept a mechanism for the protection of the legislative sphere if the Parliament—in return—would reconsider their rejection of the regulatory committee procedure or at least limit the rejection to the double safety net provision.[172] MEPs could be convinced and supported the proposal for a new comitology decision subject to some amendments. They were the same as in the second Aglietta Report except for the statement regarding the regulatory committee procedure: 'maintaining regulatory committees would be unacceptable unless the double safety-net procedures were abandoned'. For the first time the Parliament had showed some willingness to accept the regulatory committee procedure.

The Council, finally, accepted a simplification of the comitology procedures albeit not along the ambitious lines proposed by the Commission. Under the management committee procedure the restrictive variant was eliminated: the Commission could adopt a measure which would apply immediately. If the committee should give a negative opinion, the Council would be able to abolish the measure within three months (previously one month). In a declaration attached to the new Decision, the Commission also promised not to abandon its practice to secure a decision mustering the widest possible support within the committee. The regulatory committee procedure was simplified. It could still actively approve a draft before the Commission could adopt it. If not, the Commission had to submit a proposal which the Council could adopt (and amend or oppose by QMV). The latter was a novelty introduced to replace the contre-filet mechanism. The Commission would have to re-examine the proposal and either amend it or submit a new one. As regards the existing committees, the Council decided to authorize the continuous operation of the old procedures. It, however, agreed to adjust the old procedures on a case-by-case basis in the course of normal revision of legislation. The decision for the case-by-case practice could serve as an instrument to discipline the Parliament which the Council was not willing to forfeit.

The Parliament was by no means satisfied with what it had obtained in supervising implementing powers in the area of co-decision. It therefore sustained its resistance and threatened with intensified conflicts under co-decision. Member states finally conceded the Parliament the right to 'blow the whistle' if it felt that a draft implementing measure or a proposal submitted to the Council under the regulatory committee procedure was exceeding the powers conferred on the Commission in the field of co-decision.[173]

---

[172] Giving the Council the right of rejecting a proposed executive measure without proposing its own.

[173] If that was the case, the Commission would have to re-examine the measure and either submit a new draft proposal or present a proposal for normal legislation.

What mattered particularly to the Parliament was the development of systematic criteria for a distinction between legislative and implementing measures and, in the case of implementing measures, for the choice of a fixed committee procedure. Some member states were very hesitant to follow this line and proposed a case-by-case procedure. The outcome did not depart much from the Commission's proposal which had listed criteria relating to the management and safeguard procedures meant for 'management measures', and for regulatory committee procedures meant for measures of general scope designed to apply essential provisions of basic instruments or to adapt or update certain non-essential provisions of basic instruments. The advisory committee procedure, finally, should be applied in all situations where the management and regulatory procedure were not considered appropriate.

The Parliament's right of information however was replaced by a legally binding commitment that it would receive the committee agendas for draft implementing measures and the results of voting submitted within the area of co-decision.[174] Provisions to better inform the public were inserted as well: the rules for access to documents would be the same that are applied to the Commission. As regards the 'whistle-blowing mechanism', it was agreed that the Parliament could state its protest within one month after the date of receipt of the final draft of an implementing measure when it deemed that a measure was exceeding the powers conferred on the Commission.

After the adoption of the Second Comitology Decision in 1999, the Parliament released the appropriations that had been put into the reserve. It insisted, however, on the drawing up of an inter-institutional agreement defining rules of good conduct for the implementation of the Decision. The implementation rules with respect to the droit de regard were formulated as an agreement between the Commission and the Parliament (Fontaine–Prodi Agreement 2000).[175]

Theoretical Conclusion: From the Amsterdam Treaty to the Second Comitology Decision

What emerges as the most salient factor of change in this period is the reinforced *bargaining power* of the Parliament. This increased bargaining power is reflected in institutional changes favouring the Parliament. The bargaining power derives from a twofold basis: the Parliament's formal power under co-decision and its budgetary control. By skilfully linking the power in each of the arenas (co-decision and budget control) to the arena where the new

[174] It was also granted a summary record of meetings and list of the authorities and organisations to which the committee members belonged.
[175] The modus vivendi, the Plumb–Delors and Samland–Williamson agreements were thereby superseded.

comitology rules were negotiated, it could increase its influence in the latter although it formally had a mere consultative role. By threatening with 'inter-institutional conflicts' and by stalling the legislative process it obtained a for-malized droit de regard and right of whistle-blowing. This entire development can fully be accounted for by a *redistributional power-based bargaining theory of institutional change*.

H: Bargaining leverage through arena-linking
'Actor A, using a formal veto in arena X, can create a leverage in another linked arena Y in which actor A has no formal vote.'

4.6.8. From the Second Comitology Decision to the Nice Treaty and Lamfalussy Reform

Soon after the Second Comitology Decision of 1999 entered into force, the 'institutional leftovers' from Amsterdam moved centre stage. These institu-tional questions had become ever more pressing in view of the imminent large enlargement round. The more numerous and diverse member states' interests would be, the more difficult decision-making, even under QMV, and, presumably, the more delegation through decision-making in comitology would become necessary.

A significant institutional innovation of comitology decision-making occurred in the context of the Lamfalussy reform which created new con-troversies between member states, the Commission, and the Parliament. A committee chaired by Alexandre Lamfalussy,[176] presented a procedural reform which would enable speedy adoption of legislation within the field of financial securities markets. New framework legislation was to be adopted that would be linked to a delegation of powers to the Commission subject to comitol-ogy under the regulatory procedure and an enhanced consultation of market actors. Yet, some member states hesitated to so extensively delegate powers to adopt implementing measures, now that comitology procedures made it more difficult to block the Commission. They only agreed to do so after the Commission had re-committed itself not to decide against the predominant views in the Council. The Parliament, too, stated its concern and asked for a callback right if dissatisfied with the delegation, dissatisfied not just with the scope of implementing measures, but with the substance of the measures.

Only after one year of negotiations was a compromise reached: the Com-mission accepted that the Parliament should have three months to examine draft implementing measures instead of one, not just with respect to scope

---

[176] The former president of the European Monetary Institute.

but also on substance. It also promised to include a 'sunset clause' in the proposal for framework legislation, fixing a specific date at which delegation would automatically expire. The compromise reflected the Parliament's willingness to accept delegation and comitology for pragmatic reasons, but only if, in return, it would be granted a real power to exercise its responsibility for political supervision. As we will see, the sunset clause in 2005 would serve the Parliament as lever to press for a reform of the Second Comitology decision.

Theoretical Conclusions: From the Second Comitology Decision to the Nice Treaty and Lamfalussy Reform

From a *theoretical perspective* the institutional change observed between the Amsterdam Treaty (1997) and the Nice Treaty (2001)/Lamfalussy reform clearly fits the explanatory pattern of a functionally driven need for reform caused by external changes (i.e. enlargement and the speeding up of decision-making in the rapidly changing internationalized financial markets). This reflects the claim:

H: Exogenous functional pressure and institutional change
'If due to an external event the benefits of rule A have decreased, the rule will be changed, if the gains of the altered rule B including the transaction costs will be higher.'

The particular content of the institutional rule may be accounted for by a *power-based redistributive bargaining theory*. By using its power under co-decision, the Parliament could take influence on the framework directive defining the Lamfalussy reform and introduce a sunset clause allowing for the reconsideration of the entire framework after a certain period of time. This corresponds to the hypothesis:

H: Bargaining leverage through arena-linking
'Actor A, using a formal veto in arena X, can create a leverage in another linked arena Y in which actor A has no formal vote.'

The delegation of decision-making tasks to the Lamfalussy committees can also be theoretically interpreted as an act of delegation of decision-making powers under *principal–agent theory*. The principals, Council, and Parliament, delegate decision-making power to the committees (Varone et al. 2006). The principals, in particular, the Parliament, sought to ensure an adequate control over the agent by establishing institutional rules, that is the sunset clause and the droit de regard. This corresponds to the hypothesis:

H: Agency loss as a cause of institutional change
'If the divergence between the principal's and the agent's preferences has become too large, the principal will redesign the contract, i.e. change the institutional rules, in order to rein in the agent.'

4.6.9. From the Nice Treaty/Lamfalussy Reform to the Convention/Constitutional Treaty and the Revised Second Comitology Decision

Given the extensive enlargement, the call for further institutional reforms had by no means abated. Two further debates, one of smaller scale, the other of a large scale, had an impact on the institutional rules governing comitology: the Commission's White Paper on Governance and the Constitutional Treaty. In the *White Paper* the Commission called for a reform of its implementing powers along the model previously proposed. Legislation would be reduced to essential principles and framework legislation, called 'laws', to be jointly adopted by Council and Parliament. The regulations or decisions necessary to implement legislation would be adopted by the Commission, subject to the supervision by the Council and the Parliament by means of a 'call-back system'.

Another effort at reform in 2002 proposed amendments to the Second Comitology Decision. This Commission proposal basically sought to transform comitology from an arena of member states' participating in the exercise of implementing powers, into an arena for the 'legislature' (Council and Parliament) supervising the 'executive' (the Commission) whose autonomy was to be strengthened (House of Lords Select Committee 31st Report 1.7.2003). More specifically, the Commission proposed to more rigorously define the criteria for the choice of committee procedure. The regulatory committee should be used whenever the executive measures are designed to implement essential aspects of the basic instruments, that is laws, or adapt certain aspects of them; the advisory committee procedure was to be used when the executive measure has an individual scope. The new regulatory committee procedure would have two phases: the 'executive phase' is the same as the under the Second Comitology Decision of 1999, with the only difference that, in case of an unfavourable or no opinion of the committee, the Commission would not have to submit a proposal to the Council; during one further month the committee, using QMV as a decision-making rule, should make another attempt to come to a solution. In the 'supervisory' phase, the final draft would be submitted to the Parliament and the Council. If objections were raised[177] the Commission

---

[177] With absolute majority in the Parliament and QMV in the Council within one month extendable to two months.

would be left with two options: to enact the measure, possibly amending its draft to take account of objections, or to present a legislative proposal under the co-decision procedure.[178] The Commission submitted its proposal to the Council. One month later, the Parliament initiated the consultation process and immediately rejected the provision that the Commission *could*, but *did not have to* take into account the amendments of the Parliament and the Council. The Commission was not willing to yield on the regulatory committee procedure and the Parliament refused to accept that the Commission was free to adopt an implementing measure even if it was not in line with the views of the legislator. However, somewhat surprisingly it then accepted the Commission's proposal, very likely because it placed all its hopes in the imminent Convention. The revised Commission proposal stated that, in case of the Parliament and the Council objecting to a draft measure, the Commission may choose between (*a*) a modification of the draft, (*b*) the presentation of a legislative proposal, (*c*) the adoption of its draft without change, or (*d*) the withdrawal of the draft measure (Commission proposal April 2004).

In the *Convention*, the working group chaired by Giuliano Amato proposed a classification of legal instruments that would be clear to the European public: basic laws should be called framework laws and laws, regulations, and decisions should be reserved for implementation. The most prominent views were stated by Jean Claude Piris (Council), Michel Petite (Commission), and Koen Lenaerts (ECJ). Piris did not advocate a radical reform, but supported a mere renaming of the legal instruments, arguing that, given the existing convolution of legislative and executive authority, a radical reform would cause an imbalance between the Council, Commission, and Parliament. Petite supported a clear separation of power and the introduction of a hierarchy of legal acts while Lenaerts proposed to categorize procedures according to their being suited for legislative or executive functions. Legislative acts would contain the essential elements and should be adopted by the Council jointly with the Parliament. Executive acts should comprise delegated legislation or executive acts in the strict sense and would include specific subcategories: (*a*) the updating and modifying of legislative acts; for technical adaptation the Commission would be responsible on the basis of power granted in legislative acts and (*b*) the day-to-day management would be in the hands of the Commission. Under both procedures comitology would be applied. For executive acts in the strict sense, 'light comitology' would suffice, for delegated legislation 'heavy comitology' should be used including a strict control of the Parliament with a 'call-back'

---

[178] Moreover, the existing provision allows the Parliament an 'ultra vires' statement, i.e. a measure exceeding implementing powers would be abolished because the Parliament—under co-decision—could object both on scope *and* substance to a draft implementing measure.

right in certain cases. The final report of the Amato working group, which was to impact the final text of the Draft Constitutional Treaty adopted by the Convention, proposed a hierarchy of legal acts: legislative acts, called laws and framework laws, and non-legislative acts, that is delegated acts and implementing acts taking the form of regulations and decisions. The working group introduced the delegated acts as a 'new category'.[179]

While the working group had proposed that implementing decisions would be the only acts in which comitology would continue to apply, the presidium insisted that comitology would have to take into account that the Council was not any longer the only legislator, but that the Parliament is the co-legislator. Therefore, the procedure for defining the principles and rules of comitology should be shifted to co-decisions. This would have important implications: not only was the most controversial question discussed under comitology cut out and re-introduced under delegated acts,[180] but also what was left required principles and rules which the Parliament had to agree to. As a result, this meant that comitology was likely to be stripped of everything but its purely advisory functions.

In the plenary discussion the Chairman of the presidium noted that there was a broad agreement to adopt a hierarchy of legal acts and a distinction between legislative and non-legislative acts. At the same time, though, diverging views on details were expressed, many of them relating to delegated regulations. However, only some of the amendments induced the presidium to incorporate changes in its original draft. This draft was adopted by the plenary in June 2003. The text provided that the legislative acts would have the form of laws or framework laws, the non-legislative acts regulations or decisions. To control the executive there would be (*a*) a mechanism of control on a case-by-case basis through a right of 'call-back', that is to retrieve the right to legislate by the Council or Parliament; (*b*) a period of tacit approval: if the Council and the Parliament have not raised objections, the delegated acts will enter into force; and (*c*) a sunset clause: delegated acts would have a limited period of duration to be extended by the Parliament *and* the Council.

During the IGC, the hierarchy of legal acts was not taken up and renegotiated. The final version now states in Art. I-36 that, where uniform conditions for implementing legally binding Union acts are needed, European laws and framework laws may delegate to the Commission the power to adopt delegated European regulations to supplement or amend non-essential elements of the laws and framework laws, or in duly justified cases in Article I-40 to the Council. The essential elements are reserved to laws and framework laws.

---

[179] However, all decisions under these acts can also be made in acts covered by implementation, i.e. to flesh out the details or amend certain elements of existing acts under Art. 202.

[180] Which are subject to different types of controls, see above p. 221.

European laws and framework laws shall lay down the conditions to which delegation is subject, these conditions include the Council's and Parliament's right to revoke the delegation. The delegation regulation may enter into force only if no objection has been expressed by the Parliament or the Council within a period set by law or framework law. For this purpose, European laws shall lay down in advance the rules and general principles of controlling the Commission's implementing powers.

What is new with the introduction of the new hierarchy ('essential' v. 'non-essential' elements) is to define the most controversial group of measures currently covered by the notion of implementation, that is those which supplement or amend non-essential elements of legislative acts, as a new subcategory to non-legislative acts, the *delegated acts*. However, the matters to be dealt with in delegated acts are already dealt with in acts adopted under the arrangements of Art. 292 (ex 145) EC. The important difference between the existing type of delegated acts and those foreseen in the Constitutional Treaty relates to procedures and, in particular, the mechanisms of political control. Today, the acts are adopted, either by the Council itself (in specific cases) or, most commonly, by the Commission subject to comitology and the most restrictive procedure: the regulatory committee procedure. If the Constitutional Treaty should enter into force many of these acts will be adopted by the Commission alone (those which supplement or amend non-essential elements). Therefore, the new hierarchy of legal acts constitutes far more than a mere 'simplification'. It will have the effect of bringing about a fundamental reform of the arrangement in Article 202. This is what the Parliament and the Commission wanted, but the Council rejected. In short, one reading of this outcome is that—unnoticed by most Convention members because hidden behind the complexity of the Treaty provisions—the distinction between delegated and implementing acts under the category of non-legislative acts, helped the Commission achieve a considerable increase of competences in comitology by practically getting rid of a long-time thorn in its flesh, the regulatory committee procedure. However, as Bergström (2005) alternatively argues, there is nothing in the new provisions formally excluding comitology with respect to both implementing *and* delegated acts.

Given the failed confirmation of the Constitutional Treaty in 2005, the *revision of the Second Comitology Decision* became relevant again. The Parliament, by refusing to renew the Lamfalussy framework legislation under the sunset clause and by blocking individual financial market legislative items under the Lamfalussy system,[181] exerted pressure for a re-submission of a proposal for

---

[181] In the decision on Basel II on capital adequacy regulation (Report Radwal) the Parliament accepted only an abbreviated sunset clause until 2008. In 2008 the Lamfalussy framework legislation will expire and will be reconsidered (Interview Parliament February 2006). Richard Corbett in his report to the EP on the revision of the Second Comitology Decision stated: 'Time passed

the revision of the Second Comitology Decision. The urgency of the matter was underlined by a decision of the Parliament to withhold part of the budget for committees (Interview EP February 2006). The Commission resubmitted its proposal (of 2002) seeking to shift the logic of comitology from being national input into the exercise of implementing powers, to being supervision by the 'legislature' over the 'executive', and in line with that, to strengthen the autonomy of the Commission. But according to the Commission itself, the main objective of its proposal was to 'take account of the European Parliament's position as a co-legislator ... placing on an equal footing the European Parliament and the Council as supervisors of the Commission's exercise of the implementing powers' (Expl. Memorandum for Commission Proposal of 11.12.2002).[182] The central features of the proposal were found in the inclusion of criteria for the choice of committee procedure and a reform of the regulatory committee procedure which would provide the two arms of 'the legislature' with equal opportunities of control. The exercise of implementing powers would be split into two parallel regimes: one for matters falling outside co-decision and another for matters falling inside. This is indeed what the Parliament had always been asking for since the birth of the co-decision procedure. But the envisaged reform of the regulatory committee procedure would open up a new possibility to the Commission itself to adopt implementing measures regardless of objections from either the Council or the Parliament. The Council would no longer be permitted to prevent a proposal from being adopted (the contre-filet mechanism) (Commission Draft Nov. 2005). As noted by the then British Minister for Europe, Denis McShane, the Commission has tried in the past to 'secure this licence', but the Council has always resisted (House of Lords Select Committee on the EU, 22.3.2004: 20/21).

The Council[183] while it was aware that some sort of reform had to be undertaken to please the Parliament and 'buy' support for another period, in particular with respect to the Lamfalussy deadlines/sunset clauses, was rather sceptical with respect to the Commission's intentions. There was close to unanimous agreement in the Council that there should only be a limited reform focused on regulatory committees and the question of normative quality. In particular, it emphasized the need to meet the Parliament's wishes to define criteria to delimit the scope for implementing measures of 'legislative' or 'quasi-legislative' quality, but at the same time wished to preserve room for

and the Council did not progress with the Commission proposal ... until the Parliament started to introduce ... "sunset clauses" ... especially in the financial markets sector ... ' and 'Parliament increased pressure on the negotiations as branch of the budgetary authority by withholding funding of comitology committees' (Corbett 2006: 7–8).

[182] For the Council Decision amending Decision 99/468/EC.

[183] The matter is dealt with in the 'Friends of the Presidency Group on Comitology'. This entity is conducting the negotiations which formulate the Council's formal opinion (Interview Council February 2006).

manoeuvre for itself. It was willing to concede in the case of quasi-legislative decisions, that is where not purely executive decisions are at stake, that the Parliament (and the Council) should be granted more competences to block a decision or some *ex post* opportunity of control (Interview Council Feb. 2006) extending the period from one to three month(s).[184]

But there was profound unwillingness to extend the Parliament's right to review matters dealt with under the regulatory committee procedure from procedural into substantive (Interview Council February 2006). Support for this position is found in a recent opinion from its Legal Service which reasserts the Council's treaty based right to exercise delegated 'executive' functions and not merely 'legislative' functions (thus contesting the 'separation of powers' logic of the Parliament and the Commission). Importantly, a corresponding right is lacking for the Parliament (Interview Council February 2006).[185] The proposal of MEPs attending committee meetings was rejected as well.

In July 2006 the Council in its Decision agreed to introduce the 'regulatory procedure with scrutiny, which allows the legislator to oppose the adoption of draft measures ... where the drafts exceeds the implementing powers provided for in the basic instrument ...' (Council Decision 2006/512/EC).[186]

Theoretical Conclusions: From the Nice Treaty to the Third Comitology Decision

Looking at the period from the Nice Treaty 2000 to the revised Comitology Decision of 2006 through *theoretical lenses*, how can the change of comitology rules theoretically be accounted for? Under the impression of the imminent enlargement by ten/twelve new members, the pressure of revising institutional rules in order to allow for decision-making among a larger and increasingly diverse number of actors, the Commission put forward its White Paper and indeed the Convention was scheduled to propose a reform of the Treaty. A *functionalist (re)design explanation*, therefore, does play a role.

H: Functionalist transaction cost-based argument
'Given an exogenous event raising the costs of the institutional rule A, the rule will be changed if the net gains expected of a changed institution B, including the transaction costs of both negotiating the institutional revision, collecting information and maintaining the new institution, are higher than the benefits of the existing institution A.'

---

[184] It is interesting to note that the Council has broached the idea to ask the President of the Parliament for a commitment in return for any concessions, such as a statement 'we have now ended the conflict over comitology'.

[185] Art. 202 excludes a delegation of executive power to the EP.

[186] Since the Decision comprises several ambiguous terms, e.g. whether a regulatory procedure with scrutiny covers the specification of existing basic instruments, it very likely will be subject to bargaining in daily application and interpretation by the ECJ.

The Parliament being consulted on the contents of the White Paper was not quite happy with the extensive comitology reform proposed by the Commission clearly strengthening the latter's position. With the prospect of the imminent *higher-level negotiations* in the Convention, however, it muted its doubts and placed all its eggs in the Convention basket. The Convention process represents a new institutional rule of redefining higher-order institutional rules. Under these new rules the Parliament, for the first time, would have a full-blown formal role in the renegotiation of the Treaty and therefore more clout in changing the institutional rules governing the comitology procedure. This calculation is reflected in:

H: Changing levels/arenas changes outcomes
'Changing the arena/level of decision-making with different formal institutional rules changes the outcomes of the decision-making process.'

And, indeed, the hopes of the Parliament were borne out. The working group on the hierarchy of norms proposed a revision of comitology rules which, because of the complexity of the provisions and the higher saliency of other institutional issues, such as the Commission and Council Presidencies, was not unravelled in the IGC negotiations. It amounted to a significant shift of power in favour of the Commission and the Parliament by practically doing away with the regulatory committee procedure. What we observe here is an *institutional change through obfuscation* which went unobserved by most participants. By shifting a type of delegated implementing decision into the exclusive remits of the Commisson, and thereby abolishing the supervision power of the Council, the Commission (and the Parliament) gained considerable institutional ground in comitology.

The failed referenda in France and the Netherlands cut this institutional development short. In the absence of a new Constitutional Treaty, the Parliament revived the plans of a reform of the Second Comitology Decision. The Commission's proposal, one more time clearly geared towards an increase of its own competences, utilized its—by now—classic set of strategic tools to take influence on the contents of the proposal: it froze comitology funds and blocked decisions in related legislative arenas. By blocking issues in another related arena and redefining the possible choice of options, the Parliament successfully influenced the outcome of the revision of the Second Comitology Decision. This strategy of influencing institutional change is reflected in the hypothesis:

H: Bargaining leverage through arena-linking
'Actor A, using a formal veto in arena X, can create a leverage in another linked arena Y in which actor A has no formal vote.'

4.6.10. Conclusion: Comitology

The dominant pattern which emerges when one scrutinizes the institutional change in comitology over this period of more than forty years is a pattern of *exogenous functional pressure* that induces actors to engage in institutional re-design. The particular form this institutional change takes can be explained in terms of a *power-based distributive bargaining process* producing specific institutional rules. While member states as the *designing actors* with the sole formal decision-making right clearly held the upper hand in these negotiations, the Parliament, by withholding its acquiescence to decisions in other linked arenas (budget matters and co-decision), increasingly managed to take influence on the outcome. It would also make the utmost to exploit the adopted formal rules by renegotiating them and *modifying them endogenously* in their daily application to its own advantage by taking hostage of issues in other, linked arenas.

If conflicts over institutional change could not be handled through bargaining processes, and stalled, one of the involved actors, usually the less powerful one, *turned to third-party dispute resolution*, that is the court, hoping for a verdict favouring its own institutional interests. The authoritative statement of the appropriate interpretation of the rule in question or the confirmation of a choice of one of several possible rules (*procedural politics*) by a third party would then guide the subsequent rule application.

Periodically, under the condition of a strong functional exogenous pressure, the weaker negotiation partner also advocated the shifting of the institutional reform to a higher-order, that is the Treaty level, in order to improve the prospects of realizing her own institutional targets.

Finally, observing different *levels* of decision-making simultaneously, it emerged throughout the period that if decision-making processes stalled at the legislative level, the producing of decisions at the lower implementation level remained steady or increased, suggesting a compensatory relationship between the two levels.

5

Conclusion: Explaining Institutional Change in Europe . . . and Beyond

This book set out to raise questions about the causes, processes, and outcomes of institutional change in the European Union. Different theories were presented and discussed that focus on different causes and processes of institutional change. None of these theories claims to account for institutional change under any and all circumstances. Rather, the explanatory power of a particular theory comes to bear under particular scope conditions typical for the context in which the change takes place and typical for the object of change. The change of institutional rules in the European Union occurs under relatively clear-cut circumstances and the objectives of change are relatively well defined, the number of actors is limited, they interact frequently and are expected to do so well into the future. These circumstances are reflected in the assumptions of the theories which have been discussed to account for institutional change, that is rationalist institutionalist theories.

In discussing the different theories a number of perspectives were taken that may be helpful in viewing institutional change over a longer period of time: The first perspective relates to the underlying *process* of change and its theorization. Is the process of change triggered by *exogenous* factors or *endogenous* factors? What drives the change? How do different types of changes link over time and add up to typical sequences? From a 'structural' perspective the question has been raised whether the change cuts across *different levels and arenas* of institutional rule-making and what *types of actors* are involved in the process of change. These two perspectives describe the *process and structure* of institutional change.

In the empirical part, the empirical stories of change of important decision-making rules in Europe were scrutinized through the lenses of the theories discussed in the first chapter. The question raised was: considering the empirical development of this particular rule, which theoretical interpretation(s) of change discussed in the third chapter has or have most explanatory traction to account for what happened in the instance of this particular rule development? The five institutional rules that were studied are not representative in the statistical sense for the totality of institutional rules in Europe. However, they constitute key institutional rules governing the decision-making process in the European Union and they differ in their attributes. While most of the institutional rule changes are redistributive in nature, that is shifting power from one actor to another, others are efficiency enhancing, that is all involved actors benefit from the institutional rule change. Their developments over a longer time period (almost fifty years) offer insights into institutional changes under varying external circumstances.

The aim of this chapter is to draw conclusions from the theoretical interpretation of the five empirical cases. In the following I (*a*) briefly outline the typical features of the longer-term change of each case and its theoretical explanations; (*b*) compare the developments of the institutional rules across cases; (*c*) point out which important aspects of the empirical stories were not exhibited by any of the theories discussed in the first chapter; and finally (*d*) I indicate the scope conditions of the theories that have been employed and raise the question whether the theoretical insights gained on the basis of the five case studies may be extended to processes of institutional change beyond the European Union.

5.1. THE LONG-TERM INSTITUTIONAL CHANGE OF THE FIVE RULES

5.1.1. Institutional Rule One: The Change of the Parliament's Role in Legislation

What, in a nutshell, were the main driving forces behind the significant, if not speedy, expansion of the Parliament's rights in legislation from consultation to co-decision over a period of almost fifty years? From the *process* perspective, typical patterns appear in the long chain of changes. A first typical *sequence A* of linked changes that is labelled *endogenous formal/informal/formal (adjudication) rule change* consists of (*a*) an extant formal institutional rule leading to (*b*) a negotiation of informal rules that are guiding the application of the formal rule; ensuing conflicts over the informal rules are (*c*) authoritatively settled through third-party dispute resolution which subsequently guides the application of the formal rule; or alternatively (*d*) the informal institutional rule is formalized. A *distributive power-based bargaining theory of endogenous institutional change* may explain the first step in this sequence. Thus, by exploiting given formal rights to the widest possible extent, that is by delaying decision-making processes, the Parliament was able to gain some informal institutional territory. The practice of the Parliament gave rise to a conflict between Parliament and Council and was submitted to third-party dispute resolution, that is the ECJ. The Court decided in favour of the Parliament in the Isoglucose case; the rule change occurred through third-party dispute resolution over a conflicting rule interpretation. The authoritative interpretation became the reference point for the further rule development. This step in the sequence of changes is well grasped by the *theory of rule development through adjudication.*

A second pattern, *sequence B,* labelled *exogenous functional pressure/redesigning formal/informal/formal rule change* emerges from the empirical story. It starts out from a strong *exogenous* problem pressure leading to (*a*) a functional redesigning of the formal institutional rule; the latter is followed (*b*) by an endogenous renegotiation of the formal rule with the aim of introducing an informal rule. This informal rule (*c*) may subsequently be formalized or not in a formal treaty revision. More specifically, exogenous factors, such as the completion of the internal market and monetary union and various enlargement rounds triggered rounds of redesigning of existing formal rules. This corresponds to the *functionalist argument* that new tasks alter the cost–benefit calculations regarding existing institutional rules and, after calculating transaction costs, actors may be willing to redesign the existing institutions. Once these rules have been formally adopted in a treaty revision, the daily application of the rule engenders new informal rules which in a next round of formal rule revision may be confirmed in a *bargaining process* in the context of *unanimity rule.*

A slight variation of *sequence B* is *sequence C,* labelled *exogenous functional pressure/informal rule/formal rule change.* It equally starts out from a functional problem pressure which leads to the emergence of an informal rule alteration that may subsequently be formalized, depending on the power constellation underlying the bargaining process. To give an example: under the new co-decision rule, the necessity to attend to the large bulk of items in which the Parliament now played a role, spurred early agreements as an endogenous informal institutional rule speeding up the process. The terms of the early agreement procedure were negotiated in a power-based bargaining process and subsequently formalized under the Amsterdam Treaty.

What this case shows, as well, is that—given a high external functional pressure—an immediate scheduling of another higher-order rule revision tends to *reduce the attempts of endogenous informal rule changes.* There were, for instance, no attempts of the Parliament to informally extend its competences between the Amsterdam and the Nice treaties; its ambitions of rule change were entirely focused on the formal higher-order rule level. Similarly, the Nice Treaty being immediately followed by the Convention and IGC of 2004 siphoned off efforts at an endogenous rule change.

From a *structural perspective* (*levels and arenas of change and types of actors*), the case demonstrates that the *multilevel* aspect of change plays an important role for the dynamics of institutional transformation. The Parliament, tired of the only modest success obtained at the level of intra-treaty changes, shifted its ambitions of institutional reform to the higher-order level and, indeed, the meta-rules, that is the rules about higher-order rule-making. It was successful in setting the agenda for a treaty revision by constantly reiterating its requests for a treaty revision and was supported in these claims by the new functional requirements of the Single Market Project. Moreover, the Parliament strongly advocated the Convention method under which it obtained the status of a designing actor and engaged in the changing of treaty provisions. However, the shift to another level or arena as such would simply open up another opportunity of change, but by no means the guarantee of a change in the desired direction.

In order to exert some pressure on the direction of formal institutional change in an arena without a formal voice, such as the IGCs, the Parliament took recourse to a linked-arena veto. It established a link between the arena of redesign and another arena in which it does have a formal vote. By withholding or rejecting the decision in the latter, it exerted pressure on the decision in the first. To give an example: the Parliament, by delaying its decision in an arena of daily Community policymaking (refusing budgetary means, delaying the delivery of an opinion in consultation) or by forming an alliance with other formal veto-players (national parliaments or individual member state governments), attempted to influence the decision in a higher-order rule arena. This strategy of influencing institutional change is well captured by *strategic bargaining theory in a given institutional context.*

The distinction of actor types offers further insights. The *designing actors* of higher-order institutional change are the member states only. The Parliament is only an *implementing actor.* Because it does not have a voice in the designers' arena, it has an incentive to engage in a process of *endogenous institutional change between* treaty revisions to shift powers in its own favour. At the same time it constantly sought to gain direct access to the table of the designing actors. But it was not until the Nice IGC that the Parliament was informally accepted 'at the table', but only in the preparatory phase. Under the Convention process it finally gained the status of a formal designing actor in drafting the Constitutional Treaty.

Alternatively to the rational institutionalist account of the expanding role of the Parliament in legislation, one could hypothesize that a normative socialization process has occurred in the course of which the democratic legitimation argument convinced the Council and the Commission to yield power to the Parliament. Being the only directly elected political body and, therefore, able to refer to its direct democratic legitimation did help the Parliament to push its cause. This reflects the argument of *sociological institutionalism* that a change of institutional rule comes about through the force of normative ideas. Yet, bearing in mind the multiple obstacles the Parliament had to overcome in order to achieve its institutional objectives and to how many bargaining and pressure strategies it resorted to in order to achieve its purpose, makes it seem questionable whether the normative power explanation by itself would be sufficient. The democratic legitimation argument was certainly used by the Parliament to push its goals. This explanation would be perfectly compatible with the argument of strategic bargaining. What becomes evident is that the *functional causes* of rule change, that is the new exigencies of the Single Market Programme and the democratic legitimation arguments were linked in a bargaining process. Some member states were only willing to shift the competencies necessary for the completion of the internal market to the supranational level if this shift would be connected to a strengthening of the power of the Parliament.

5.1.2. Institutional Rule Two: Council Presidency

The most pervasive *process* feature of the change of the rules governing the Presidency is a relatively smooth adjustment to new external functional demands. This adjustment primarily occurred through the development of informal rules which subsequently were formalized without much controversy. Why was such a smooth development possible?

We predominantly find *sequence C exogenous pressure/informal/formal rule change*, consisting of an external problem pressure (*a*) giving rise (*b*) to an informal rule which, in turn, (*c*) was formalized. The change of this rule was driven by the external pressure of increasing policy tasks and widened membership. They gave rise to the incremental emergence of informal rules. In some instances the informal institutional rules were subsequently formalized, such as in the agenda-setting function of the Presidency or the submitting of a Presidency's programme.

Viewing the *process/sequence* through theoretical lenses, a *functionalist redesign explanation to save transaction costs* seems plausible. Crucially, the institutional change did not imply a redistribution of power. This is because of the rotation principle which limits the power purveyed on the Presidency to six months. By equally distributing the power of the Presidency among member states, large or small, the rotation rule prevents the decision-making process from being subject to conflicts. As a consequence, the adjustment of the institutional rules in the face of new challenges occurred effortlessly in incremental informal steps which, subsequently, sometimes were formalized, but again without great difficulty. One may conclude, therefore, that the informal rules served to *increase the efficiency* of the Council decision-making process in view of increased exogenous demands.

Charging the Presidency of the Council with chairing the decision-making procedure within the Council can also be theoretically interpreted in terms of *principal–agent theory*: member states delegated this task to the Presidency. With delegation, the principals also seek to ensure that the preferences of principals and agents do not diverge too much, therefore, some measures of control were introduced to control the agent's activities and to secure the credibility and continuity of policymaking, for example by introducing the troika, and a long-term strategy programme.

From the *structural perspective*, if the informal rules that had been developed in daily application would subsequently be formalized at the level of higher-order rules, the institutional change occurred across levels, for example when the Presidency's right to set the agenda was formalized. As regards the *types of actors* involved, the *designing actors*, that is member states, are also the *implementing* actors. Due to this and the fact that a coordination problem was at issue, there was no incentive for the designing/implementing actors to engage in an attempt at endogenous interstitial institutional change to shift power.

The empirical account points to two general features that were not theorized in the first chapter on theories of institutional change. One concerns the change of the institutional rules originating in increased interorganizational interaction. Pressure to change the rules within the Council resulted from increased interaction with other Community bodies in particular with the Parliament. With increasing interactions under the cooperation and co-decision procedures, the Presidency gained in power because the bargaining with the Parliament is centred in the Presidency. Increasing interaction with another organization in joint decision-making strengthens the actor controlling the exchange of information with the other organization. Again—thanks to the rotation principle—the other member states allowed for this concentration of power in the Presidency.

This general insight can also be conceived of in terms of unexpected effects between two institutional rules. A new institutional rule (co-decision) contributed to a change of the internal rule within the Council. This was reinforced by another impact of co-decision: the Commission's need to incorporate the Parliaments positions into its draft diminished the latter's role in acting as broker among member states in the Council. This in turn contributed to the strengthening of the role of the Presidency of the Council as a broker between diverse member states' interests.

5.1.3. Institutional Rule Three: the Parliament's Investiture of the Commission

The Parliament, virtually 'out of nothing', obtained a formal voice in the investing of the Commission, that is it achieved its institutional objectives in this redistributive question at the cost of the relative power of the Council. The main factor prompting the change was the Parliament's determined institutional self-promotion combined with a linked-arena veto, that is an endogenous mechanism of change. The typical pattern corresponds to *sequence A endogenous formal/informal/formal rule change* consisting of (*a*) a given formal rule as a starting point which is followed by (*b*) the extensive unilateral interpretation of this rule by the Parliament and the implicit bargaining of an informal rule with the Commission. In this bargaining process the Commission yielded because the Parliament, by applying a linked-arena veto, had the upper hand; (*c*) then member states, depending on their preferences, and the given decision-making rule would accept or reject the informal rule.

This sequence follows two theoretical explanations: the first explanation is based on the *distributive power-based bargaining explanation* arguing that within a given formal institutional rule, the daily application of this rule consists of an implicit bargaining process among the involved actors and that this process gives rise to an *endogenously driven informal change of institutional rule* in which the actor with the better fallback position prevails. The second step of the sequence, that is the formalization or non-formalization of the new informal rule, may, again, be interpreted in terms of *distributive power-based bargaining theory*.

From the *structural* viewpoint (types of actors and levels/arenas), institutional change clearly occurred across levels: the informal institutional change was bargained at the level of rule application. The latter, subsequently, was decided on at the level of higher-order rule change (treaty revision). What is noticeable from the perspective of the involved actors are two things: in the first part of the sequence (formal/informal) none of the designing actors was involved, only the implementing actors, that is the Commission and the Parliament. The Parliament unilaterally 'issued' a change of rule in the parliamentarian rules of procedure, then, by using pressure and threatening to delay the process by withholding its opinion, forced the Commission to accept the new informal rule. Once the Commission had obliged, it gained practical importance. In the second part of the sequence, the *designing actors*, the member states, entered the stage and, as the sole designing actors, decided about whether or not to formalize the informal rule. This pattern of informal change, initiated by *implementing actors* (Parliament and Commission), which then, in order to be formalized, must be accepted by a different set of actors, the *designing actors* (the member states), is a recurring feature in the long-term change of the Parliament's role in the investiture of the Commission. The *disconnection* between implementing actors seeking a change and the designing actors overwhelmingly resisting change plays an important role in spurring change.

We can also identify *sequence B*, that is *exogenous functional pressure/redesigning formal/informal/formal rule change*. (a) The scheduled formal change responds to an external problem pressure (enlargement) and prompted the Parliament to strong lobbying activities in order to obtain an institutional change in its favour at a higher-order rule level; once the new treaty provisions had been adopted, (b) attempts at endogenous rule change were initiated through the formal-informal dynamic; and, finally, (c) a (non)formalization of the endogenously developed informal rule was decided by the designing actors. More specifically, the Parliament supported in its lobbying by some formal veto-players at the national level (national parliaments), influenced the agenda of the formal treaty revisions. The diverging preferences of member states in the negotiations of the Maastricht Treaty were accommodated in a compromise between member states. Once formalized under the Maastricht Treaty, the new formal rules were endogenously changed by the Parliament which, in an implicit bargaining process with the Commission, transformed the right of consultation into a de facto vote of confidence. The Parliament drew its bargaining power from its formal right of a vote of confidence on the *entire* Commission, that is applied a linked-arena veto. Since member states had split preferences and the Parliament exerted pressure through its veto-right, the outcome of the formal negotiations under the Amsterdam Treaty was moderately beneficial to the Parliament. The President, previously nominated solely by governments after consulting the Parliament, was now to be nominated by common accord of the governments of the member states, with the nomination having to be approved by the Parliament.

From a theoretical perspective, this *sequence B* begins with a functionalist explanation of a problem-driven (re)designing of existing formal rules. The type of rule change is explained on the basis of distributive power-based bargaining which unfolds in a given institutional context. Once the formal rules were adopted, a process of endogenous change set in, which again is interpreted as an implicit bargaining process, in which the Parliament gained leverage through arena-linking, that is threatening to block the decisions in a linked arena (the confirmation of the Commission in its entirety).

The *structure (types of actors and levels)* of institutional change is characterized by a disjunction of *designing and implementing actors*. The *implementing actor* undertook continuous and systematic efforts to endogenously change the rule at the level of rule application in such a way as to gain power, and then pressed the *designing actors* to formalize the rule at the higher-order treaty level.

Another such *sequence B* of *endogenous formal/informal/formal rule change* occurred after the Amsterdam Treaty. The Parliament unilaterally changed the rule of 'approbation' of the Commission President into a right of 'election'. It also set out to secure a right to confirm individual Commissioners, using the vote of confidence for the entire Commission as an expedient. By threatening not to confirm the Commission as a whole, it informally obtained a quasi-right of investiture of the individual Commissioners. The question of whether to formalize this informal rule (along with others) was moved to a higher level of rule change in the Convention. Here the Parliament held the status of a designing actor allowing it to take more influence on the higher-order rule change.

The theoretical explanations used to account for this renewed occurrence of *sequence B* are the same as above, except for the last step, that is the formalization of the informal institutional rule by the Convention. The formalization of some of these gains under the Convention method may in part be attributed to arguing and persuasion following rules of deliberation that are described in sociological institutionalist theories. The same process of deliberation, however, could also be regarded as a first integrative bargaining phase in which actors are trying to push out the Pareto frontier and find solutions benefiting all concerned before passing on to status quo oriented defensive bargaining. Even if in some working groups of the Convention deliberation may have prevailed, the fact that the difficult redistributive institutional issues were bracketed and shifted to the IGC, shows that these questions were not subject to a solution through deliberation resulting in convergent actors' preferences.

Cutting across *levels and arenas* played an important role in bringing change about. The fact that the Parliament established a link between different issue arenas (selection of the Commission President and the selection of the Commission as a whole) proved to be very effective in extending its rights in the investiture of the Commission.

As regards the types of actors involved, there was no rule-shaping asymmetry between 'designing' and 'implementing actors' under the Convention method; rather implementing actors acted as designing actors, too.

From a different theoretical viewpoint than distributive bargaining theory, it could be argued that the Parliament's success in obtaining increasing rights in the investiture of the Commission could be traced back to the *normative pressure of democratic norms*, that is the expectation to democratize the European decision-making processes. As argued above, however, if this had been the crucial influence, one would need to explain why the competencies were not much more readily granted and why the Parliament had to fight so tenaciously for these rights, deploying all possible strategies to reach its goals.

5.1.4. Institutional Rule Four: The Composition of the Commission

The rule governing the composition of the Commission has been remarkably stable in spite of considerably changing demands of the external environment. How can this be accounted for? What emerges from the analysis of the development or lack of development of the rule over time is that the change of a rule, such as the composition of the Commission which is so clearly redistributive in its content, does not lend itself to hidden incremental change. The formal rule clearly determines the number of Commissioners per member state and cannot possibly be transformed informally through a creative interpretation and modification of content. As a result, we do not find long-term changes of the *type A sequence endogenous formal/informal/formal rule change*, but a series of separate, failing attempts to reform the rule in the light of strong exogenous problem pressure, that is various rounds of enlargement. In the bargaining process under unanimity rule no actor was willing to yield ground in this redistributive question, therefore institutional change was unlikely to happen. The widening of the agenda and the inclusion of further redistributional institutional issues, that is the reweighting of Council votes and the extension of QMV, did not facilitate the negotiations over the composition of the Commission. The two last issues are just as contested and prone to polarize the political arena. It was only under the impression of the absolute immediacy of enlargement including another ten (eight plus two) members and the overwhelming impression of a lack of practicability that a compromise between two controversial redistributive issues, the composition of the Commission and the reweighting of Council votes, could finally be thrashed out. In sum, there is no 'gliding change' of the type of sequence A in which rules are subject to endogenous subtle change. Rather, under the impression of exogenous pressure, the process consisted of a number of 'go and stop' efforts at institutional change which, due to the redistributive nature of the issue and the extant decision-making rule, mostly failed. The functionalist efficiency argument as such did not suffice to bring about the required institutional change; over an extended period of time, the old rule successfully resisted change although its inefficiency was constantly deplored.

The *structural* aspects of change (types of actors and levels/arenas) show that designing and affected/implementing actors were identical. Member states decide how to change the treaty provisions regarding the composition of the Commission and the weighting of Council votes and they are the ones to apply these rules, as well. Every loss a member state incurred in negotiations had to be borne directly by this member state, that is the costs of redistribution could not be externalized to affected/implementing actors.

The level of rule change was the higher-order level exclusively. With one exception where, under the Convention, the meta-rules, that is the rules about how to change higher-order rules were included and altered as well. This shift of arena introducing new types of *designing actors* was sought because the IGC method had failed to produce viable solutions in difficult redistributive institutional questions. The Convention serving as an 'integrative bargaining phase' was supposed to prepare the agenda and develop new strategic options for the IGC and to overcome the decision-making impasses of the past. As it turned out, however, in the case of the composition of the Commission and the reweighting of votes, the Convention was not able to achieve a break-through in these hotly contested issues.

In short, a rule like the composition of the Commission, involving clear stakes with redistributive implications, where designing actors are identi-cal with implementing/affected actors, can only be changed in a bargaining process by designing actors themselves at the higher-order rule level. It does not lend itself to incremental, informal changes by affected and implementing actors at the application level. Too much is at stake for the designing actors. But in the negotiations at the highest level, the high saliency and the clear zero-sum character of the issue, under conditions of unanimity, render an easy bargaining result unlikely, even when confronted with strong exogenous functional pressure.

5.1.5. Institutional Rule Five: Comitology

Comitology, the institutional rules developed to control the implementing powers of the Commission, emerged slowly in the beginning then spread fast across different policy areas. The Parliament was very slow in gaining influence in the process. The long-term changes may best be captured by *sequence B exogenous pressure/formal/informal rule change*: (*a*) an exogenous functional pressure led to the (re)designing of institutions in a power-based distributive bargaining process both at the lower and higher-order; (*b*) once the formal rule had been adopted, an endogenous change set in, based on a renegotiation and ensuing modification of the formal rules in daily application producing an informal rule. To augment its bargaining position, the Parliament 'took hostage' of issues in other linked arenas. The changes of the informal insti-tutional rules were subsequently (*c*) formalized or not, depending on the preferences of the designing actors, that is governments, and the outcome of the bargaining process in the context of unanimity rule. This sequence B repeated itself several times over a period of more than forty years.

When conflicts over institutional change within *sequence B* could not be handled through a normal bargaining processes, and fell into gridlock, one of the involved actors, usually the less powerful ones, turned to third-party dispute resolution, that is the ECJ, hoping for a verdict favouring its own institutional interests (*sequence A adjudication*).

The process of change under *sequence B* may be explained on the basis of *functionalist theory accounting for institutional change in the face of exogenous problem pressure.* The particular institutional form this institutional change took can be interpreted on the basis of a *power-based distributive bargaining process.* If third-party dispute resolution was included in the development (*sequence A*), the *theory of rule development through adjudication* accounts for the last phase.

The comitology case directs the attention to yet another *sequence D* consisting of an *endogenous formal choice/adjudication/formalization of rule change:* (*a*) if a higher-order rule allows for a choice among several lower-order rules, (*b*) this may lead to a conflict over the selection of the lower-order rule; (*c*) adjudication may be sought to settle this conflict. This in turn may be followed by (*d*) a formalization of the appropriate choice under a subsequent higher-order rule revision. The choice of a particular committee procedure, as we have seen, was very much contested throughout the period under scrutiny since the relative competencies of the Council and the Commission vary across committees.

The establishing of committees to control the Commission's implementing powers may also interpreted in the terms of *principal–agent theory*. The principals, member states, delegated powers of implementation to the agent, the Commission, but only under the condition that the Commission be subject to rules allowing member states to control the agent in order to prevent agency loss. While principal–agent theory mainly explains the nature of these institutional rules in efficiency terms, the theory employed here accounts for these rules in terms of *distributional power-based bargaining* theory.

From the *structural* perspective (types of actors, levels/arenas), member states, as the *designing actors*, for a long time were the sole actors 'in the driving seat' until the Parliament, an indirectly affected actor,[1] increased its pressure to be included in the process. By increasingly withholding its acquiescence to decisions in other *linked arenas* (comitology budget matters and

---

[1] Through its right of political supervision of the Commission and its role as a co-legislator under co-decision.

co-decision), it managed to gain some influence on the bargaining outcome on the comitology rules, and make the delimitation of legislation and delegation a major issue of institutional debate.

From the level perspective, another aspect arises pointing to a *compensatory function* of comitology procedures: When Council legislation stalled in the years of relative paralysis (empty chair crisis and Luxembourg compromise), the decision-making machinery in comitology committees functioned smoothlessly, allowing for the further development of policies and the deepening of integration at a *lower level* in spite of the deadlock *at the higher level*.

5.2. THE FIVE RULES IN COMPARISON

When we compare the five rules from the perspectives of problem type, process and structure, the following general pattern emerges: distinguishing between *redistributive and coordination problems*, that is rule changes that imply a shift of power from one actor to another and rule changes from which all gain equally and which save transaction costs, the rules 'Parliament in legislation', 'Composition of the Commission', 'Comitology', and 'Investiture of the Commission', all are rules in which a redistribution of competences is at stake. In the case of 'Parliament in legislation' we are faced with a redistribution of competencies from the Council to the Parliament; in the case of 'Comitology' from the Council to the Commission (and vice versa) and from the Council and Commission to the Parliament; in the case of 'Composition of the Commission' a shift of power between member states is at risk; and in the case 'Investiture of the Commission' a redistribution of competencies between the Council and the Parliament. The rule 'Presidency of the Council', on the contrary, does not involve such a redistribution of power. The temporary shift of power to the Presidency is not considered to be a zero-sum game because the Presidency is limited in time and subject to the rotation principle. It is, therefore, dealt with as a coordination problem. The type of problem that a particular rule is facing has important implications for the process and structural aspects of change to which a rule is subject over time.

From the process perspective a number of typical *sequences* of change were identified when analysing the empirical stories of the five cases of long-term rule change:

- *Sequence A: endogenous formal/informal/formal (adjudication) rule change* consisting of (*a*) an extant formal institutional rule leading to (*b*) a negotiation of informal rules that are guiding the application of the formal rule; ensuing conflicts over the informal rules between actors lead (*c*) to an authoritative settlement through third-party dispute resolution guiding the subsequent application of the thereby formalized rule; or, alternatively, (*d*) to a higher-order formalization of the informal rule.

- *Sequence B: exogenous functional pressure/redesign formal/informal/formal rule change* consisting of exogenous problem pressure leading to (*a*) a functional redesigning of the formal institutional rule; this is followed (*b*) by an endogenous rebargaining of the formal rule with the aim of introducing an informal rule. This informal rule (*c*) may subsequently be formalized or not in a following formal treaty revision.

- *Sequence C: exogenous functional pressure/informal rule/formal rule change* consisting of (*a*) a functional problem leading (*b*) to the emergence of an informal rule change that (*c*) is subsequently formalized or not.

- *Sequence D: endogenous formal choice/adjudication/formal rule change* which consists of (*a*) a higher-order rule allowing for a choice among several lower-order formal rules; (*b*) a conflict over this selection, and (*c*) a turn to adjudication in order to settle the conflict, (*d*) followed by a possible formalization of the appropriate choice under a subsequent higher-order formal rule revision.

Comparing the typical processes driving institutional change across the five cases, it becomes apparent that in the rule developments of 'Parliament in legislation', 'Comitology', and 'Investiture of the Commission', the *sequences B functional pressure formal/informal/formal rule change, and A existing formal/informal/formal adjudication rule change* are prevalent. In comitology we find both of these, but also *sequence D formal choice/adjudication/formalization of rule change*. In the case of 'Presidency in the Council' the prevailing sequence is C *functional pressure informal/formal rule change*.

What we may observe in these four cases are long chains of changes spurred by functional demands, the (re)designing of formal rules in the light of these demands, followed by endogenous interstitial informal rule changes that subsequently may be adopted as formal rules or not (depending on the bargaining power constellation and underlying institutional rule), or, in case of conflict, may lead to third-party dispute resolution. These sequences are theoretically well expressed by functionalist theories of institutional change (principal–agent theory being one variant of functionalist theory), redistributive power-based bargaining theory and rule interpretation through adjudication theory. In one case, 'comitology', the battle over competences may also be conceived of as a relationship of delegation. Member states, as the principals, delegated a task to the Commission, the agent, who is to be kept under control. These rules of control have been very much contested, though, and are interpreted on the basis of power-based distributive bargaining theory.

In all these three *redistributive* cases, 'Parliament in legislation', 'Comitology', and 'Investiture of the Commission', these theories capture well the long drawn-out contests about competencies in which the less powerful *implementing and affected actors*, the Parliament (and the Commission) sought to gain institutional territory and wrench competences from the *designing actor*, the Council. In these endeavours, they brought into play various strategies to exert pressure on the designing actor, one particularly effective one being the 'linked-arena veto': by withholding a formal decision in a related issue arena, the implementing actor (Parliament) sought to influence the outcome in the designing actors', that is member states' arena. The disjunction between designing and implementing actors marks a line of conflict successfully exploited by implementing actors to push for endogenous informal and formal change.

In the other *redistributive* case, 'Composition of the Commission', designing actors (the member states) and implementing actors are identical. The issue at stake is of high political saliency and entails a clear, distributional conflict that could only be decided in a high-level bargaining process among member states. The issue being redistributive and the decision-making rule used being unanimity, the probability of gridlock was very high. The outcome was institutional stability or lack of change in spite of high external functional pressure, that is enlargement. Under the impression of strong problem pressure, there were several attempts at redesigning the rule, attempts which all failed. The identity of designing and implementing actors and the clear redistributive nature of the issue, precluded interstitial informal changes initiated by a separate set of implementing actors, as in the cases of 'Parliament in Legislation', 'Comitology', and the 'Investiture of the Commission'.

The patterns of change in the case dealing with a *coordination problem*, that is 'Presidency of the Council', were different altogether. We encounter a repeated occurrence of *sequence C*: swift and smooth adjustments to *external functional challenges* by the development of *informal rules* that subsequently were sometimes *formalized*, sometimes not. Due to the rotation principle there were *no redistributive conflicts* about the shifting of competences. The rules were changed responding to a higher need of coordination with the only purpose of reducing transaction costs, not shifting power between actors. There was no disjunction and no conflict between *designing* and *affected/implementing* actors, the two are identical. The changing rules governing the Presidency may also be interpreted as an act of delegation on the part of member states (the principals) to the Presidency (agent). Since the delegation constitutes only a temporary act, that is the function of the agent is rotating among principals, the formulation of the rules of control over the agent were not contested although involving a temporary redistribution of competences.

Looking at the different sequences and their theoretical explanations from the angle of *exogenous and endogenous* processes of change, it becomes apparent that all sequences are characterized by a combination of the two, but differ with respect to the starting point which, in one instance, is an exogenous factor (*sequences B and C*), in the other, an endogenous factor (*sequences A and D*). A first phase of change may be set off by an *exogenous* pressure giving rise to a designed change of institutional rules. Once instituted, the rule is subject to an *endogenous* dynamic of change, driven by the mechanism of formal/informal or the mechanism of formal/and choice among several possible rules; the outcomes may subsequently be formalized when renewed *external* pressure calls for another event of institutional redesign (IGC).

In short, all sequences are characterized by a *combination of exogenous and endogenous explanations* of institutional change. Institutional rules frequently are drawn up as an answer to a collective action problem in response to *exogenous pressure*. Once the rules have been introduced, they may respond both to exogenous *and* endogenous demands. There may be changes due to the effects of institutions on 'the non-institutional outcomes and change due to the effects of institutions on institutional change' (Caporaso forthcoming: 18) or exogenous factors setting in motion change. In the first case, institutions have an impact on the external socio-economic environment which, in turn, constitutes a renewed exogenous factor of institutional change. In the second case, institutions have an impact on institutions themselves and their operation which, in turn, prompts a need for a renewed institutional change. In the third case, completely independent socio-economic factors set off institutional change. Only the second instance constitutes an *endogenous change in the strict sense.*[2] Several examples of such an endogenous institutional change in the strict sense have been discussed in this book. But it has also been shown that exogenous factors regularly play an important role in spurring institutional change.

5.3. THEORETICAL LACUNAE AND MODEL SPECIFICATION

The account of the empirical cases shows that an important part of the development may be captured by using the explanatory potential of theories of

---

[2] Greif and Laitin (2004), by contrast, argue that an impact of institutions on the non-institutional environment, i.e. economic and social aspects, which in turn feed back on the functioning of the institutional rules, is a form of endogenous institutional change as well.

functionalist institutional redesign, principal–agent theory, and distributive power-based bargaining theory. However, the empirical accounts also point to patterns of change which had not been conceived of theoretically in the third chapter. One of these blind spots is the institutional changes deriving from the unanticipated effects of the *relationship between two or more institutional rules.* When one rule is changed, it may induce a change in another rule, possibly with an impact on the existing distribution of competences. The impact of such a change will be fought off by the actor whose competencies are being impinged on by this indirect effect; thus, the Parliament saw its right of polit-ical supervision of the Commission at danger when the Council established comitology to control the implementing powers of the Commission. Or to give another example: co-decision leading to an increased legislative interaction between the Council and the Parliament reinforced the role of the Presidency within the Council. These dynamics between distinct institutional rules are only captured when the analysis focuses on the entire institutional architecture of a polity, a perspective which has not been taken in this longitudinal analysis of the change of individual institutional rules over a longer period of time. However, the link between rules is indirectly included when the focus rests on the formal (re)designing of the individual rule as part of an entire treaty revision.

5.4. CONCLUSION: SCOPE CONDITIONS
AND GENERALIZABILITY

The five institutional rules discussed in this book all are characterized by certain features: the issues which are at stake are clearly defined, that is more or less competencies of the Parliament in legislation and in comitology; more or less Commissioners for a member state; more or less competences for the Presidency of the Council; and more or less competences for the Council in controlling the Commission's implementing powers. Moreover, the number of actors which have been involved is limited and the actors are clearly defined. And, importantly, the conditions under which these actors interact are clearly defined. The conditions of interaction have been institutionalized several decades ago and are likely to persist well into the future. All these features reflect the specific boundary conditions for the applicability of the theories which have predominantly been used here. The latter show considerable power to account for the change of institutional rules in the European Union. By implication, would I have chosen to analyse the change of institutional rules of unclear stakes, in an 'anarchic' international environment in which the number of participant actors is high, not well defined and fluctuating, the goals of interaction uncertain and repeated interaction unlikely, the theoretical explanations offered would have had less explanatory traction.

What about alternative explanations building on entirely different theories based on different assumptions, such as behaviour guided by the logic of appropriateness? The explanation of the change of some rules indicates that—while the outcome of an institutional change may plausibly be accounted for by a distributive power–based argument—in some instances a *sociological institutionalist* argument, that is the pressure of normative ideas, contributes to the explanation as well, for example for the widening decisional power of the Parliament. However, at a closer glance, the sole application of the normative power of legitimation argument does not seem plausible. If the argument would hold, the normative pressure should have swept away all the institutional obstacles and actors' resistance against the deployment of the full parliamentarian power. As the empirical accounts show, this was by no means the case. To be the only directly electorally legitimated actor certainly helped the Parliament to realize its objectives, but it still had to fight 'tooth and nail' for the expansion of its power using all classical tools of implicit negotiations, such as delaying, holding hostage, and so on. Hence, the sociological institutionalist explanation is considered of subordinate importance for the change of institutional rules under analysis here.

Bearing the theoretical boundary conditions outlined above in mind, the question arises as to what extent the theoretical explanations of institutional change proposed for the long-term change of the five rules under consideration may be generalized across the change of institutional rules outside the European Union? The answer would be that, if the same boundary conditions are given, the explanations for a long-term change developed here, would equally be applicable and hold explanatory power. If the number of actors and types of actors are clearly defined and limited, if the gains and losses of the issues at stake are clear, and if coordinative issues are at stake which are beneficial to all actors concerned and save transaction costs, institutional change will happen as a rather smooth informal or formal process adjusting the existing institutional rules to new exogenous functional demands. If, on the contrary, redistributive issues are at stake where an institutional change will imply the gain of one actor and the loss of another, several developments may follow: if the losers are formal designing actors in the arena of change and if there is unanimity rule, they will either block the institutional change, in which case institutional stability would be the outcome; or they may be compensated by gains in another institutional issue or substantive policy issue through issue linkages or package deals. This presupposes that the agenda comprises several institutional or substantive policy issues. Under this condition, even an institutional change redistributing competencies may be agreed on. If a redistributive institutional issue is at stake, and the costs of change are not borne by the designing actors, but by affected and implementing actors, the latter may have an indirect means of clawing back power. By establishing a linked-arena veto, that is withholding a formal decision in a linked arena where they have a formal decision-making right, they may impact on the designing actors' decision.

References

Abbott, K. and Snidal, D. (2000). 'Hard Law and Soft Law in International Governance', *International Organization*, 54: 421–56.

Aghion, P. and Tirole, J. (1997). 'Formal and Real Authority in Organizations', *Journal of Political Economy*, 105(1): 1–29.

Alchian, A. A. (1950). 'Uncertainty, Evolution, and Economic Theory', *Journal of Political Economy*, 58, 211–24.

Alchian, A. A. (1965). 'Some Economics of Property Rights', *Il Politico*, 30(4): 816–29.

—— and Demsetz, H. (1972). 'Production, Information Costs, and Economic Organization', *American Economic Review*, 62: 777–95.

Alston, L. J., Eggertsson, T., and North, D. C. (1996). 'Introduction', in L. J. Alston, T. Eggertsson, and D. C. North (eds.), *Empirical Studies in Institutional Change*. Cambridge: Cambridge University Press.

Armstrong, K. A. and Bulmer, S. J. (1998). *The Governance of the Single European Market*. Manchester, UK: Manchester University Press.

Arrow, K. J. (1985). 'The Economics of Agency', in J. W. Pratt and R. J. Zeckhauser (eds.), *Principals and Agents: The Structure of Business*. Cambridge: Harvard Business School Press.

Bartolini, S. (2005). *Restructuring Europe: Centre Formation, System Building and Political Structuring between the Nation State and the European Union*. New York: Oxford University Press.

Bates, R. H. (1988). 'Contra Contractarianism: Some Reflections on the New Institutionalism', *Politics and Society*, 16(2–3): 387–401.

Beach, D. (2005). *The Dynamics of European Integration. Why and When EU Institutions Matter*. Basingstoke, UK: Palgrave Macmillan.

Benz, A. (1992). 'Mehrebenen-Verflechtung: Verhandlungsprozesse in verbundenen Entscheidungsarenen', in A. Benz, F. W. Scharpf, and R. Zintl (eds.), *Horizontale Politikverflechtung*. Frankfurt am Main, Germany: Campus Verlag.

—— Scharpf, F. W., and Zintl, R. (eds.) (1992). *Horizontale Politikverflechtung*. Frankfurt am main, Germany: Campus Verlag.

Bergström, C. F. (2005). *Comitology. Delegation of Powers in the European Union and the Committee System*. Oxford: Oxford University Press.

Bertram, C. (1967–8). 'Decision Making in the EEC: The Management Committee Procedure', *Common Market Law Review*, 5: 246–64.

Boucher, S. (2006). *Exploring Leadership Effectiveness: The Presidency of the European Commission*. Ph.D. dissertation Mscr. Florence, Italy: European University Institute.

Bourlanges, J. L. (1996). 'Achieving a New Balance Between Large and Small Member States', In *A Larger EU, Can All Member States be Equal?* Brussels: Philip Morris Institute.

Bradley, K. S. C. (1997). 'The European Parliament and Comitology: On the Road to Nowhere?', *European Law Journal*, 3(3): 230–54.

Brousseau, E. and Fares, M. (2000). 'Incomplete Contracts and Governance Structures: Are Incomplete Contract Theory and New Institutional Economics Substitutes or Complements?', in C. Ménard (ed.), *Institutions, Contracts and Organizations: Perspectives from New Institutional Economics*. Cheltenham, UK: Edward Elgar.

Budden, P. (1994). 'The United Kingdom and the European Community, 1979–1986. The Making of the Single European Act'. D.Phil. thesis. Oxford: Oxford University Press.

—— (2002). 'Observations on the Single European Act and "Relaunch of Europe": A Less Intergovernmental Reading of the 1985 Intergovernmental Conference', *Journal of European Public Policy*, 91: 76–97.

Bulmer, S. J. and Wessels, W. (1987). *The European Council. Decision-Making in European Politics*. Basingstoke, UK: Macmillan.

Calvert, R. L. (1992). 'Leadership and Its Basis in Problems of Social Coordination', *International Political Science Review*, 13(1): 7–24.

—— (1995). 'Rational Actors, Equilibrium, and Social Institutions', in J. Knight and I. Sened (eds.), *Explaining Social Institutions*. Ann Arbor, MI: University of Michigan Press.

Caporaso, J. A. (2003). 'Democracy, Accountability, and Rights in Supranational Governance', in M. Kahler and D. A. Lake (eds.), *Global Governance in a Global Economy. Political Authority in Transition*. Princeton, NJ: Princeton University Press.

—— (forthcoming). 'Promises and Pitfalls of an Endogenous Theory of Institutional Change', in H. Farrell and A. Héritier (eds.), *Contested Competences in Europe. Incomplete Contracts and Interstitial Institutional Change. West European Politics* (Special Issue).

Carey, J. M. (2000). 'Parchment, Equilibria, and Institutions', *Comparative Political Studies*, 33(6–7): 735–61.

Checkel, J. T. (2001a). 'Why Comply? Social Learning and European Identity Change', *International Organization*, 55(3): 553–88.

—— (2001b). 'Constructing European Institutions', in M. Aspinwall and G. Schneider (eds.), *The Rules of Integration: Institutionalist Approaches to the Study of Europe*. Manchester, UK: Manchester University Press.

—— (2001c). 'From Meta- to Substantive Theory? Social Constructivism and the Study of Europe', *European Union Politics*, 2(2): 219–26.

Christiansen, T. and Jorgensen, K. E. (1999). 'The Amsterdam Process: A Structurationist Perspective on EU Treaty Reform', *European Integration online Papers (EIoP)*, 3(1).

Coase, R. (1960). 'The Problem of Social Cost', *Journal of Law and Economics*, 3(1): 1–44.

Corbett, R. (1993). *The Treaty of Maastricht: From Conception to Ratification. A Comprehensive Reference Guide*. Harlow, UK: Longman Group.

—— (1998). *The European Parliament's Role in Closer EU Integration*. Basingstoke, UK: Macmillan.

——Jacobs, F., and Shackleton, M. (2000). *The European Parliament*. London: John Harper Publisher.

Cortell, A. P. and Peterson, S. (2001). 'Limiting the Unintended Consequences of Institutional Change', *Comparative Political Studies*, 34(7): 768–99.

Crawford, S. E. S. and Ostrom, E. (1995). 'A Grammar of Institutions', *American Political Science Review*, 89(3): 582–600.

Crouch, C. and Farrell, H. (2004). 'Breaking the Path of Institutional Development: Alternatives to the New Determinism in Political Economy', *Rationality and Society*, 16(1): 5–43.

Crum, B. (2004). 'The EU High Representative and the EP: Resisting the 'Ratchet Effect', Mscr. Vrije Universiteit, Amsterdam.

Dahrendorf, R. (1977). *Homo Sociologicus. Ein Versuch zur Geschichte, Bedeutung und Kritik der Kategorie der Sozialen Rolle*. Opladen, Germany: Westdeutscher Verlag.

Davignon, E. (1995). 'Die Herausforderungen, vor denen die Kommission steht', in The Philip Morris Institute for Public Policy Research (ed.), *Wie sieht die Zukunft der Europäischen Kommission aus?* Brussels: The Philip Morris Institute for Public Policy Research.

Davis, C. L. (2004). 'International Institutions and Issue Linkage: Building Support for Agricultural Trade Liberalization', *American Political Science Review*, 98(1): 153–69.

de Ruyt, J. (1989). Acte Unique Européen. Brussels: Editions de L'ULB.

de Schoutheete, P. (1988). 'The Presidency and the Management of Political Cooperation', in A. Pijpers, E. Regelsberger, and W. Wessels (eds.), *European Political Cooperation in the 1980s. A Common Foreign Policy for Western Europe?* Dordrecht, Germany: Martinus Nijhoff Publishers.

Dehousse, F. (1999). Amsterdam: The Making of a Treaty. London: London European Research Centre.

Demsetz, H. (1988). *The Organization of Economic Activity*. Oxford: Basil Blackwell.

Devuyst, Y. (1998). 'Treaty Reform in the European Union: The Amsterdam Process', *Journal of European Public Policy*, 5(4): 615–31.

Diermeier, D. and Krehbiel, K. (2003). 'Institutionalism as a Methodology', *Journal of Theoretical Politics*, 15(2): 123–44.

DiMaggio, P. J. and Powell, W. W. (1991). 'Introduction', in W. W. Powell and P. J. DiMaggio (eds.), *The New Institutionalism in Organizational Analysis*. Chicago, IL: University of Chicago Press.

Dinan, D. (1999). *Ever Closer Union? An Introduction to the European Union*. London: Macmillian.

——and S. Vanhoonacker (2000). IGC 2000 Watch (Part 1–4). Europ. Community Studies Assoc. 13/2–4.

Dowding, K. M. (2000a). 'How Not to Use Evolutionary Theory in Politics. A Critique of Peter John', *British Journal of Politics and International Relations*, 2(1): 72–80.

——(2000b). 'Institutional Research on the European Union. A Critical Review', *European Union Politics*, 1(1): 125–44.

Dyson, K. and Featherstone, K. (1999). *The Road to Maastricht. Negotiating Economic and Monetary Union*. Oxford: Oxford University Press.

Edwards, G. and Wallace, W. (1976). *A Wider European Community? Issues and Problems of Further Enlargement*. London: Federal Trust for Education and Research.

Eggertsson, T. (1996). 'A Note on the Economics of Institutions', in L. J. Alston, T. Eggertsson, and D. C. North (eds.), *Empirical Studies in Institutional Change*. Cambridge.

Eising, R. (2002). 'Policy Learning in Embedded Negotiations: Explaining EU Electricity Liberalization', *International Organization*, 56(1): 85–120.

Elster, J. (1989a). *The Cement of Society. A Study of Social Order*. Cambridge: Cambridge University Press.

——— (1989b). *Nuts and Bolts for the Social Sciences*. Cambridge: Cambridge University Press.

Farrell, H. and Héritier, A. (2003). 'Formal and Informal Institutions under Codecision: Continuous Constitution Building in Europe', *Governance*, 16(4): 577–600.

——— ——— (2004). 'Interorganizational Negotiation and Intraorganizational Power in Shared Decision Making. Early Agreements under Codecision and Their Impact on the Parliament and the Council', *Comparative Political Studies*, 37(4): 537–56.

——— ——— (eds.) (forthcoming). *Contested Competences in Europe. Incomplete Contracts and Interstitial Institutional Change. West European Politics* (Special Issue).

——— ——— (forthcoming). Codecision and Institutional Change, in H. Farrell and A. Héritier, eds., *Contested Competences in Europe. Incomplete Contracts and Interstitial Institutional Change*, Special Issue, *West European Politics*, 33 pp.

Fearon, J. D. (1998). 'Bargaining, Enforcement, and International Cooperation', *International Organization*, 52(2): 269–305.

Finnemore, M. and Sikkink, K. (1998). 'International Norms Dynamics and Political Change', *International Organization*, 52(4): 887–917.

Fisher, R. and Ury, W. (1981). *Getting to Yes*. London: Hutchinson.

Fligstein, N. (1997). 'Social Skill and Institutional Theory', *American Behavioral Scientist*, 40(4): 397–405.

Foss, P. (ed.) (1995). *Economic Approaches to Organizations and Institutions: An Introduction*. Aldershot, UK: Dartmouth.

Frieden, J. A. (1999). 'Actors and Preferences in International Relations', in D. A. Lake and R. Powell (eds.) *Strategic Choice in International Relations*. Princeton, NJ: Princeton University Press, 39–76.

Furubotn, E. G. and Richter, R. (1997). *Institutions and Economic Theory: The Contribution of the New Institutional Economics*. Ann Arbor, MI: University of Michigan Press.

Galloway, D. (2001). *The Treaty of Nice and Beyond. Realities and Illusions of Power in the EU*. Sheffield, UK: Sheffield Academic Press.

Gardner, R. and Ostrom, E. (1991). 'Rules and Games', *Public Choice*, 70(2): 121–49.

Gazzo, M. (ed.) (1985). *Towards European Union. From the 'Crocodile' to the European Council in Milan*. Brussels, Belgium: Agence Europe.

Gazzo, M. (ed.) (1986). *Towards European UnionII: From the European Council in Milan to the Signing of the Single European Act.* Brussels–Luxembourg: Agence Europe.

Geertz, C. (1980). *Negara: The Theatre State in Nineteenth-Century Bali.* Princeton, NJ: Princeton University Press.

Gerring, J. (2005). 'Causation: a Unified Framework for the Social Sciences, *Journal of Theoretical Politics*, 17(2): 163–98.

Goldmann, K. (2005). 'Appropriateness and Consequences: The Logic of Neoinstitutionalism', *Governance*, 18(1): 35–52.

Goodin, R. E. (2000). 'Institutional Gaming', *Governance*, 13(4): 523–33.

———— (2004). 'Sequencing Deliberative Moments'. Paper presented at the conference 'Empirical Approaches to Deliberative Politics', Florence, Italy: European University Institute, 21–22 May 2004.

Gourevitch, P. A. (1999). 'The Governance Problem in International Relations', in D. A. Lake and R. Powell (eds.), *Strategic Choice and International Relations*. Princeton, NJ: Princeton University Press, 137–64.

Granovetter, M. S. (1985). 'Economic Action and Social Structure: The Problem of Embeddedness', *American Journal of Sociology*, 91(3): 481–510.

Gray, M. and Stubb, A. (2001). 'Keynote Article: The Treaty of Nice—Negotiating a Poisoned Chalice?', *Journal of Common Market Studies*, 39: 5–23.

Greif, A. (1994). 'Cultural Beliefs and the Organization of Society: A Historical and Theoretical Reflection on Collectivist and Individualist Societies', *Journal of Political Economy*, 912–50.

———— (2006). *Institutions and the Path to the Modern Economy. Lessons from Medieval Trade.* Cambridge: Cambridge University Press.

———— and Laitin, D. D. (2004). 'Theory of Endogenous Institutional Change', *American Political Science Review*, 98(4): 633–52.

Grieco, J. M. (1988). 'Anarchy and the Limits of (International) Cooperation: A Realist Critique of the Newest Liberal Institutionalism', *International Organization*, 42(3): 485–507.

Grunhage, J. (2001). 'The Institutional Reforms of Amsterdam: A View from the European Parliament', J. Monos and W. Wessels, eds. The European Union after Treaty of Amsterdam, Publ. Continuum Internal.: 31–44.

Haas, E. B. (1958). *The Uniting of Europe: Political, Social, and Economic Forces, 1950–1957.* Stanford, CA: Stanford University Press.

Habermas, J. (1987). *The Theory of Communicative Action.* Boston, MA: Beacon Press.

Hayek, F. A. von. (1967). *Studies in Philosophy, Politics and Economics.* London: Routledge & Kegan Paul.

Hayes-Renshaw, F. and Wallace, H. (2006). 'The Council of Ministers', 2nd ed. Basingstoke: Palgrave Macmillan

Heckathorn, D. D. and Maser, S. M. (1987). 'Bargaining and the Sources of Transaction Costs: The Case of Government Regulation', *Journal of Law, Economics, and Organization*, 3: 69–98.

Heiner, R. A.(1990). 'Imperfect Choice and the Origins of Institutional Rules', *Journal of Institutional and Theoretical Economics*, 146: 720–6.

Helmke, G. and Levitsky, S. (2004). 'Informal Institutions and Comparative Politics', *Perspectives on Politics*, 2(4): 725–40.

Héritier, A. (1999). *Policy-Making and Diversity in Europe. Escape from Deadlock.* Cambridge: Cambridge University Press.

—— (2001). 'Differential Europe: National Administrative Responses to Community Policy', in M. G. Cowles, J. A. Caporaso, and T. Risse (eds.), *Transforming Europe. Europeanization and Domestic Change.* Ithaca, NY: Cornell University Press.

Hix, S. (2002). 'Constitutional Agenda-Setting through Discretion in Rule Interpretation: Why the European Parliament Won at Amsterdam', *British Journal of Political Science*, 32(2): 259–80.

Homans, G. C. (1950). *The Human Group.* New York: Harcourt, Brace and World.

Ibanez, A. G. (1992). 'Spain and European Political Union', in F. Laursen and S. Vanhoonacker (eds.), *The Intergovernmental Conference on Political Union.* Maastricht: European Institute of Public Administration.

Immergut, E. M. (2005). 'Historical Institutionalism in Political Science and the Problem of Change', in A. Wimmer and R. Kossler (eds.), *Understanding Change: Models, Methodologies and Metaphors.* New York: Palgrave Macmillan.

Jacobs, F., Corbett, R., and Shackleton, M. (1995). *The European Parliament.* London: Cartermill.

Jenkins, R. (1991). *A Life at the Centre.* London: Macmillan.

Jensen, M. C. and Meckling, W. (1976). 'Theory of the Firm: Managerial Behavior, Agency Costs, and Ownership Structure', *Journal of Financial Economics*, 3(4): 305–60.

Joergensen, C., Kock, C., and Roerbech, L. (1998). 'Rhetoric That Shifts Votes: An Exploratory Study of Persuasion in Issue-Oriented Public Debates', *Political Communication*, 15: 283–99.

Joerges, C. and Neyer, J. (1997). 'From Intergovernmental Bargaining to Deliberative Political Processes: The Constitutionalisation of Comitology', *European Law Journal*, 3(3): 273–99.

Jones, B. D. (2001). 'Politics and the Architecture of Choice: Bounded Rationality and Governance.' Chicago: Chicago University Press.

Jonsson, H. and Hegeland, H. (2003). 'Konventet Bakom Kulisserna—Om Arbetsmetoden Och Förhandlingsspelat I Europeiska Konventet', SIEPS Working Paper 2003:2u.

Judge, D. (1995). 'The Failure of National Parliaments', *West European Politics*, 18(3): 79–100.

Jupille, J. (2004*a*). *Procedural Politics. Issues, Influence, and Institutional Choice in the European Union.* Cambridge: Cambridge University Press.

—— (2004*b*). 'Forum Shopping and Global Governance', Paper presented at the 'Workshop on Forum Shopping and Global Governance', Florence, Italy: European University Institute, 23–24 April 2004.

Kaiser, J. H. (1966). 'Das Europarecht in der Krise der Gemeinschaften', *Europarecht*, 1: 4–24.

Kaldor, N. (1939). 'Welfare Propositions of Economics and Interpersonal Comparisons of Utility', *The Economic Journal*, 49: 549–52.

Karagiannis, Jean-Antoine (2006). 'The Politics of EU Competition Law: Delegation, Control, and the Progress in the Most Supranational Policy', Ph.D. thesis manuscript. Florence, Italy: European University Institute.

Kay, A. (2002). 'Evolution in Political Science: A reply to Kerr', *British Journal of Politics and International Relations*, 5(1): 102–11.

Keohane, R. O. (1984). *After Hegemony: Cooperation and Discord in the World Political Economy*. Princeton, NJ: Princeton University Press.

Kerr, P. (2003). 'Keeping It Real! Evolution and Political Science: A Reply to Kay and Curry', *British Journal of Politics and International Relations*, 5(1): 118–28.

Kiser, L. L. and Ostrom, E. (1982). 'The Three Worlds of Action. A Metatheoretical Synthesis of Institutional Approaches', in E. Ostrom (ed.), *Strategies of Political Inquiry*. Beverly Hills, CA: Sage.

Knight, J. (1992). *Institutions and Social Conflict*. Cambridge: Cambridge University Press.

—— (1995). 'Models, Interpretations, and Theories: Constructing Explanations of Institutional Emergence and Change', in J. Knight and I. Sened (eds.), *Explaining Social Institutions*. Ann Arbor, MI: University of Michigan Press.

—— and Sened, I. (1995). *Explaining Social Institutions*. Ann Arbor, MI: University of Michigan Press.

Koremenos, B. (2005). 'Contracting around Uncertainty', *American Political Science Review*, 99(4): 549–65.

Krasner, S. D. (1988). 'Sovereignty: An Institutional Perspective', *Comparative Political Studies*, 21(1): 66–94.

—— (1991). 'Global Communication and National Power: Life on the Pareto Frontier', *World Politics*, 43(3): 336–66.

Kreppel, A. (2000). 'Rules, Ideology and Coalition Formation in the European Parliament: Past, Present and Future', *European Union Politics*, 1(3): 340–62.

Lake, D. A. (1999). 'Global Governance: A Relational Contracting Approach', in A. Prakash and J. A. Hart (eds.), *Globalization and Governance*. New York: Routledge.

—— (2004). 'Finding Pareto', Paper presented at the conference 'Forum Shopping, Global Governance, and International Security Institutions'. 23–24 April 2004.

—— and Powell, R. (1999). Strategic Choice and International Relations. Princeton, NJ: Princeton University Press.

Lanzara, G. F. (1998). 'Self-Destructive Processes in Institution-Building and Some Modest Countervailing Mechanisms', *European Journal of Political Research*, 33: 1–39.

Lauth, H.-J. (2000). 'Informal Institutions and Democracy', *Democratization*, 7(4): 21–50.

Lax, D. A. and Sebenius, J. K. (1986). *The Manager as Negotiator: Bargaining for Cooperation and Competitive Gain*. New York: Free Press.

Levi, M. (1988). *Of Rule and Revenue*. Berkeley, CA: University of California Press.

Lichbach, M. I. (2003). *Is Rational Choice Theory All of Social Science?* Ann Arbor, MI: University of Michigan Press.

Lieberman, R. C. (2002). 'Ideas, Institutions, and Political Order: Explaining Political Change', *American Political Science Review*, 96(4): 697–712.

Lindberg, L. N. (1963). *The Political Dynamics of European Economic Integration.* Stanford, CA: Stanford University Press.

Lodge, J. (1998). Negotiations in the European Union in the 1996 Intergovernmental Conference, *International Negotiation*, 3: 481–505.

Lohmann, S. (2003). 'Why Do Institutions Matter? An Audience-Cost Theory of Institutional Commitment', *Governance*, 16(1): 95–110.

Lubell, M., Schneider, M., Scholz, J. T., and Mete, M. (2002). 'Watershed Partnerships and the Emergence of Collective Action Institutions', *American Journal of Political Science*, 46(1): 148–63.

Ludlow, P. (2002). *The Laeken Council.* Brussels: EuroComment.

—— (2004). *The Making of the New Europe. The European Councils in Brussels and Copenhagen 2002.* Brussels: EuroComment.

Lupia, A. and McCubbins, M. D. (2000). 'Representation or Abdication? How Citizens Use Institutions to Help Delegation Succeed', *European Journal of Political Research*, 37: 291–307.

McAllister, R. (1997). *From EC to EU. An Historical and Political Survey.* London: Routledge.

McCubbins, M. D. and Schwartz, T. (1984). 'Congressional Oversight Overlooked: Police Patrols Versus Fire Alarms', *American Journal of Political Science*, 28(1): 165–79.

McDonagh, B. (1998). *Original Sin in a Brave New World: The Paradox of Europe. An Account of the Negotiation of the Treaty of Amsterdam.* Dublin: Institute of European Affairs.

Magnette, P. and Nicolaidis, K. (2003). 'Large and Small Member States in the European Union: Reinventing the Balance', *Notre Europe. Research and European Issues*, vol. 25 (May 2003).

Mahoney, J. (2000). 'Path Dependence in Historical Sociology', *Theory and Society*, 29(4): 507–48.

Mantzavinos, C. (2001). *Individuals, Institutions, and Markets.* Cambridge University Press.

March, J. G. and Olsen, J. P. (1989). *Rediscovering Institutions: The Organizational Basis of Politics.* New York: Free Press.

—— (1998). 'The Institutional Dynamics of International Political Orders', *International Organization*, 52(4): 943–69.

Martin, L. L. (1992). 'Interests, Power, and Multilateralism', *International Organization*, 46(4): 765–92.

Mateo Gonzalez, G. (2004). 'Un Análisis Institucional de las Conferencias Intergubernamentales en la Unión Europea: De Amsterdam a Niza', PhD dissertation, Universidad Autónoma de Barcelona.

Mattli, W. (1999). *The Logic of Regional Integration. Europe and Beyond.* New York: Cambridge University Press.

—— and Slaughter, A.-M. (1995). 'Law and Politics in the European Union: A Reply to Garrett', *International Organization*, 49(1): 183–90.

Maurer, A. (1999). *What Next for the European Parliament?* London: Federal Trust.

_____ (2002). The European Parliament, in F. Laursen, ed. *The Amsterdam Treaty: National Preference Formation, Interstate Bargaining and Outcome*. Odense: Odense University Press.

_____ (2003). 'The Legislative Powers and Impact of the European Parliament', *Journal of Common Market Studies*, 41(2): 227–47.

Mayntz, R. (2002). *Akteure—Mechanismen—Modelle: Zur Theoriefähigkeit Makro-Sozialer Analysen*. Frankfurt am Main, Germany: Campus.

Meyer, J. W. and Rowan, B. (1991). 'Institutionalized Organizations: Formal Structure as Myth and Ceremony', in W. W. Powell and P. J. DiMaggio (eds.), *The New Institutionalism in Organizational Analysis*. Chicago, IL: University of Chicago Press.

Middlemas, K. (1995). *Orchestrating Europe. The Informal Politics of the European Union, 1973–95*. London: Fontana.

Milgrom, P. and Roberts, J. (1990). 'Bargaining Costs, Influence Costs, and the Organization of Economic Activity', in J. E. Alt and K. A. Shepsle (eds.), *Perspectives on Positive Political Economy*. New York: Cambridge University Press.

Mitchell, R. B. and Keilbach, P. M. (2001). 'Situation Structure and Institutional Design: Reciprocity, Coercion, and Exchange', *International Organization*, 55(4): 891–917.

Moe, T. M. (1982). 'Regulatory Performance and Presidential Administration', *American Journal of Political Science*, 26: 197–224.

_____ (1984). 'The New Economics of Organizations', *American Journal of Political Science*, 28(4): 739–77.

_____ (1990). 'Political Institutions: The Neglected Side of the Story', *Journal of Law, Economics, and Organization*, 6 (Special Issue): 213–61.

_____ (2005). 'Power and Political Institutions', *Perspectives on Politics*, 3(2): 215–33.

Moravcsik, A. (1991). 'Negotiating the Single European Act: National Interests and Conventional Statecraft in the European Community', *International Organization*, 45(1): 19–56.

_____ (1993). 'Preferences and Power in the European Community: A Liberal Intergovernmental Approach', *Journal of Common Market Studies*, 31(4): 473–524.

_____ (1998). *The Choice for Europe: Social Purpose and State Power Form Messina to Maastricht*. Ithaca, NY: Cornell University Press.

_____ (2001). 'Bringing Constructivist Integration Theory out of the Clouds: Has It Landed Yet?', *European Union Politics*, 2(2): 226–49.

_____ and Nicolaïdis, K. (1999). 'Explaining the Treaty of Amsterdam: Interests, Influence, Institutions', *Journal of Common Market Studies*, 37(1): 59–85.

Nelson, R. R. and Winter, S. G. (1982). *An Evolutionary Theory of Economic Change*. Cambridge, MA: Harvard University Press.

Nicoll, W. (1998). 'The Evolution of the Office of the Presidency'. Paper presented at the conference 'The Presidency of the European Union', Dublin, 15–16 Oct 1998.

Norman, P. (2003). *The Accidental Constitution. The Story of the European Convention*. Brussels, Belgium: EuroComment.

North, D. C. (1981). *Structure and Change in Economic History*. New York: Norton.

North, D. C. (1990*a*). *Institutions, Institutional Change and Economic Performance.* Cambridge: Cambridge University Press.

———(1990*b*). 'A Transaction Cost Theory of Politics', *Journal of Theoretical Politics*, 2(4): 355–67.

———(1996). 'Epilogue: Economic Performance through Time', in L. J. Alston, T. Eggertsson, and D. C. North (eds.), *Empirical Studies in Institutional Change.* Cambridge: Cambridge University Press.

Nugent, N. (2000). The European Commission. Basingstoke: Palgrave Macmillan.

Nuttall, S. (1992). 'European Political Cooperation.' Oxford: Clarendon.

Olson, M. (1965). *The Logic of Collective Action. Public Goods and the Theory of Groups.* Cambridge, MA: Harvard University Press.

Orren, K. and Skowronek, S. (1994). 'Beyond the Iconography of Order: Notes for a "New Institutionalism"', in L. C. Dodd and C. Jillson (eds.), *The Dynamics of American Politics: Approaches and Interpretations.* Boulder, CO: Westview.

———(2000). 'History and Governance in the Study of American Political Development', Paper presented at the 'Annual Meeting of the American Political Science Association', Washington, 31 August–3 September 2000.

Ostrom, E. (1986). 'An Agenda for the Study of Institutions', *Public Choice*, 48(1): 3–25.

———(1990). *Governing the Commons: The Evolution of Institutions for Collective Action.* Cambridge: Cambridge University Press.

———(1999). 'Institutional Rational Choice: An Assessment of the Institutional Analysis and Development Framework', in P. A. Sabatier (ed.), *Theories of the Policy Process.* Boulder, CO: Westview Press.

Ostrom, V. (1980). 'Artisanship and Artifact', *Public Administration Review*, 40(4): 309–17.

Oye, K. A. (1992). *Economic Discrimination and Political Exchange: World Political Economy in the 1930s and 1980s.* Princeton, NJ: Princeton University Press.

Palayret, J. M., Wallace, H., and Winand, P. (eds.) (2006). *Visions, Votes and Vetoes. The Empty Chair Crisis and the Luxembourg Compromise. Forty Years On.* Frankfurt am Main, Germany: Peter Lang.

Parsons, T. (2001). *Toward a General Theory of Action: Theoretical Foundations for the Social Sciences.* New Brunswick, NJ: Transaction.

Petersen, T. (1995). 'Transaction Cost Economics', in P. Foss (ed.), *Economic Approaches to Organizations and Institutions. An Introduction.* Brookfield, WI: Dartmouth.

Petite, M. (1998). 'Treaty of Amsterdam', Jean Monnet Working Papers 2/98. New York: NYU School of Law.

Pierson, P. (1993). 'When Effect Becomes Cause: Policy Feedback and Political Change', *World Politics*, 45(5): 595–628.

———(1996). 'The Path to European Integration: A Historical Institutionalist Analysis', *Comparative Political Studies*, 29(2): 123–63.

———(2000*a*). 'Three Worlds of Welfare State Research', *Comparative Political Studies*, 33(6–7): 791–821.

———(2000*b*). 'Increasing Returns, Path Dependence, and the Study of Politics', *American Political Science Review*, 94(2): 251–67.

Pollack, M. A. (2003). 'The Engines of European Integration. Delegation, Agency and Agenda-Setting. Oxford: Oxford University Press.

Powell, W. W. and DiMaggio, P. J. (eds.) (1991). *The New Institutionalism in Organizational Analysis*. Chicago, IL: University of Chicago Press.

Przeworski, A. (2004). 'Institutions Matter?', *Government and Opposition*, 39(4): 527–40.

Putnam, R. D. (1988). 'Diplomacy and Domestic Politics: The Logic of Two-Level Games', *International Organization*, 42(3): 427–60.

Püttner, U. (2003). 'Informal Circles of Ministers: A Way out of the EU's Institutional Dilemma', *European Law Journal*, 9(1): 109–24.

Radaelli, C. M. and Schmidt, V. A. (2005). *Discourse and Policy Change in Europe*. London: Routledge.

Raiffa, H. (1982). *The Art and Science of Negotiation*. Cambridge, MA: Harvard University Press.

Rasmussen, A. (2006). 'Delegation and Political Influence: Conference Committees in the European Union and the USA', Ph.D. dissertation Department of Political Science, University of Copenhagen.

Rawls, J. (1971). *A Theory of Justice*. Cambridge, MA: Harvard University Press.

Reh, C. (forthcoming). 'Pre-Cooking the European Constitution? The Group of Government Representatives and Delegated Pre-Decisions in EU Treaty Reform'. *Journal of European Public Policy*. 33 pp.

Riker, W. H. (1980). 'Implications from the Disequilibrium of Majority Rule for the Study of Institutions', *American Political Science Review*, 74(2): 432–46.

―― and Sened, I. (1996). 'A Political Theory of the Origin of Property Rights: Airport Slots', in L. J. Alston, T. Eggertsson, and D. C. North (eds.), *Empirical Studies in Institutional Change*. Cambridge: Cambridge University Press.

Risse, T. (2000). 'Let's Argue! Communicative Action in World Politics', *International Organization*, 54(1): 1–39.

―― and Wiener, A. (1999). 'Something Rotten and the Social Construction of Social Constructivism: A Comment on Comments', *Journal of European Public Policy*, 6(5): 775–82.

Rittberger, B. (2003a). 'Endogenizing Institutional Change: Moving Beyond the Institutionalist Holy Trinity', University of Oxford, Nuffield College, unpublished manuscript.

―― (2003b). 'The Creation and Empowerment of the European Parliament', *Journal of Common Market Studies*, 41(2): 203–25.

―― (2005). *Building Europe's Parliament. Democratic Representation Beyond the Nation State*. Oxford: Oxford University Press.

Ross, G. (1995). *Jacques Delors and European Integration*. New York: Oxford University Press.

Rothstein, B. (1996). 'Political Institutions: An Overview', in R. E. Goodin and H-D. Klingemann (eds.), *A New Handbook for Political Science*. Oxford: Oxford University Press.

Sabatier, P. A. and Jenkins-Smith, H. C. (1993). *Policy Change and Learning: An Advocacy Coalition Approach*. Boulder, CO: Westview Press.

Sandholtz, W. and Stone Sweet, A. (2004). 'Law, Politics, and International Governance', in C. Reus-Smit (ed.), *The Politics of International Law*. Cambridge: Cambridge University Press.

Scharpf, F. W. (1991). 'Political Institutions, Decision Styles, and Policy Choices', in R.
M. Czada and A. Windhoff-Héritier (eds.), *Political Choice. Institutions, Rules and
the Limits of Rationality*. Boulder, CO: Westview.

—— (1997). *Games Real Actors Play. Actor-Centered Institutionalism in Policy Research*.
Boulder, CO: Westview.

Schickler, E. (1999). 'Disjointed Pluralism and Congressional Development: An
Overview', Paper presented at the 'Annual Meeting of the American Political Science
Association', Atlanta, 2–5 September 1999.

Schiffauer, P. (2004). 'Die Gestaltungskraft des EP im Prozess der Entstehung einer
Verfassung der Europ.', Union, EP, Abtlg. Internat. und Konstitutionelle Angelegen-
heiten, Brussel.

Schimmelfennig, F. (2001). 'International Socialization in the New Europe: Rational
Action in an Institutional Environment', *European Journal of Political Research*, 6(1):
109–39.

Schotter, A. (1981). *The Economic Theory of Social Institutions*. Cambridge: Cambridge
University Press.

Schout, A. and Vanhoonacker (2001). 'The Presidency as a Broker? Lessons from Nice
Paper delivered at 4th PanEuropean IR Conference, Canterburg, 8–10 Sept.

Scott, W. R. (1995). *Institutions and Organizations*. Thousand Oaks, CA: Sage.

—— and Meyer, J. W. (1994). *Institutional Environments and Organizations: Structural
Complexity and Individualism*. Thousand Oaks, CA: Sage.

Scully, R. (1997). 'The European Parliament and the Co-Decision Procedure: A
Reassessment', *Journal of Legislative Studies*, 3(3): 58–73.

Sebenius, J. K. (1992). 'Challenging Conventional Explanations of International Cooperation: Negotiation Analysis and the Case of Epistemic Communities', *International
Organization*, 46(1): 323–65.

Sened, I. (1991). 'Contemporary Theory of Institutions in Perspective', *Journal of
Theoretical Politics*, 3(4): 379–402.

Shackleton, M. (2000). 'The Politics of Codecision', *Journal of Common Market Studies*,
38(2): 325–42.

—— and Raunio, T. (2003). 'Codecision since Amsterdam: A Laboratory for Institutional Innovation and Change', *Journal of European Public Policy*, 10(2): 171–87.

Sherrington, P. (2000). *The Council of Ministers. Political Authority in the European
Union*. London: Pinter.

Simon, H. A. (1957). *Models of Man*. New York: John Wiley & Sons.

—— (1982). *The Science of the Artificial*. Cambridge, MA: MIT Press.

—— (1987). 'Politics as Information Processing', *LSE Quarterly*, 1(4): 345–70.

Sjöblom, G. (1993). 'Some Critical Remarks on March and Olsen's "Rediscovering
Institutions"', *Journal of Theoretical Politics*, 5(3): 397–407.

Snidal, D. (1996). 'Political Economy and International Institutions', *International
Review of Law and Economics*, 16(1): 121–37.

_____ (2004). 'Shopping for Concepts and Concept of (Forum) Shopping', Paper presented at the 'Workshop on Forum Shopping and Global Governance'. Florence, Italy: European University Institute, 23–24 April 2004.

Spence, D. (2000). 'Plus Ça Change, Plus C'est La Même Chose? Attempting to Reform the European Commission?', *Journal of European Public Policy*, 7(1): 1–25.

Spruyt, H. (1994*a*). 'Institutional Selection in International Relations: State Anarchy as Order', *International Organization*, 48(4): 527–57.

_____ (1994*b*). *The Sovereign State and Its Competitors: An Analysis of Systems Change.* Princeton, NJ: Princeton University Press.

Stacey, J. and Rittberger, B. (2003). 'Dynamics of Formal and Informal Institutional Change in the EU', *Journal of European Public Policy*, 10(6): 858–83.

Steiner, J., Bächtiger, A., Spörndli, M., and Steenbergen, M. R. (eds.) (2004). *Deliberative Politics in Action. Analysing Parliamentary Discourse.* Cambridge: Cambridge University Press.

Stigler, G. J. (1961). 'The Economics of Information', *Journal of Political Economy*, 69(3): 213–25.

Stinchcombe, A. L. (1968). *Constructing Social Theory.* New York: Harcourt, Brace and World.

Stone Sweet, A. (1998). 'Rules, Dispute Resolution, and Strategic Behavior. A Reply to Vanberg', *Journal of Theoretical Politics*, 10(3): 327–38.

_____ (1999). 'Judicialization and the Construction of Governance', *Comparative Political Studies*, 32(2): 147–84.

_____ and Sandholtz, W. (1997). 'European Integration and Supranational Governance', *Journal of European Public Policy*, 4(3): 297–317.

Streeck, W. and Thelen, K. (eds.) (2005). *Beyond Continuity: Institutional Change in Advanced Political Economies.* Oxford: Oxford University Press.

Sugden, R. (1986). *The Economics of Rights, Co-Operation and Welfare.* Oxford: Basil Blackwell.

Sunstein, C. (2000). 'Deliberative Trouble? Why Groups Go to Extremes', *Yale Law Journal*, 110(1): 71–119.

Svensson, A.-C. (2000). *In the Service of the European Union. The Role of the Presidency in Negotiating the Amsterdam Treaty, 1995–97.* Uppsala, Sweden: Acta Universitatis.

Tallberg, J. (2006). *Leadership and Negotiation in the European Union.* Cambridge: Cambridge University Press.

Taylor, M. (1987). *The Possibility of Cooperation.* Cambridge: Cambridge University Press.

_____ and Singleton, S. (1993). 'The Communal Resource: Transaction Costs and the Solution of Collective Action Problems', *Politics and Society*, 21: 195–214.

Thelen, K. (2003). 'How Institutions Evolve. Insights from Comparative–Historical Analysis', in J. Mahoney and D. Rueschemeyer (eds.), *Comparative Historical Analysis in the Social Sciences.* Cambridge: Cambridge University Press.

Tsebelis, G. (1990). *Nested Games. Rational Choice in Comparative Politics.* Berkeley, CA: University of California Press.

Tsebelis, G. (1995). 'Conditional Agenda-Setting and Decision-Making inside the European Parliament', *Journal of Legislative Studies*, 1(1): 65–93.

Varone, F., de Visscher, C., and Maiscocq, O. (2006). *Governance and the EU Securities Sector: Agency or Fiduciary Relationships between European Institutions and Market Actors?*, Mscr. Workshop Cluster 2, NewGov Framework Six Integrated Project. Florence, Italy: European University Institute, 29 Jan. 2006.

Walton, R. E. and McKersie, R. B. (1991). *A Behavioral Theory of Labor Negotiations. An Analysis of a Social Interaction System*. Ithaca, NY: ILR Press.

Weidenfeld, W. (1994). Europa '96: Reformprogramm für die Europäische Union, Gütersloh Bertelsmann.

Weingast, B. R. and Marshall, W. J. (1988). 'The Industrial Organization of Congress; or, Why Legislatures, Like Firms, Are Not Organized as Markets', *Journal of Political Economy*, 96(1): 132–63.

Wendt, A. (2001). 'Driving with the Rearview Mirror: On the Rational Science of Institutional Design', *International Organization*, 55(4): 1019–49.

Wessels, W. (2001) 'Nice Results: The Millennium IGC in the EU's Evolution', *Journal of Common Market Studies*, 39(2): 197–219.

Westlake, M. (1994). A Modern Guide to the European Parliament. London: Pinter.
—— (1999). The Council of the European Union, 2nd ed. London: John Harper.

White, J. P. (2003). 'Theory Guiding Practice: The Neofunctionalists and the Hallstein EEC Commission', *Journal of European Integration History*, 9(2): 111–31.

Williamson, O. E. (1975). *Markets and Hierarchies: Analysis and Antitrust Implications*. New York: Free Press.
—— (1985). *The Economic Institutions of Capitalism. Firms, Markets, Relational Contracting*. New York: Free Press.

Zucker, L. G. (1983). 'Organizations as Institutions', *Research in the Sociology of Organizations*, 2: 1–47.

Official Documents

Intergovernmental Conference (1996). *Report from the Chairman of the Reflection Group of 5 December 1995 on the 1996 Intergovernmental Conference: A Strategy for Europe*. Luxembourg: Office for Official Publications of the EC.

European Commission (1970). *Third General Report on the Activities of the European Communities*. Luxembourg: Office for Official Publications of the EC.
—— (1971). *Fourth General Report on the Activities of the European Communities*. Luxembourg: Office for Official Publications of the EC.
—— (1985). 'Proposal to the IGC 1985' (Bulletin EC Sep 1985, point 1.1.1 et seq.).
—— (1989). 'Report to the European Parliament of 28 September 1989: Delegation of Executive Powers to the Commission' (SEC (89) 1591 final).
—— (2004). 'Amended Proposal of 22 April 2004 for a Council Decision Amending Decision 1999/468/EC Laying Down the Procedures for the Exercise of Implementing Powers Conferred on the Commission' (COM(2004) 324 final).

European Council (1974). 'Report by Mr. Leo Tindemans, Prime Minister of Belgium, to the European Council' (Bulletin of the European Communities Supplement 1/76).

_____ (1979). *Report on European Institutions of 8 November 1979 Presented by the Committee of Three to the European Council.* Luxembourg: Office for Official Publications of the EC.

_____ (2003). 'A Secure Europe in a Better World: European Security Strategy' (Solana Report) (12 December 2003).

_____ (2006). 'Council Decision of 17.7.2006 Amending Decision 1999/468/EC Laying Down the Procedures for the Exercise of Implementing Powers Conferred on the Commission' (2006/512/EC).

European Commission (1968–93). *Bulletin of the European Communities.* Luxembourg: Office for Official Publications of the EC.

_____ (1994–). *Bulletin of the European Union.* Luxembourg: Office for Official Publications of the EC.

Agence Europe (1953–). Europe: *Bulletin Quotidien.* Luxembourg: Agence internationale d'information our la presse.

European Court of Justice (1970). 'Case 25/70 Einfuhr- und Vorratsstelle für Getreide und *Futtermittel v. Köster, Berodt & Co.*' (2 ECR 1161).

_____ (1970). 'Case 41/69 *ACF Chemiefarma NV* v. *Commission*' (ECR 661).

_____ (1977). 'Case 5/77 *Carlo Tedeschi* v. *Denkavit Commerciale S.R.L*' (ECR 1555).

_____ (1977). 'Case 5/77 *Pretura Di Lodi* v. *Italy*' (ECR 1555).

_____ (1988). 'Case 16/88 *Commission* v. *Council*' (ECR 3457).

_____ (1988). 'Case 302/87 *European Parliament* v. *Commission*' (ECR 5615).

_____ (1995). 'Case C-156/93 *European Parliament* v. *Commission*' (ECR I-2019).

_____ (1995). 'Case C-417/93 *European Parliament* v. *Coluncil*' (ECR I-1185).

House of Lords (2003). 'House of Lords Select Committee on the European Union: Reforming Comitology', Session 2002–03, 31st Report (1 July 2003).

Council of Ministers (1962). 'Council Regulation 17/62/EEC of 6 February 1962 Implementing Articles 85 and 86 of the EEC Treaty' (OJ 1962 P 13/204).

_____ (1962). 'Council Regulation 19/62/EEC of 4 April 1962 on the Progressive Establishment of a Common Organisation of the Market in Cereals' (OJ 1962 30/933).

_____ (1962). 'Council Regulation 20/62/EEC of 4 April 1962 on the Progressive Establishment of a Common Organisation of the Market in Pork' (OJ 1962 30/945).

_____ (1962). 'Council Regulation 21/62/EEC of 4 April 1962 on the Progressive Establishment of a Common Organisation of the Market in Eggs' (OJ 1962 30/953).

_____ (1962). 'Council Regulation 22/62/EEC of 4 April 1962 on the Progressive Establishment of a Common Organisation of the Market in Poultry' (OJ 1962 30/959).

_____ (1962). 'Council Regulation 23/62/EEC of 4 April 1962 on the Progressive Establishment of a Common Organisation of the Market in Friut and Vegetables' (OJ 1962 30/965).

_____ (1962). 'Council Regulation 24/62/EEC of 4 April 1962 on the Progressive Establishment of a Common Organisation of the Market in Wine' (OJ 1962 30/989).

Council of Ministers (1972). 'Council Directive 72/156/EEC of 21 March 1972 on Regulating International Capital Flows and Neutralising Their Undesirable Effects on Domestic Liquidity' (OJ 1972 L 91/13).

—— (1981). 'Report on European Political Cooperation (London, 13 October 1981)' (Bulletin of the European Communities Supplement 3).

—— (1987). 'Council Decision 87/373/EEC of 13 July 1987 Laying Down the Procedures for the Exercise of Implementing Powers Conferred on the Commission' (OJ 1987 L 197/33).

—— (1996). 'Council Directive 96/62/EC of 27 September 1996 on Ambient Air Quality Assessment and Management' (OJ 1996 L 296/55).

European Parliament (1962). 'Rapport du 5 Octobre 1962 fait au nom du comité des présidents sur le cinquième rapport général sur la l'activité de la communauté économique européenne (Rapporteur: Arved Deringer)' (EP Doc 74/62).

—— (1968). 'Rapport du 30 Septembre 1968 fait au nom de la Commission juridique sur les procédures communautaires d'exécution du droit communautaire dérivé (Rapporteur: Léon Jozeau-Marigné)' (EP Doc 115/68).

—— (1983). 'European Parliament Resolution of 16 September 1983 on the Cost to the EC Budget and Effectiveness of Committees of a Management, Advisory and Consultative Nature' (OJ 1983 C 277/195).

—— (1986). 'Debates of the European Parliament on 9 July 1986' (OJ 1986 Annex 2-341/130).

—— (1986). 'European Parliament Resolution of 23 October 1986 Closing the Procedure of Consultation for the European Parliament on the Proposal from the Commission to the Council for a Regulation Laying Down the Procedures for the Exercise of Implementing Powers Conferred on the Commission' (OJ 1986 C 297/94).

—— (1991). 'European Parliament Resolution of 19 April 1991 on Infant Formulae and Follow-up Milks' (OJ 1991 C 129/226).

—— (1994). 'Résolution sur l'investiture de la Commission (21 April 1994)' (OJ 1994 C 128/358).

—— (1995). 'Report of 4 May 1995 on the Functioning of the Treaty on European Union with a View to the 1996 Intergovernmental Conference: Implementation and Development of the Union. Committee on Institutional Affairs (Rapporteurs: Bourlanges/Martin)' (EP Doc A4-0102/95).

—— (1996). 'Report of 5 March 1996 on (I) Parliament's Opinion on the Convening of the IGC and (II) Evaluation of the Work of the Reflection Group and Definition of the Political Priorities of the European Parliament with a View to the Intergovernmental Conference. Committee on Institutional Affairs (Rapporteurs: Dury/Maij-Weggen)' (EP Doc A4-0068/96).

—— (1998). 'Debates of the European Parliament on 15 September 1998' (OJ 1998 C 313/17).

—— (1998). 'European Parliament Resolution of 17 December 1998 on the Draft General Budget of the European Union for the Financial Year 1999 as Modified by the Council' (OJ 1999 C 98/212).

—— (1999). 'Debates of the European Parliament on 5 May 1999' (OJ 1999 C 279/160).

—— (2002). 'Report of 28 January 2002 Drawn up on Behalf of the Committee on Constitutional Affairs on the General Revision of the Rules of Procedure (Rapporteur: Richard Corbett)' (EP Doc A5-8/02).

—— (2003). 'Report of 11 July 2003 Drawn up on Behalf of the Committee on Constitutional Affairs on the Proposal for a Council Decision Amending Decision 99/468/EC Laying Down the Procedures for the Exercise of Implementing Powers Conferred on the Commission (Rapporteur: Richard Corbett)' (EP Doc A5-266/03).

—— and European Commission (2000). 'Agreement between the European Parliament and the Commission of 17 February 2000 on Procedures for Implementing Council Decision 1999/468/EC of 28 June 1999 Laying Down the Procedures for the Exercise of Implementing Powers Conferred on the Commission' (OJ 2000 L 256/19).

—— 'Report on the Draft Council Decision 1999/468/EC (2006) Laying Down the Procedures for the Exercise of Implementing Powers Conferred on the Commission (Repporteur: Richard Corbett)' (EP A6-0236/2006).

Index